I Only Read It for the Cartoons

I Only Read It for the Cartoons

The New Yorker's
Most Brilliantly Twisted Artists

RICHARD GEHR

New Harvest
Houghton Mifflin Harcourt
BOSTON   NEW YORK
2014

This edition published by special arrangement with Amazon Publishing

For information about permission to reproduce selections from this book,
go to www.apub.com.

www.hmhco.com

Library of Congress Cataloging-in-Publication Data
Gehr, Richard, date.
I only read it for the cartoons : the New Yorker's most
brilliantly twisted artists / Richard Gehr.
pages cm
ISBN 978-0-544-11445-6 (hardback)
1. Cartoonists—United States—Biography.
2. New Yorker (New York, N.Y. : 1925) I. Title.
NC1305.G45 2014
741.5'69730922—dc23
[B]
2014016711

Printed in the United States of America
DOC 10 9 8 7 6 5 4 3 2 1

For my parents

Contents

Foreword

View of *The New Yorker* from Portland, Oregon

I FELL IN LOVE with *New Yorker* cartoons before I could read. I remember being four years old, crawling on the carpet through the hovering living-room dust motes to the bookshelf behind my cartoonist dad's easy chair. There a treasure trove of oversized hardback anthologies of magazine cartoons was kept conveniently on the bottom shelf, easy for me to grab and scribble in. With a mix of awe and bafflement, I pored through *"The New Yorker" 1950–1955 Album; "The New Yorker" Twenty-Fifth Anniversary Album, 1925–1950;* Helen E. Hokinson's *The Ladies, God Bless 'Em!;* James Thurber's *Fables for Our Time* and *The Thurber Carnival;* Charles Addams's *Monster Rally, Addams and Evil,* and *Homebodies;* Syd Hoff's *"Oops! Wrong Party!";* and Peter Arno's *Sizzling Platter, Hell of a Way to Run a Railroad,* and *Man in the Shower. Man in the Shower*'s cover particularly unnerved me—that's the one with the hapless underwater naked guy gesticulating to his wife to open the shower door.

Throughout my childhood I returned to those cartoon books (along with memorable collections by *Punch* magazine contributors Ronald Searle and Rowland Emett), but learning to read the captions only wised me up slightly to the real meanings of these strange and beautiful and sometimes sexy drawings. In fourth grade my precocious pal Duncan Smith clued me in to the genius of Saul Steinberg, and we would sit in the adult art-book room at the Multnomah County Library in downtown Portland, Oregon, trying to copy Steinberg from his books *The Passport* and *The Labyrinth.* (Duncan's illustrations were great—I couldn't draw a straight line.) I also spent countless hours in the basement at home among the piles of *New Yorker*s, never bothering with the long columns of snoozy print, only reading it for the cartoons. It wasn't until high school and college that I started digging the non-cartoon content, but the *New Yorker* thing I still remember most from those years is Steinberg's 1976 cover "View of the World from 9th Avenue."

My grown-up love of *New Yorker* cartoons continues unabated. *New Yorker* cartoonists have always been fascinating creatures, toiling away in solitude and self-effacing about their subtle brilliance. I think I understand most of their cartoons these days, although I admit a few still bewilder me, which is enjoyable in its own perverse way. (That Ed Koren cartoon with the crashed car—"It's a narrative I didn't intend"—remains a stumper.) In 2004 I bought *The Complete Cartoons of "The New Yorker"* ("includes two CDs with all 68,647 cartoons ever published in the magazine"), but the CDs were kind of balky. A couple of years later I got the eight-DVD *Complete "New Yorker,"* which proved even more annoying than the CDs; so I coughed up three hundred bucks for *The Complete "New Yorker" Portable Hard Drive,* which kind of worked until I lost it in a drawer someplace. And now here we are in the spectacular future and the whole *New Yorker* archive is online for subscribers . . . hooray!

My longtime friend and Boy Scout troop mate Richard Gehr has done a terrific job with the profiles in this book. He is possibly even more besotted with *New Yorker* cartoon mania than me, if the issues he packed on camping trips are any indication. His knowledge of the history and culture of the magazine and his incisive, revealing interviews make for great reading, and you can tell the cartoonists are tickled by his informed questions. *New Yorker* cartoonists, like almost all less exalted cartoonists, are a pretty unpresuming lot, but, man, are they quirky, sly, and funny. When Roz Chast, George Booth, Ed Koren, and all the rest read this book, I think they will be delighted—as will you.

—MATT GROENING

SANTA MONICA, CALIFORNIA

JANUARY 2014

Introduction

How to Read a *New Yorker* Cartoon

I F YOU THINK entering *The New Yorker*'s weekly Caption Contest is a hoot, try competing with a roomful of cartoon fans and an open bar. A live version of the Cartoon Caption Contest is among the more popular events of the annual New Yorker Festival, and in 2012 I found myself sitting at one of several tables in Condé Nast Publications' executive dining room, where participants enjoyed executive snacks and the opportunity to have their captions judged by the pros: George Booth, Harry Bliss, Kim Warp, and *New Yorker* editor-cartoonist Robert Mankoff. The tables competed against one another for copies of the recently published *The Big "New Yorker" Book of Dogs*. Not coincidentally, all three of the captionless images we were required to enhumor also involved canine situations. A captioning newbie, I quickly got the hang of this kartoon karaoke and was soon amusing myself, if no one else. (The one about Laika and the dating service was especially killer.) *What is* wrong *with these people?* I thought, as lesser efforts were rewarded.

The Caption Contest is an immensely popular feature. Some five thousand entries a week suggest that a good portion of the magazine's readers imagine that they could step up to the plate and knock gags out of the park with these Yankees of Yucks. But, of course, that's only half the battle, insofar as relatively few of us can draw as well as quip. For much of the magazine's run, outside writers supplied artists with their material. Today, however, drawing a *New Yorker* cartoon is rarely a two-person proposition.

In reality, cartooning for *The New Yorker* is mostly an exercise in rejection. Cartoon editor Mankoff and editor in chief David Remnick nix hundreds of cartoons for every one they publish in the magazine. One regular contributor, Matthew Diffee, has taken the iniquity in hand by publishing a series of Rejection Collection volumes devoted to "Cartoons You Never Saw, and Never Will See, in *The New Yorker*." And when I asked staff writer Calvin Trillin for his thoughts on the state of *New Yorker* cartooning, he prefaced his response by saying it would be prejudiced by the fact that not a single one of his many cartoon ideas had ever made it into the magazine.

Two days after the festival, I was in Lawrence, Kansas, recounting my afternoon of shame to Jack Ziegler, one of *The New Yorker*'s more inventive and frequently appearing cartoonists. I suppose I expected a little sympathy. Instead, Ziegler went about as straight-faced as I'd seen him get all afternoon.

"Now you know how *I* feel," he said.

But there's a lot more to a *New Yorker* cartoon than a clever caption, and it takes an artist like Ziegler to complete the equation. Like a pop single, every cartoon creates its own little universe in which you can linger. In fact, says single-panel virtuoso Dan Piraro, whose *Bizarro* comic appears in some 350 outlets daily, a cartoon is the *only* way certain ideas can be expressed. "You see a small slice of time, and a few words, and your mind must put together what has just happened to lead to this, or what is about to happen moments later. If you take almost any given single-panel gag and spell it out long form, be it a comic strip or actors fleshing out the scene on video, the joke is completely ruined."

Ivan Brunetti, a cartoonist and a comics scholar to boot, insists that "whether it's minimal or dense with detail, a cartoon instantly puts you somewhere, and you're picking up so much narrative without even realizing it. You're entering a world the cartoonist creates." A cartoon is a collaboration between artist and reader and a tiny vacation from sad, boring reality.

The timing of the first *New Yorker* cartoons couldn't have been better in this respect. The Roaring Twenties were about to give way to the Great Depression. In the magazine's first issue—dated February 21, 1925—founding editor Harold Ross wrote, "*The New Yorker* starts with a declaration of serious purpose but with a concomitant declaration that it will not be too serious in executing it. It hopes to reflect metropolitan life, to keep up with events and affairs of the day, to be gay, humorous, satirical but to be more than a jester." Little could Ross have imagined that he would be publishing an entire issue devoted to John Hersey's "Hiroshima" just twenty years later. Or, for that matter, imagine Hersey marrying Charles Addams's first wife, which he did.

The first *New Yorker* cartoon appeared on the same page as Ross's credo. In Alfred Frueh's drawing, a disheveled subway rider wearing an overcoat and fedora holds on to a strap with one hand (a lunch bucket draped over his arm) while the other assiduously wipes a clear view through a dirty window. Beside him, a sign implores PLEASE! HELP KEEP THE "L" AND SUBWAY CLEAN. The cartoon's caption consists of a single word: "Co-operation." With a couple of small changes, that image might have been published in this week's issue—perhaps swapping in a handlebar-mustached nostalgist from Williamsburg carrying a bento box. There's a timeless appeal to the best cartoons, which this one, filled as it is with local meaning, still possesses.

Cartoons are essential to *The New Yorker*'s identity. They're what—admit it—you look at first upon opening its pages, and they constitute what Roz Chast calls "a magazine within a magazine." They're a gateway (drug) to both the magazine's long-form journalism and the world at large. Growing up in Oregon during the fifties and sixties, I learned everything I *really* needed to know about New

York City from *New Yorker* cartoons and Howard Smith's Scenes column in my closet-bohemian father's copies of the *Village Voice*. Charles Addams's famous drawing of a skier's legs creating *ünheimlich* parentheses around an obstructing tree shattered my notion of reality as effectively as Jack Kirby. And here in Brooklyn, where I've lived for seventeen years, I fondly recall my two young daughters leafing through each week's issue, annotating every image according to the quality and/or comprehensibility of its humor—e.g., funny, not funny, don't get. Sadly, however, *The New Yorker* is the only general-interest magazine that still publishes single-panel cartoons on an ongoing basis, and the world is less charming for it.

Modern cartooning's roots lie in Egyptian hieroglyphs, Greek friezes, medieval tapestries, and the British and French satirical-art traditions. At the turn of the twentieth century, cartoons and Sunday comics—the funnies—composed a mass medium that cut across age and class. By 1950, cartoonists could make a decent living drawing for the stag and wholesale gag mags and for general-interest outlets, such as *Look, Collier's,* and the *Saturday Evening Post,* with *The New Yorker* at the top of the ladder.

For its first year or so, the magazine published illustrations large and small, caricatures, and cartoons. The latter consisted mostly of sequential narrative cartoons, with and without captions, and full- or half-page drawings. These included art director Rea Irvin's *Social Errors* series, e.g., "The Man Who Used the Wrong Spoon" and "The Man Who Actually Ate Dinner" (at a nightclub). John Held Jr. translated old American songs into ironic wood engravings, and Carl Rose employed proto-expressionist techniques. It was fun stuff, but it ran its course quickly.

By the following summer, Harold Ross and Rea Irvin began concentrating on the special hybrid of word and image the magazine would become renowned for. Captions shrunk; art and text synergized in ironic fashion; and drawings appeared in novel shapes and proportions, often leaping from page to page. During the thirties, the wit of early humorists such as Dorothy Parker, Robert Benchley, and

James Thurber extended more forcefully into the cartoon realm, often thanks to ideas provided by the magazine's writers and editors. In one famous *New Yorker* cartoon, written by E. B. White and drawn by Carl Rose in 1928, a very proper mother informs her equally prim daughter that "It's broccoli, dear," to which the child replies, in words that have echoed through the decades, "I say it's spinach, and I say the hell with it."

Peter Arno (born Curtis Arnoux Peters) was the magazine's clown prince. Arno, Robert Benchley wrote, "may not have been the first to make use of the overheard remark as a basis for a drawing, but he has made himself the High Priest of the school." Arno's decades at the magazine produced some choice interactions between Harold Ross and his art department. In a 1949 memo, Ross informed art editor James Geraghty that Arno "is going to lay in for the next two or three weeks and finish fifteen or twenty drawings, he says, and that would mean we would have to use almost one drawing a week . . . I said I'd buy him an unlimited meal if he'd do this." The artist-editor relationship remained a work in progress, even after twenty-five years. "In other words," ran another 1949 memo, "the Arno caption sheet goes through the regular procedure, except that Ross IS NOT SUPPOSED TO CHANGE ARNO CAPTIONS AFTER THEY'VE BEEN BOUGHT." The process was solidified the following year, when art department staffer Louis Forster suggested the following procedure to Geraghty:

> All captions for Arno drawings are to be O.K.'d by Mr. Ross before Mr. Arno begins work. Mr. Geraghty is to give Mr. Lobrano sheets bearing the tentative captions for drawings that Arno is to do. Mr. Lobrano will take these to Mr. Ross with the regular batch of caption sheets that he takes in to Mr. Ross on Wednesdays. When Mr. Ross inititals [*sic*] and releases the Arno sheets, we (in Forster's dept.) are to copy them. We are to send copies to Mr. Geraghty and hold the originals ourself. When the drawings are completed by Mr. Arno and inititalled [*sic*] by Mr. Ross, we are to make sure that the captions on them are the same as the ones Mr. Ross O.K.'d.

Arno's stylized socialites were generally younger, though no less iconic, than Helen Hokinson's images of New York women at home, in shops, and at play. And Mary Petty, whose long-lined depictions of the older upper class anticipated Bruce Eric Kaplan's sly inversions of children's and adults' observations, was another notable exception to the predominantly male cartoon cabal. Charles Addams brought his elegantly macabre sensibility to the magazine in the early thirties. Romanian-born immigrant Saul Steinberg added a high-art sensibility, even as he labored ferociously on countless commercial jobs, to Harold Ross's rich mix. Bronx-raised William Steig and New Jersey native George Price (the magazine's most prolific artist, with some twelve hundred images to his credit) brought a working-class sensibility to *The New Yorker*.

Artists like William Crawford Galbraith, Wallace Morgan, and Carl Rose drew eye-boggling full-page cartoons full of subtle shadings and written by someone else. In later years, that someone else might have been someone like Richard McCallister or Peter De Vries, who translated some of his *New Yorker* experiences into his comic novel *The Tunnel of Love*. De Vries's Augie Poole is an aspiring cartoonist desperate to get into the pages of his friend Dick's *New Yorker*–like magazine, *The Townsman*. De Vries makes the hierarchy of artist and joke man clear in this exchange from his novel's theatrical adaptation:

> DICK. (*Arm on AUGIE's shoulder.*) Look, my boy, I'm not an art critic, I'm an editor—and an editor is merely a panderer who brings the artist and his public together. That's what I'm trying to do. So why don't you break down and sell us your ideas and then instead of being an artist who doesn't sell his work, you'll be an idea man who *does*.
>
> AUGIE. "Idea man"—a euphemism for "gag man."—Is that my fate? *Gag man?*—turning out jokes for other artists to draw?
>
> DICK. (*Quickly.*) I think of you as a social satirist, like George Bernard Shaw . . .
>
> AUGIE. (*Grimly.*) Sure, Shaw was a helluva cartoonist.

James Stevenson, a more successful version of Augie Poole, began supplying gags to artists while interning as an office boy in the forties. Several years later, Geraghty, a former gag writer hired as an editor in 1939, hired Stevenson as an in-house joke man, assigned him an office, but forbade him from revealing his duties. Stevenson eventually graduated to full-time cartooning.

Geraghty succeeded Rea Irvin, who contributed immeasurably to *The New Yorker* aesthetic after drafting its look with Ross in 1925. Lee Lorenz succeeded Geraghty as the magazine's cartoon editor in 1973. With editor William Shawn, who succeeded Ross in 1952, Geraghty launched the golden age of *New Yorker* cartooning that extended into the early eighties. The early greats overlapped with the avant-garde during this period. Shawn and Geraghty may have butted heads, as has been reported, but they drafted most of the artists in this book into the magazine during their years together, along with Sam Cobean, Charles Saxon, Saul Steinberg, and many other celebrated inksters.

Your favorite *New Yorker* cartoonists reveal your personality, and the refrigerator door where their works hang provides a map of your soul. They take ancient concepts—of love, war, cats—and recast them in contemporary forms. Each weekly mixture provides a glimpse into the zeitgeist. Thus the artists are something like soothsayers, peering into the collective unconscious to retrieve images and ideas that appear to have been meant for each other alone. How often have you looked at a Caption Contest winner and thought: *Of course! How could it have been otherwise?* Which is precisely the lightbulb moment each and every cartoonist aspires to, week after week.

The New Yorker, however, has always been about aspiration of a different sort. Most of its readers don't live in any of the five boroughs, although many probably wish they did. *New Yorker* cartoons taught us what life in New York City was like—and much more. These deceptively innocent images are like modern cave drawings. There's the commuter, artist, prophet, punk, financier, husband, wife, clergyman, matron, ne'er-do-well, and panhandler. (These characters, like their creators and editors, are rarely nonwhite, alas.) Beside translating New York to the world, the magazine's cartoonists mock our vanities while suggesting a thousand and one ways to spend time on a desert island, at Heaven's gates, in front of a judge, with a couple of guys in a bar, hanging from the walls of a prison, or in any of the other archetypal scenarios *The New Yorker* has made part of our hive mind.

And after more than eighty thousand cartoons, the gags keep on coming, with no end in sight and a somewhat lucrative aftermarket. Condé Nast, the magazine's corporate owner, sells framed prints for $125 a pop or so through the Cartoon Bank, which markets and licenses *The New Yorker*'s vast cartoon archive, repurposing these sketches as umbrellas, beach towels, shower curtains, watches, iPhone cases, and more. The most widely distributed *New Yorker* cartoon—Peter Steiner's 1993 drawing of two dogs at a computer with one saying, "On the Internet, nobody knows you're a dog"—has generated more than $100,000 in licensing and reprint fees alone. Cartoons may no longer be the mass medium they once were, but they're still earning their keep.

Let's hope the same can be said for the fine artists behind them, most of whom toil in relative obscurity. Behind the drawings and gag lines are flesh-and-blood artist-writers whose sensibilities have helped define the magazine. *The New Yorker*'s cartoons may reflect an institutional aesthetic, but its artists' best work comes from somewhere deep inside them, often over the course of decades, without proper acknowledgment. Unfortunately, as in the greater comics industry, many of the medium's finest talents have disappeared without receiving their due. And biographies, when they arrive, do so long after the Grim Reaper shows up at the door.

And speaking of which, *my* favorite Grim Reaper cartoon is the one by David Sipress, where the scythe-bearing man in black offers a card to a startled occupant while saying, "Don't freak out—it's just a save-the-date."

· · ·

A note on the illustrations found herein: Most *New Yorker* cartoons can be enjoyed online via the Cartoon Bank. That being the case, I asked each artist to choose a favorite or particularly representative image to represent his or her work for the magazine. The rest consists of previously unpublished roughs, rejects, and sketchbook material I hope will illuminate the cartoonist's process.

I Only Read It for the Cartoons

The Editor with a Horn: Lee Lorenz

"Now look what you've done!"

STANDING FRONT AND center on the bandstand at Arthur's Tavern, where he has performed nearly every Sunday night for more than three decades, Lee Lorenz is an incongruous jazzman from another era. Surrounded by his bandmates, he has the comfortable demeanor of the contented semirural Connecticut resident he is; Lorenz could be a professional golfer or advertising account executive. You know that he has to love the gig, because he certainly isn't in it for the money; his Creole Cooking Jazz Band plays for tips at this obscure portal into Greenwich Village's bohemian heyday. And the glory is, shall we say, modest, with a small yet constant stream of delighted tourists and regulars drifting in and out during the evening.

Lorenz represents the free-flying spirit of a music that sounds dated while still epitomizing the improvisational whimsy informing so much modern art—not least of all the single-panel gag cartoon.

From 1973 to 1998, Lorenz presided over a supersession of *New Yorker* cartoonists. Only the magazine's second art editor since its 1925 launch, he shepherded his department's transition from the William Shawn era through its purchase by Condé Nast and subsequent editorships of Robert Gottlieb and Tina Brown. As a cartoonist himself, Lorenz earned a *New Yorker* contract in 1958 and still contributes to the magazine.

Published in 1995, Lorenz's *The Art of "The New Yorker," 1925–1995* is a remarkable contribution to the history of both the magazine and the art form it nurtures. As art editor, Lorenz often took it upon himself to memorialize the talents of his departed colleagues in elegant obituaries. "On paper," he wrote upon George Price's passing, "the Pricean line was whiplike and beautifully finished; when lasers came along, they at last provided an image that befitted such exactitude." He possesses an encyclopedic knowledge of the weekly's artist contributors, which probably didn't hurt when it came time to consider a successor to its only other art editor, James Geraghty.

Lorenz's brushstrokes provide a rich contrast to the pen-preferring cartoonists who dominate *The New Yorker*'s pages. Like the abstract expressionists he studied at Carnegie Tech and Pratt Institute, Lorenz's lines radiate a lively, in-the-moment quality. He often captures characters in motion, momentary slices of time that may make you laugh out loud while pondering their befores and afters. The improvised aspect of his work suggests a sort of jazz, which he began devoting himself to as a teenager. "I was much more interested in music than art," says Lorenz of his adolescent self, "and was more knowledgeable about music, especially early jazz."

The artist's Easton, Connecticut, home has a rustic, extemporized feel. Wood sculptures that he's constructed, folk art that he's acquired, and found items that may or may not be art are scattered about. A detached garage has been transformed into a painting studio Lorenz admits has never quite served its intended function. Canvases lie stacked on the floor, on countertops, and against walls.

"So much for kinetic art, eh, Leo?" a slim espresso-sipping bohemiette asks an artist friend, spinning wildly, in a 1965 Lorenz cartoon.

Chair sculpture by Lee Lorenz

Many of Lorenz's best drawings caricature the modern-art world from which one might say he escaped—note the resemblance to the artist's own name in that cartoon—to become one of *The New Yorker*'s more influential staffers, albeit not without a couple of bumps along the way.

Lorenz wasn't management's first choice to replace Geraghty. And while other aspiring replacements mounted serious lobbying efforts for the job, Lorenz was not among them. Writer-editor Roger Angell was offered the position first, says Lorenz. The magazine's star baseball reporter did not accept the gig as offered, however. "Roger's got a very short fuse," says Lorenz, who suspects the job required more patience than the writer could muster. Angell and the magazine finally couldn't come to terms on money; though the magazine's profits were exceptional at the time, "they were very cheap," says Lorenz. The lawyer who negotiated Lorenz's contract, for example, suggested that whatever Lorenz earned as an artist be deducted from his editor's salary. Lorenz refused that part of the deal and continued to augment his pay with cartoons. "It was not a big salary, but they kept bumping it up a little bit," he says.

Money wasn't Lorenz's prime motivation when deciding whether to take the job: "My real anxiety was about working with the artists." He transitioned into the position slowly, working beside Geraghty until he grew comfortable enough to fly solo. Even then, the pilot seat remained occupied. "Geraghty didn't want to leave! They had instituted a retirement age, and he was dragging it out. I told Shawn that if I was going to do the job, Geraghty's got to leave at some point. He didn't want to—he stayed in the office while I was sitting in his chair! He wanted to keep his hand in. He was very angry and began talking as if I had deliberately pushed him out of the job, which had no truth to it whatsoever. I'd never thought about replacing him because he was a very good editor."

Harold Ross hired Geraghty largely for his gag-writing skills. And staff member Rea Irvin, the artist-designer who created cover mascot Eustace Tilley and the magazine's signature typeface, never relished dealing with the magazine's artists. Someone from Katherine White's fiction department would usually act as an intermediary, attending art meetings, where cover and cartoon decisions were made, and communicating with the artists themselves. "I think Peter Arno suggested they ask Geraghty if he'd like to do it," Lorenz recalls, "because Geraghty had sold a lot of ideas directly to Arno." Geraghty grabbed the reins and whipped the ragged department into shape. He gradually took responsibility for both cover and small spot illustrations in addition to cartoons, which became Lorenz's job as well.

Unlike Lorenz, Geraghty had no formal artistic training. "I could see what was wrong with a drawing right away," says Lorenz. "Any artist could do that because it's easy to see what's wrong with someone else's drawing. It's no special skill. But it was a useful skill at *The New Yorker*, and the artists were very happy to work with me." Lorenz could edit both captions and drawings, but he says the magazine's stars rarely needed editing. "If you wanted to suggest something to Steinberg, he would listen, but he rarely had to change anything. The

only people who made problems were those at the bottom of the totem pole. Not contract artists, but people who only occasionally sold to the magazine. They'd always bellyache about this and that."

The only complaint Lorenz had with the regulars was their perfectionism. "They always had second thoughts: 'I could do it better.'" Lorenz would tell them the work had already gone to press or "they'd just keep doing it over and over again." He could understand, possessing the same impulse himself. Between shadowing Geraghty and consulting with colleagues, Lorenz gradually became comfortable working with the magazine's artists, who were "very responsive" overall.

Like many incoming editors, Lorenz found himself balancing tradition with innovation. He relished working with *New Yorker* mainstays such as George Price and Charles Addams. He could be "very prickly, but not with me," Lorenz says of Price, who was "just like all those wiseacres in his cartoons." And Addams was "one of the most gracious and charming men you could ever meet. He was the only artist who never reworked anything. He did his drawings, brought them in, they were always beautiful, and that was it. Then he went off to have drinks with some gorgeous woman. He was less anxious about his work than any artist I know."

The most painful aspect of Lorenz's job was dealing with Whitney Darrow Jr., Alan Dunn, and other artists approaching the ends of their careers. "Their ideas just weren't fresh anymore," admits Lorenz ruefully. Darrow's material began to seem dated even to longtime fans. Dunn, meanwhile, "would send his stuff down by messenger on tiny pieces of paper." Unable to find ideas the magazine could use, Lorenz had to deliver the bad news to Dunn every week by phone. "He was very gracious about it," Lorenz says. "What made it even harder was that I think he sold more ideas to *The New Yorker* than anyone. He was wonderfully prolific." As at any job, the veterans would see fresh faces arrive and fear they were being phased out. "It wasn't like that, but I think that's every cartoonist's anxiety," Lorenz says.

Just as Geraghty had brought in a younger group of cartoonists that included Charles Barsotti, George Booth, and his own replacement, Lorenz was eager to make his mark by hiring his own roster of up-and-comers. Over the course of Geraghty's tenure, the magazine went from nearly always illustrating gag writers' ideas to printing cartoons written and drawn by the same person almost exclusively. "Geraghty effected that change," says Lorenz. At least part of the reasoning behind it, he speculates, may have been that "it was such a pain in the ass to go through written cartoons to find ideas for somebody else to draw."

When Roz Chast first dropped off her work at the magazine's office, in 1978, Lorenz showed it to Shawn, who said, "I think we should go for a contract right away," later adding, "Do you think she can keep it up?" She did keep it up, of course. "But there was such an uproar when she started appearing in the magazine," Lorenz recalls. "People think I'm making this all up—but no! The artists didn't like her work and said she couldn't draw." Until then, the model *New Yorker* cartoon was a finely crafted image, and plenty of such craftsmen contributed to the magazine. "But hers weren't funny in the same way and they weren't drawn in the same way. It was a radical departure."

Lorenz found bringing new artists into *The New Yorker* to be the most satisfying aspect of his job. His first discovery was Jack Ziegler, who arrived at the magazine in 1973. Ziegler imported elements of comic strips into the single-panel gag cartoon, often by moving captions into the panel as insets. "It became interesting to see how quickly other artists picked up on that and incorporated it into what they were doing," says Lorenz of Ziegler's zaniness. Suddenly cartoonists like the prolific Robert Kraus, who specialized in dark charcoal drawings, were adding talking kitchen utensils to their toolbox.

While *New Yorker* cartoons have evolved continuously since the 1920s, one thing about them has remained constant: Nobody finds the magazine's cartoons as funny as they used to be, whether that means last year or several decades ago. Geraghty's usual response to the claim was that the magazine "was never that funny!" His point, of course, was that readers tend to recall what *they* consider hilarious while conveniently erasing everything else. However, he added, "If you get three or four terrific ideas in an issue, you're doing fine."

"I want a distinctive point of view," Lorenz replies when asked what he was looking for in a *New Yorker* cartoonist. Gags were not enough. A point of view—personality plus style—could be as elegantly simple as Bruce Eric Kaplan's inverted view of society, in which adults act like children, and vice versa, or as complex as Steinberg's cartoon cubism. Most cartoonists, however, rely first and foremost on jokes. "There were always people who thought they could be the next George Booth or Gahan Wilson—but we already *had* George Booth and Gahan Wilson," says Lorenz. "I wanted artists who could bring something new to the mix."

When Geraghty was editor, younger artists would drop off their batches of roughs on Tuesday, even if they had contracts; Wednesday was reserved for the senior group, who'd join the editor for lunch after showing him their work. Lorenz, however, let anyone who'd sold a drawing, or whom he felt *could* sell a drawing, come in to see him on Tuesdays; contract artists alone came in on Wednesdays. This system was an improvement, he believed, "because a lot of the younger artists thought they were being discriminated against. Geraghty only saw the contract artists."

The first person to mention Austrian bodybuilder and future governor of California Arnold Schwarzenegger to Lorenz was his boss, William Shawn, with whom he selected each issue's cartoon lineup. "Shawn was full of interesting stuff," says Lorenz. "He loved Johnny Carson's *Tonight Show* and claimed he could identify the different writers who wrote his opening monologues. And once, when we were talking about some new building in New York, he told me, 'It's no good. Its atrium is too shady and they have uncomfortable aluminum chairs.' He'd already checked it out. He was interested in *everything*." Not that Lorenz and Shawn spent all afternoon chatting about TV and architecture. "It was strictly business, but he *loved* the cartoons," Lorenz recalls. "He'd tell me how much he looked forward to doing the cartoons every week. He'd ask about the cartoonists and was very aware when some guy wasn't doing well. He'd suggest we buy something we didn't really need to help get him back on track. He was very generous and would always try to be helpful. He made my job extraordinarily enjoyable." According to Gigi Mahon's *The Last Days of "The New Yorker,"* paying for articles and cartoons that never ran "was a means for Shawn to be loved by starving writers or by friends."

In 1985, Advance Publications (Condé Nast's parent company) bought *The New Yorker* from Raoul H. Fleischmann's F-R Publishing Company. Several months later, it replaced the eighty-year-old Shawn with Knopf books editor Robert Gottlieb. A petition was circulated by staff members who opposed Gottlieb's hiring, and the repercussions of the changeover were felt in the art department no less than on the editorial floor. "I found out after the fact that Condé Nast's biggest concern was that the artists would go on strike," Lorenz recalls, "and some artists wanted to strike. I discouraged them from doing that because they weren't salaried and I thought they would be risking too much. I didn't sign the petition against Gottlieb that went around, either."

In retrospect, Lorenz believes Shawn misplayed the opportunity to choose his own successor, which Condé Nast owner Samuel Irving "Si" Newhouse Jr. had already agreed to in writing. "But Shawn kept coming up with people who were unacceptable to the rest of the staff," Lorenz says. "It just lingered on and on. So when he got to Chip [Charles] McGrath, who everybody agreed would be a very good editor, he sort of moved the goal line by saying he wanted to stay on as senior editor. Shawn simply did not want to go! He made it very difficult, and somebody eventually had to budge." Newhouse eventually made a move, "and it was ultimately Newhouse's decision to make," Lorenz says.

Bob Gottlieb's and William Shawn's working relationships with Lorenz couldn't have been more different. A words man best known for buying and editing Joseph Heller's *Catch-22* for Simon & Schuster in 1957, Gottlieb, to Lorenz's dismay, initially had trouble finding any cartoons he liked at all. "If we don't start buying, we won't have any cartoons within twelve weeks" was the gist of a memo Gottlieb received from Lorenz, who complains that "he just didn't like stuff!"

The British absurdist Glen Baxter, whose pastiche style combined pop culture references with a look borrowed from wartime books for boys, was one of Gottlieb's few cartoonist hires. "He brought this guy from England he liked very much—a guy whose work I didn't like. So I said, 'You'll have to edit him because I can't.' I didn't *get* Glen Baxter," admits Lorenz, "and nobody we printed was like Glen Baxter. So we went through a very bad time."

For a while, Gottlieb rejected "everything." One cartoon he especially liked, however, was set in the Middle Ages and showed giant toasters launching spear throwers toward a castle. "Someday man will find a peaceful use for my machines," says the inventor to the soldier beside him. "It's the extravagant, off-the-wall kind of stuff [Gottlieb] liked," Lorenz says of that Bill Woodman image. "But he finally figured out that everything couldn't be like that. We had to have a range of humor in the magazine."

Lorenz and his cartoonist colleagues eventually got in tune with Gottlieb's aesthetic. "Bob had a great weakness for puns, so we started buying stuff from Danny Shanahan, who used a lot of them." (In one early Shanahan panel, a criminal being walked away from the judge's bench exclaims, "We wuz robed!") Bruce Eric Kaplan came to the magazine for much the same reason. "His early drawings were all puns," Lorenz says. "That opened the gate a little bit. I found a few artists who were on Bob's wavelength, and the regular contributors somehow got on it, too, so it eventually came together. But it was very touch-and-go at the beginning."

Gottlieb also believed the magazine's covers to be overly subdued, and longtime cover artists such as Arthur Getz were laid off in his effort to enliven them. Shawn had already phased out humorous covers. "We used to print a lot of covers by cartoonists," says Lorenz, "and I guess he felt uncomfortable doing that during the Vietnam era." The magazine's covers had become deliberately nonpolitical and rarely even topical. Shawn "wanted a cover you'd be comfortable with if the magazine sat on the table for a couple of weeks"; Gottlieb commissioned splashier, juicier, more colorful covers.

Si Newhouse doubled down on his effort to shake things up at *The New Yorker* by hiring Tina Brown in 1992, which was when Lorenz heard the "mandate" verbalized for the first time in meetings. Believing advertising revenue to be keyed more to newsstand sales than to subscription numbers, Brown began commissioning covers intended to jump off the racks. These "outlandish and provocative covers," in Lorenz's words, included Art Spiegelman's image of an orthodox Jewish man passionately kissing a black Caribbean woman, and R. Crumb's portrait of a pimply, backward-baseball-cap-wearing version of Eustace Tilley contemplating a strip-club flyer in midtown for the magazine's 1994 birthday cover.

"Hold it—" yells an Eskimo holding a very large fish in his arms as an elder is set adrift on a floating chunk of ice, "we almost forgot his benefits package." In 1992, Lee Lorenz, who happened to draw this timely image, was offered a "fantastic" retirement package that had been arranged by Gottlieb prior to the latter's departure from the magazine the same year. When Lorenz informed Tina Brown of his own plans to retire, she asked him to stay on, adding, "We can work out another package later." Lorenz said no to that—"and I'm glad I did"—but agreed to remain on as cartoon editor for as long as need be, which turned out to be almost another five years. "I started working with her on covers, but it soon became pretty clear we didn't see eye to eye. That's when she hired Françoise Mouly. I went to one cover meeting with the two of them, and they were a good match. I mean, they were at it hammer and tongs the moment Françoise walked in."

In 1998, Brown replaced Lorenz with Robert Mankoff, which was fine by Lorenz. "The retirement package they gave me was fine, and I was happy to go. No, I don't have any hard feelings about Bob."

Although most cartoonists he knows wanted to draw gags from the time they were kids, Lee Lorenz didn't start cartooning until he discovered the work of Saul Steinberg in high school. Opening his Greenwich High School yearbook for me during a visit, Lorenz points to inner-cover illustrations bearing unmistakable echoes of both Steinberg and Gene Deitch. An animator by trade, Deitch illustrated prolifically for the *Record Changer,* a jazz magazine that began publishing in 1942. Young Lee's primary passion was jazz, and he bought records with whatever money he made walking dogs or delivering newspapers. It wasn't until his family moved to Greenwich, New York, when he was a junior in high school, that he was introduced to art by Lucia Cumins, a "real New England type" of teacher who in 1949 was already deeply into the abstract expressionists.

Lee Lorenz was born in Hackensack, New Jersey, on October 17, 1932. His father, Alfred, administered USO programs for the YMCA, which necessitated moving his family around the country. The Lorenzes lived in Fort Leavenworth, Kansas; White Plains, New York; and Newburgh, New York, prior to settling in Greenwich. The quality of the town's high school was a "revelation" for Lee, although he was "crushed" his first day there because "it seemed as though everybody was able to do anything." Lee's mother, Martha, was a prospective artist who never got much further than the greeting-card business, while his father was as passionate about cycling as he was uninterested in the arts.

Lorenz had been seeing William Steig's work in *The New Yorker* for years. But Lorenz viewed him with fresh eyes when Lucia Cumins lent him *Listen, Little Man,* Steig's illustrated version of radical psychoanalyst Wilhelm Reich's well-known work. "Steig's illustrations were very powerful," Lorenz says. "Mrs. Cumins taught me to look at things in a different way." In Steig, Lorenz saw an artist who brilliantly worked the Venn intersection of art, illustration, and cartooning, and his influence is apparent in a Lorenz cartoon labeled SELF-ACTUALIZER, which depicts a man-puppet hybrid pulling his own strings. (In 1998, Lorenz would collaborate with Steig on *The World of William Steig,* whose contents ultimately angered the infamously temperamental children's books star. Although Lorenz says Steig was involved with the work at every stage, Steig objected to its containing early work he had renounced.)

Early Milton Caniff–inspired cartoon

"I was not a comic book guy," Lorenz says. "In fact, when I was a kid I don't think I was allowed to have any action comics. I had Donald Duck, so cartooning to me was Walt Disney." The only comics artist to make a real impression on him, though, was Milton Caniff. Lorenz loved the "rich brush quality" and "graphic richness" of Caniff's drawings. "As a kid, I didn't know you could draw with a brush. I drew with a pen I got at the ten-cent store."

After high school, Lorenz accepted a scholarship at the Carnegie Institute of Technology but didn't stick it out. "Living in Pittsburgh was tough then," he says. He returned to New York and earned a bachelor of fine arts degree at the Pratt Institute in Brooklyn. He married a classmate shortly after graduation, which gained him a military deferment, and soon began making the rounds as a cartoonist. He was encouraged by the father of a high school classmate, Jack Morley, who had worked with Crockett Johnson on the daily comic strip *Barnaby* and with Fontaine Fox on *Toonerville Folks*. "He never did his own scripts," says Lorenz, "but he knew the business." It just so happened to be an ideal moment to move into cartooning. "There were all kinds of magazines out there, so you could probably sell." And he did.

Lorenz began selling cartoons long before he had a style to call his own, largely because gag ideas turned out to be easy for him. In time he sold to the *Saturday Evening Post, Look, True, Argosy,* and *Playboy* and its imitators. There were also magazines like *1000 Jokes* "you'd go to at the end of the day with whatever you hadn't sold. They were always sympathetic, and I'd always sell five or six drawings there for twenty dollars apiece. I was able to make a living out of this early on and did quite well." He eventually realized, however, that if you wanted to make money, you had to go to *The New Yorker*.

Geraghty initially bought a few of Lorenz's gags as material for other artists. Unlike some cartoonists, Lorenz saw no shame in selling his ideas. He sold his first gag to the magazine in 1956. Richard Taylor, a painter who also cartooned, transformed Lorenz's idea into a spectacular page depicting the Hanging Gardens of Babylon. (A visitor says to the king, "First, let me congratulate you on your green thumb.") Charles Addams and George Price drew other gags of his. Geraghty eventually agreed to let Lorenz provide his own art as well, but: "I couldn't seem to pull it off. I still wasn't quite sure what my style was." Geraghty's assistant, cartoonist Frank Modell, made suggestions, but it still took years for Lorenz to sell "a nondescript drawing of some gorgeous airhead talking to a sugar daddy. I don't even remember the caption. They were very indulgent."

"Oh lord! Here comes Mr. Forty-Eight-Hour Erection!"

Lorenz recalls being paid $25 for each gag and $150 per cartoon. But it wasn't always as simple as that. *New Yorker* contracts were notoriously complicated. At first, Ross thought artists should be paid according to how much space they took up in the magazine. Lorenz joined the magazine long after Ross's editorship, but contracts still paid a set amount per square inch of published drawing. "So, of course, everybody submitted the largest drawings they could," he says, "hoping they'd publish them at that size." It got even more complicated: "You also got a quarterly increase in your base rate and a bonus at the end of the year." Lorenz was given a contract in 1958.

Lorenz was on a streak, selling so much to the magazine that he could afford to buy a small house in Newtown, Connecticut, after his first child was born. Then psychological disaster struck. "I had a kind of breakdown in the early sixties," he says, "and I couldn't seem to finish a drawing." He could finish drawings for other publications, just not for *The New Yorker*. Geraghty and Shawn assisted him financially during his crisis by OKing a large batch of ideas and allowing him to draw from that account each month. Lorenz eventually got past it, "with some help," but he still finds his particular form of artist's block confusing. "I guess I thought there was so much more at stake with *The New Yorker*," he says. He eventually pulled out of his slump and went on to sell the magazine forty to fifty drawings per year.

He had just as much trouble finishing his paintings. "It's hard for me to just sit down and do it. I have a big studio space here, but right now it's just a pile. You couldn't work there if you wanted to." The painter Philip Guston, who taught Lorenz at Pratt, affirmed Lorenz's decision to become a cartoonist and also served as best man at his wedding. "I had lunch with him one day when I was feeling down, because I'd hoped to make some sort of career as a painter. He said, 'Let me see what you're doing.' Well, the cartoons I was doing were certainly not good or very interesting graphically. He told me, 'You shouldn't feel that way. This is a really vital and interesting art form. You should be pleased you can do this.' I thought he was pulling my leg, but he utilized a lot of cartoon clichés himself many years later," Lorenz says. Guston's outrageous 1967 break from abstract expressionism was decidedly influenced by comics, and his subsequent figurative work contained a liberal amount of cartoon figures.

Lorenz's own style emerged slowly. "I had no idea how to develop one," he says. "Once I managed to acquire an early original of mine, a rough, that somebody was selling on eBay." Purchased from the son of the new owner of a house once owned by premier *New Yorker* gag writer Richard McCallister, the piece cost him all of seven dollars. Lorenz was shocked—but not at the price. "It looked like I had drawn it with a crayon! I didn't know *what* it was. If you look at my early drawings in *The New Yorker*, I was all over the place. I worked with pen, and some of my stuff resembled Chuck Saxon's work. I didn't solidify a style until after I started working at *The New Yorker* and decided to work directly with brush."

Lorenz considers his "true" style to be a happy accident that came about when he was forced to confine his roughs to 8.5-by-11-inch drawings in order to be able to fax them to the office. "I wasn't used to working that small. But I used a paper that had a little tooth to it and was transparent enough so that I could draw over the rough and work from that, even without a light table. And that's the way I did most of my finishes for years. It's not acid-free paper or anything, but it's held up pretty well, and it was a nice surface to work on. And then they stopped making it." Once he started using brushes, he never went back to pen. "It's the Milton Caniff thing. I loved that rich brush line."

Today Lorenz's cartoons stand out from the magazine's younger artists, who tend to draw with a shaggier line. "When I started, the tradition was still nineteenth-century academic style. Those guys could all draw. Nobody comes out of that tradition anymore; it's not what [the editors] recognize as cartooning. It seems old hat, which is too bad. Some really wonderful draftsmen were working in those days. Mischa Richter would get his OKs from Geraghty the day they had the art meeting. If he had one or two, he would sit down and do the finish right there in the office. Then he'd get on an airplane back to Cape Cod."

For his roughs, Lorenz uses Marvy markers, which "dry out in a hurry" but give a line that's a little like a brush. "I just sketch them out in pencil and tidy them up with the markers. Then I erase some of the pencil, put on the caption, and fax them in. When I get an OK, I have a sketch to work from, and that's about it." He's always bought the cheapest brushes he could find. "A really good brush is always an extravagance." He buys Jerry's Artarama brushes by the handful, uses them for half a dozen drawings, and throws them away. He prefers any paper with a rough vellum surface. "Nothing fancy; I always used the cheapest stuff." He also throws away a lot of drawings, even finished ones. "I do them again and again. Yesterday I did a drawing that had to go out immediately. They were in a rush. I wasn't satisfied with it but I turned it in. Then this morning I got up and did it again just for my own satisfaction." He likes to work in a hurry, for freshness' sake, incorporating improvements between small sketches and the larger sheets on which Lorenz finishes his panels for publication.

His lines are gentle yet precise, smooth but loose. His characters all have a vulnerable roundness to them. Both the prosperous and the wanting suffer alike. "Any time you get tired of flagellating yourself, I'd be happy to take over," oozes a middle-aged matron to her cringing, anxious spouse. His characters are befuddled when not peeved, irked when not angry, triumphantly smug, or cheerfully oblivious—such as the hosts at a party introducing their young friend as "one of those fabulously charming right-wing sociopaths you've been reading about." His work often deals with classic power relationships. "Now look what you've done!" says an angry mother hen to the surprised chick that has just burst from its egg—Lorenz's favorite cartoon, a 1971 panel he claims "saved me years of analysis." He pokes fun at the stiff Upper East Side businessman in countless cartoons. In one, a scowling newcomer to Heaven approaches St. Peter, who says, "Ah! Here you are—over on the shit list." If comedy is tragedy plus time, Lorenz reduces the interval to nil.

The sound of a neighborhood kid practicing his trumpet worked its magic on eight-year-old Lee Lorenz. "This kid in the neighborhood used to practice his trumpet in the backyard, much to the neighbors' chagrin," he recalls. "But I thought, 'Oh, God, that sounds so great!'" He was first-chair trumpet at Greenwich High School when he received a copy of *Bix & Tram*, an album of early Bix Beiderbecke 78s featuring saxophonist Frankie "Tram" Trumbauer, as a Christmas gift. "It puzzled me; I didn't understand what they were doing. It was weird, but I kept listening to it." Shortly thereafter, he discovered Columbia Records' reissues of early Louis Armstrong Hot Fives and Hot Sevens recordings, which were a "revelation." Soon he was buying Blue Note and Commodore recordings, frequenting Manhattan clubs like Central Plaza Casino and Café Society to hear Friday-night jam sessions, and playing in local bars with friends from school.

While attending Pratt, Lorenz jammed regularly at the Hotchkiss prep school with a group of contemporaries from around Greenwich. Hotchkiss's hockey coach was the father of Roswell Rudd, who would grow up to become one of the country's most renowned experimental jazz trombonists. Lorenz joined Eli's Chosen Six, the college jazz group Rudd formed at Yale University, and traveled north on weekends to play rags and stomps to club goers and drunk students. Eli's Chosen Six recorded an album for Columbia in 1955 and was featured prominently—driving around Newport, Rhode Island, in a convertible—in the 1959 concert film *Jazz on a Summer's Day.* "When I started cartooning, I was living on what I was making with Eli's Chosen Six," Lorenz says. "We were making $150 to $200 a man then. These days, if I get a gig that makes me $50 I feel pretty good about it." Like Lorenz, his current bandmates all played in college jazz bands at Yale, Princeton, and other schools.

Eli's Chosen Six continued to work together after college, traveling as far as Chicago's renowned Blue Note to perform. But travel became increasingly hard for this family man. Rooted in Connecticut, he joined a society band that played at weddings and country clubs. His current group grew out of the band he formed to play at the Place, a club across Seventh Avenue from Arthur's. "I used to have a Sunday-afternoon band there. Freddie Moore, an old-timer who went back to Jelly Roll Morton, played drums and washboards and sang with us. We also had a very good tenor player named Sammy Margolis." Lorenz assembled the Creole Cooking Jazz Band thirty years ago,

Lee Lorenz blowing at Arthur's Tavern with Joe Licari

when Arthur's needed a group to play on Sunday nights. "It's a place to play," he notes drily, adding that he also performs annually on a flatbed truck in Southington, Connecticut's Memorial Day parade.

After playing instrumental versions of "(I'd Like to Get You on a) Slow Boat to China," "I Never Knew," and "Lover Man (Oh, Where Can You Be?)," Lorenz sidles up to the mike at Arthur's for his first and only vocal of the evening, a sly take on Edgar Leslie and Walter Donaldson's 1929 hit "Tain't No Sin (to Take Off Your Skin and Dance Around in Your Bones)." A song without lyrics isn't quite the same as a cartoon without a caption, but like any good cartoonist, Lorenz aims to entertain. He recalls speaking with a young couple who frequented Arthur's. "He did all the talking and was obviously the one who liked jazz, while she just sort of sat there. So finally he asked her what she liked, and she said, 'I just can't get into music that doesn't have words.' And I thought, 'That's probably true!'"

For a time, Lorenz's musical and cartooning lives even intersected briefly. "When I got divorced the *first* time," he recalls, "we used to have jam sessions in my Manhattan loft. All kinds of musicians would come, and there were a lot of *New Yorker* guys who weren't professional level but liked jazz." These included writers Warren Miller and Paul Brodeur and even jazz critic Whitney Balliett (on drums). "They had a little band that would get together before I came to *The New Yorker*. Warren was a good trumpet player; I don't know if he still plays. Paul wasn't a very good clarinet player. A reporter named Wally [Wallace] White played piano. So there was a little crossover there. And William Shawn used to play piano and was very knowledgeable about jazz. He played in some little honky-tonk somewhere." As does Lee Lorenz, to this day.

2

Sex, Death, and Frogs' Legs: Sam Gross

"I GOT A JOB!"

AYBE IT'S A little too obvious to suggest that Sam Gross is one of the more aptly named cartoonists of our time. But why not? As with other *New Yorker* artists of his generation—including Gahan Wilson, Leo Cullum, and Lee Lorenz—Gross's career began in the pages of *Argosy, Rogue, Gent,* and other "stag mags" that flourished during the fifties and early sixties. Gross's most outlandish and bawdy material never appeared in *The New Yorker,* of course, and his work shares the traditions of aggressively outlandish men's magazine cartoonist Virgil Partch (or VIP, according to his signature) and Charles Addams.

Since his first *New Yorker* appearance in 1959, Gross has acquired a reputation among his peers as a cartooning purist who strives to be as funny as possible through image alone. As outrageous as he can be, much of his best-known work is downright cute and full of heart: A cat deposits a piece of garbage into a can marked KITTY LIT-TER; a long dachshund chases a stretch limousine down the street; or a mouse motors a rodent-sized car out of a maze as a surprised researcher looks on. But Gross takes just as much delight in offending with the type of drawings included in his subversive 1977 collection *I Am Blind and My Dog Is Dead*. Gross's edge slices deep into delicate sensibilities. His world is populated in large part by the handicapped, the homeless, and the slightly horrific. "Oh, the humanity," he seems to moan before moving on to the next everyday atrocity.

Gross's most famous image depicts a legless frog on wheels emerging from a restaurant's kitchen while wearing an expression of dismay. TRY OUR FROGS' LEGS, reads a sign beside the doorway. Gross sold the original version of this drawing on eBay for $20,000 in 2010, a solid payday for a former accountant who maintains close watch on

every image he creates and every dollar he earns. "I figured I would tie the auction in with the *National Lampoon* book that was coming out," he says, referring to comedy writer Rick Meyerowitz's *Drunk Stoned Brilliant Dead: The Writers and Artists Who Made the "National Lampoon" Insanely Great.* "I put a twenty-thousand-dollar floor on it and some people said that was too much. I said, 'Look, I can always go down but you can't go up.' I also said, 'If somebody doesn't make the floor, it's OK, I'm not gonna miss a meal.'" The drawing sold in the auction's last few seconds.

Thin and bearded, with a serious, perhaps professorial face that belies his comedic talent, Gross works out of an Upper East Side building next door to a comics store he has never visited. His doorbell displays an old family name because he doesn't want to be hassled by anyone who might have been offended by *We Have Ways of Making You Laugh: 120 Funny Swastika Cartoons,* a book he published in 2008. A relentless storyteller with a steel-trap mind, Gross works with shades drawn in what used to be a small one-bedroom apartment. A single light shines over his drawing table in the flat's former living room, and a comprehensive archive of virtually everything he has ever drawn fills multiple bookshelves. "I number and date all my drawings," he explains.

Like countless other immigrants whose names were altered, Sam's father, Mordecai Putkovic, was transformed into Max Gross upon his arrival at Ellis Island from Lithuania in 1902. Sam's mother, Sophie Goldberg, came to the United States in 1905. Max and Sophie married in 1930, and Samuel Harry Gross was born in the Bronx on August 7, 1933. "I'm named after two dead uncles, Sam and Harry," Gross says. "They were both in the diamond business and both of them died young." Max Gross grew up to become a certified public accountant, "which is why I keep fairly good track of things," says Sam.

"It's not perfect," he continues, concerning his accounting tendencies, "because if it was I wouldn't get any other work done. But I am keeping fairly good track of 27,592 drawings at the moment." Gross goes into a panic when he loses something in the mail or a client misplaces his work. He therefore releases only photocopies into the world and explains why: "Many years ago this cartoonist, Jimmy Frankfort, was sitting very despondently at the *Saturday Evening Post*. 'What's the matter?' I asked. He said, 'They lost twenty-seven of my drawings here.' I says, 'Well, geez, you have a record of it?' 'No, I don't have a record of it.' He lost twenty-seven drawings, just gone. And it made an indelible impression upon me. Things get lost; and a lot of things that get lost don't get found."

The Gross family lived on Mosholu Parkway in the Bronx, where Sam recalls drawing on his desk with crayon and ink in first grade. "Mrs. Levy, my teacher, sent me home with a note. My mother had to come to school with Kirkman soap and we had to scour the desk together." Eight years later, Sam began walking to DeWitt Clinton High School, an all-boys institution at the time, and published his first cartoons in its student newspaper, the *Clinton News*.

He also began submitting work to his favorite magazine, the *Saturday Evening Post*, which he relished for the copious cartoons in its back pages. To this day, Gross says he still looks at magazines from back to front—"except for *The New Yorker*." The *Post* paid $75 per cartoon at the time, so one day the teenager sent in ten of his best. That night, he lay in his bed in a cold sweat, fantasizing about his imminent $750 windfall. All were returned, a defeat the young artist never forgot.

His parents hoped he would become an accountant like his father, so Gross began studying business at the City College of New York. "I was supposed to be an accounting major. Then I was an advertising major. And then I basically took a lot of art and history courses because I just wanted to get the hell out of there." His cartoons began to appear in the college's student paper, the *Kicker*. He made his first professional sale to the *Saturday Review* in 1953 with a cartoon that nicely captured his ambivalence about college. It showed a scholarly looking guy being interrogated by the police. "It all began when my Phi Beta Kappa key fit into the bank vault," reads its caption.

After graduating from City College in 1954, Gross was drafted into the army and sent to Germany. A few months after his arrival, he was contacted by International Media Company (IMC), which published the *Overseas Weekly*. "We called it the 'Oversex Weekly,'" he says. Founded in 1950 by Marion Rospach, *Overseas Weekly* was read widely by enlisted men and became an increasingly influential, if controversial, publication. During the Vietnam War, Secretary of Defense Robert S. McNamara would deem the magazine "personally repulsive"—by which time the tabloid's muckraking reportage had led to the dismissal of more than three hundred military officers for various offenses. Having noticed Gross's weekly cartoon in the headquarters area command post newsletter, IMC offered to publish a book of his military cartoons. Titled *Cartoons for the GI*, his 1955 collection sold very well, and Gross began receiving monthly checks from IMC on top of his military pay. Although he was only a private first class, Gross was soon earning more than a major, "which pissed off my company commander."

Back in the States, Gross felt adrift and, he admits, a little "screwed up in the head." His reentry into civilian life didn't go smoothly. His family pressed him to find a job, preferably in accounting, and Gross succumbed to the pressure but lasted just six months at the first firm that hired him. Again unemployed, he helped out his father during tax season, which, it turned out, gave him the time and flexibility he needed to continue cartooning. Living at home, he was able to save enough money to marry his girlfriend, Isabelle Steiner, who worked for the New York State Department of Labor. Isabelle recognized Sam's artistic talent and encouraged him to make a go of it. "Isabelle said, 'You gotta give it a shot, a real serious shot,'" Gross recalls.

The newlyweds saved up enough money to survive for a year. Banking on his uncomplicated style's ability to cross borders, they decided to move to Europe, where Sam had made his first publishing connections. The couple moved to Darmstadt, Germany, to be near International Media, and bought a car so Sam could shop his work in Paris. Isabelle spoke passable French, and the couple would go from magazine to magazine, selling filler cartoons to *Pariscope*, France's version of *TV Guide*, and other outlets. Another small publisher, "a little man in a gray suit," was located across the street from

Élysée Palace. His company's two magazines, *Le Rire* (Laughter) and *Fou Rire* (Giggles), were modeled on stateside publications like *Army Laughs* and *Broadway Laughs*—cheesecake, racism, and all. Gross was paid twenty francs per cartoon, the equivalent of about five dollars, and the publisher would buy ten or fifteen of them at a time. With a hotel running him about four dollars a night, the artist was satisfied.

Gross acquired much of his professional confidence in Europe. "I learned I could get up in the morning and draw," he says. "I also found out that I could go to your office and if you looked at my stuff and gave it all back to me, I wouldn't be devastated." His resistance to rejection has served him well over the decades. "You'd be surprised how many people at *The New Yorker* even now won't go in to see Bob Mankoff. They'll just leave stuff in the pile outside his office. So although I was far from being wildly successful, I could function."

After a little more than a year in Europe, the Grosses returned to the United States in 1958. Sam began to submit his work to domestic publications while flying abroad occasionally to reconnect with clients in Germany and France. He continued to help out his father during tax season but was beginning to accrue steady work as an artist. Among Sam's first regular outlets was the Brooklyn greeting card company Charm Craft, which paid him $35 per idea. "I made $985 and change my first year back," he says. "As the old gag goes: Who gave you the change? Everybody!"

Once back in the States, Gross hit the streets with vigor and possibly inflated expectations. He began sending his cartoons to *Dude, Gent, Man's Action,* "that type of magazine." Heavy on sexual fantasias and bloody, violent accounts, the stag magazines touted features like "Trapped in a Dervish Harem" and "Crawling Death of Bad Luck Island." They sold by the millions both in the States and to overseas men in uniform. Collector Bill Devine has estimated that more than 130 men's adventure publications were released—from *Brigade* and *Cavalcade* to *Rage* and *Real.* As Johnny came marching home again, the publishing industry catered to the male libido zealously. Men who considered themselves more lovers than fighters were cultivated by *Playboy,* which came along in 1953 to steal the audience of would-be sophisticates that *Esquire* had once dominated. In 1957, a reporter for *Time* magazine counted more than forty men's adventure and *Playboy*-inspired titles on a New York newsstand, noting of the latter that "the average playkid [*Playboy* knockoff] reads less like pornography than a gay-dog college magazine put out while the dean was napping." The cartoon sections of these magazines and others like them provided ample outlets for many cartoonists of all abilities.

Gross recollects precisely the going rates for cartoons during the late fifties and early sixties. "Just to show you how stupid or naive one can be when they start out in this business," he says, *"Writer's & Artist's Yearbook* and *Writer's Digest* listed the rate for cartoons as $10 to $300 each. Somebody sent me to *Rascal* when I came back from Europe, so I figure that anyone is going to recognize my sterling, fantastic talent and say, 'Give this boy $300!' And lo and behold, when the check came in, it was for $10. I soon realized the range was pure hogwash. I asked the editor of *Rascal,* 'Does anyone ever get more than $10?' He said, 'Yeah, we pay Bill Ward $12.50 because he does cross-hatching.'"

Some couples have little to do with each other's career, and the Grosses are among them. "She doesn't help me at all," Sam says of Isabelle. "God, if she helped me we wouldn't be married." Isabelle has never even extended a career suggestion—with one exception. Sam had been unceremoniously dismissed from *Esquire* in the late fifties by Jerome Beatty Jr., its cartoon editor. Because it was such a lucrative market, Isabelle encouraged her husband to give it another go, so Sam eventually returned to Beatty's office. "He looks at the stuff and says, 'Hey, this is really good. I'm buying these two.' I said, 'Great. I got a story to tell you, though. Eleven months ago you threw me out of here.' He says, 'I did?' I says, 'Yeah, you did.' He says, 'Well, eleven months ago you were lousy!'" Adds Sam: "That's the only time she stuck her nose in."

No matter wherever else Gross sent his work, it always went to *The New Yorker* first. He describes one of the two spot illustrations from his first sale as "a lady waiting at a bus stop, and there's a kid running after a little wind-up toy." The other he can't quite recall—"Believe me, there are things you do that you prefer to forget"—although he does remember receiving $125 for the pair of drawings. Gross's long-term break into the magazine would not come until much later. Beginning in 1968, his cartoons appeared sporadically, twice a year or so. A decade later, during Robert Gottlieb's tenure as editor in chief, art editor Lee Lorenz began buying more of Gross's work.

Who gets paid how much at *The New Yorker* has always been one of the institution's great mysteries, particularly during William Shawn's editorship. Gross's professional pride extends from how long he's been drawing for the magazine to the amount he's been paid for doing so. When he began appearing on a semiregular basis, it was at a favorable rate he believes was higher than the magazine's contract rate at the time. "The contract rate started below my special rate and went up incrementally, for each five you sold, until they would be way ahead of my rate," he says. "Then it would go back down again at the beginning of the year. There was also a signature fee, a quantity bonus, and a pension. None of this do they have now."

Like other *New Yorker* contributors during the sixties, Gross also sold the magazine gags that were illustrated by other artists. He found himself providing ideas for Charles Addams, the artist Gross claims exerted the greatest influence on his own work and taught him how "to create a mood and get involved" with the characters. "I did a Puss in Boots gag some years ago," he says. "The cat is wearing these high leather boots with stiletto heels and has a whip. A guy is looking at the cat and saying something like 'This is not the Puss in Boots I knew as a child.' I could tell there was something wrong with my sketch, though, and it finally dawned on me that the guy I drew had never read a book in his life; he looked like he drove a truck or something. I had to draw somebody bookish to make it work."

Cartooning is a disposable medium and only a small percentage of drawings maintains an afterlife—although *The New Yorker*'s Cartoon Bank retail outlet and the Internet are changing that. Despite passing on in 1988, Addams continues to work full steam ahead—at least as far as his Addams Family creations are concerned. In addition to two popular television series (1964–66 and its 1998–99 remake) and two animated TV series, there have also been Addams Family movies and a Broadway musical, video games and a pinball machine, a recipe book, calendars, and coffee cups. That's a long marketing trail for a clan depicted in only 139 cartoons, about half of which appeared originally in *The New Yorker*, and whose originals now sell for what even Addams himself might consider frightening amounts.

During a visit to the Cartoon Bank office, Gross learned that an Addams drawing had been sold to a collector for $10,000. When he saw the drawing—a group of shrunken heads, one of which has a smiley face—he couldn't help but notice that Addams had created it from an idea Gross had sold to the magazine for $200 sometime in the sixties. That's when Gross decided to put his frogs' legs drawing up for auction.

Gross was no hippie during the sixties. "I was learning my trade," he says of his work during that decade, "doing some wild stuff." Yet Gross never felt like part of the counterculture; he never joined a commune or took LSD. "No, no, no," he says emphatically. "Why would I do that?" (His sister, on the other hand, was a Buddhist and followed an unnamed Russian mystic for a spell.) Neither was he enthralled by

"THIS IS SHIT, WE'RE GOING TO PUBLISH IT."

Published originally in National Lampoon

the work of R. Crumb or any of the other underground experimentalists associated with *Zap Comix* on the West Coast or New York's *East Village Other.*

National Lampoon, which debuted in April 1970, turned out to be a perfect outlet for his transgressive sensibility. Gross had been working for the counterculture magazine *Cheetah* and the *Diners Club Magazine,* which were published by former Diners Club executives Leonard Mogel and Matty Simmons's company, Twenty-First Century Communications. *Cheetah* failed, but the partners went on to found *National Lampoon,* whose influence and comedic worldview eventually extended to institutions such as *Saturday Night Live, The Simpsons,* and some horrible Chevy Chase movies. Gross's frogs' legs cartoon appeared in the magazine's December 1970 issue, and he became a frequent contributor.

In *Drunk Stoned Brilliant Dead,* Rick Meyerowitz described Gross's amphibious image as the magazine's "ur-cartoon." It embodied the *Lampoon* sensibility perfectly, and the magazine slapped Gross's image onto posters, T-shirts, blow-in subscriptions cards, renewal notices, and elsewhere. Gross, however, had drawn it with no expectations.

"I had no idea what I was doing," he says. "Not only did I not know what I was doing, I didn't spend any time trying to figure out what I was doing. Because you can't. When you sell reprints or the original art, you're not really selling the art; you're selling the button or whatever it is you pressed. So I pressed a button with the frogs' legs cartoon, although I really have no idea what that button is. I do know one thing, though," he adds with a laugh. "Nobody draws a better frog than me."

Gross is convinced that sometimes "you get an idea and it glows." This happened to him in 2008 with a cartoon that, coincidentally or not, echoes his earlier masterpiece. The scene is a kitchen in a French restaurant. A cook reaches into a bin full of frogs as a big pot boils in the background. "We will always have Paris," says one frog to the rest, quoting *Casablanca*. (A copy editor attempted to change his caption to the more colloquial, though less accurate, "We'll always have Paris.") Gross submitted the cartoon to *The New Yorker*, where it was held for a while until Bob Mankoff sent it back to him.

"I have it on my board for two weeks," Gross recalls. "What the hell am I gonna do with this? *Gourmet* isn't buying cartoons anymore, and the *Lampoon* is gone. Finally, I brought it back to Bob and said, 'I'm gonna give you and Remnick another chance on this thing.' I got to hand it to him; he took it and now it's pumping money—but nothing like some of the others."

At the *Lampoon*, Gross was part of a cartooning stable that included his good friend Charles Rodrigues, Ron Barrett, Arnold Roth, Ed Subitzky, and Gahan Wilson. Gross was encouraged to be his most extreme, provocative self, and he delivered. He tells the story of another politically incorrect highlight of his *Lampoon* years: "I was heading up to the *Lampoon* one day, and there was a black guy holding a sign that said 'Blind since birth.' I stopped to look at him for a couple of minutes and thought, 'He's blind from birth. Does he have any concept that he's black?' Like every artist, I have an obsession about my eyes. So I mulled this over for a day or two and came up with this gag about a guy on the street with a sign that said 'Blind, and I think I may be black.' When I came in to the next *Lampoon* editorial meeting, I got my only standing ovation for it."

The handicapped figure prominently in Gross's cartoon vocabulary. One of his first big sales after he returned from Europe was a spread of drawings called "Humor of the Handicapped" for Paul Krassner's *Realist,* an obvious *Lampoon* precursor. The paper "got a lot of letters both ways," according to Gross, "but handicapped people loved it."

When it comes to taste, good or bad, *New Yorker* colleague Ed Koren feels Gross "is right at the borderline," adding, "I can't draw that. I can't make fun of people who are in distress, who just hit the bottom of life's goodies. I like to go for the other end, the over-enfranchised and overindulged. It's much more fun. But he's so brash about it; his drawings are brash, like he is. And I enjoy them."

"The thing about transgressive cartoons is that they cut to the core," says Ivan Brunetti, a Columbia College Chicago comics scholar and an outrageous cartoonist in his own right. "You can try to rationalize them later, or pretend it wasn't as funny as it was, but they get at something kind of deep and true. And sometimes you *should* be ashamed of yourself for laughing."

Although he never identified himself as strongly with the magazine as others did, shameless Gross became *National Lampoon's* cartoon editor in 1985. "I was never a part of any scene except *my* scene," he says, "which is one reason I survived." In 1989, actor Tim Matheson and producer Dan Grodnik bought the *National Lampoon* in hopes of resuscitating the flagging publication. When their newly chosen executive editor, Billy Kimball, took over, he told Gross to inform his artists that they would need to provide pencil sketches prior to receiving formal assignments. According to former executive editor Larry "Ratso" Sloman, Gross replied, "Pencils! Cartoonists don't do no stinkin' pencils. [Charles] Rodrigues will tell you to go fuck yourself rather than show you a pencil. Oh, and by the way, you *can* go fuck yourself." This exchange marked the end of Gross's stint as the magazine's cartoon editor, but he continued to sell cartoons to the *Lampoon* until its final issue in 1998.

A good cartoon editor, in Gross's opinion, is simply "somebody who can see—and he doesn't necessarily have to have a great sense of humor." He mentions a cartoon Rodrigues once did depicting *The*

Protocols of the Elders of Zion as a paperback book. "I said, 'No, that's conceivable; let's go all the way and make it a pop-up book.'" Combining talent with trust, *Lampoon* cartoonists took advantage of an editorial freedom one would be hard-pressed to find in any contemporary publication. Once the artist M. K. Brown called Gross to say she'd had a rough time at the dentist. "I'm sorry to hear that," he commiserated. "But I can get three to five pages out of it," she added. Gross went to Sloman and said, "Larry, I got M. K. on the phone. She was at the dentist and can do three to five pages. But we got to nail it down so you need to decide how many right now." Sloman gave her five.

A consummate professional, Gross doesn't miss deadlines. But he's no cartooning speedball, either. "Sometimes I have to give a drawing a lot of thought after drawing it," he says. "I may look at it for two weeks if I'm trying to sell it to *The New Yorker*—or three weeks if it's really bothering me."

When it comes to inspiration, Gross's muse knows precisely when and where to find him. Every Wednesday, he says, "I just clear everything, sit down, and trip. I don't draw for markets like *The New Yorker* or anyone else at all. I just trip. I'm doing stuff as if *National Lampoon* still existed." Gross will come up with sixteen or seventeen drawings during a typical day of artistic brainstorming. As he works, he numbers and dates each of his drawings, which he photocopies onto forty-

"I ORDER MY ROCKS ON-LINE."

four-pound paper stock. He then punches three holes into each sheet and puts them into black loose-leaf books shelved about his office. "I think I got 27,592 cartoons now," he told me.

When money comes in, Gross documents its receipt in an index correlated to his drawings. He knows "pretty much to the nearest dollar" what each drawing has earned and for now is rather pleased with the aftermarket his *New Yorker* work earns through the Cartoon Bank. Where he once pursued advertising work for which he might have earned $3,000 for a drawing, similar assignments currently only pay about half as much, without the possibility for reprints or royalties. He'd rather take a chance on editorial work, where "it's not uncommon for me to make six or seven thousand dollars on a drawing."

Some of his books, mostly those featuring cats, have sold well; others have not. "I draw a good cat," Gross admits. While visiting a Metropolitan Museum of Art exhibit of Leonardo da Vinci drawings with cartoonists Nick Downes, Peter "P. S." Mueller, and Phillipe Cohen, Gross called his friends over to look at a collection of cat sketches. "Look at that," he said to his friends. "I draw a cat better than he does." Not all animals are created equally funny in Gross's universe. "I don't think horses are funny at all," he says. "Possums are funny. Anteaters are funny. Cats, dogs, and chickens are funny. Guys in chicken outfits, they're funny. If a guy's in a chicken outfit handing out something, I always take it. I figure anyone reduced to being in a chicken outfit deserves my patronage."

While many good cartoonists have also been excellent artists, Leonardo-level drawing skills are not required. Style, on the other hand, is the thing that lets a cartoonist get away with dodgy lines. One good thing about cartoons, according to Gross, is that "if you can't draw something, you draw it your way." When Ed Koren draws a horse, it's not just any horse: "It's *his* horse, and it's a funny, funny horse." For Gross, "a horse is something I have an awful time with. It's usually the legs. Sometimes I'll put the horse in some tall grass—the taller the better." So while Leonardo wins when it comes to horses, Gross still draws better cats.

The most frequently extended advice found on any shelf's worth of writers' guides is "know your market." But Gross has never drawn with *The New Yorker, National Lampoon,* or any other specific outlet in mind. "My work hasn't changed because of *The New Yorker,*" he explains. "I don't do things for *The New Yorker;* I do things for me." Working independently of both "scenes" and markets has been a point of pride for Gross. It's also his primary survival strategy, a way to avoid the political and economic hazards of being tied to any particular publication or editor. "I operate on the premise that Bob Mankoff can be there today and gone tomorrow, and the same with David Remnick. Somebody else could come along with a totally different outlook and I will either fit in or not. If I've geared my work toward the people who were there before, I'm basically embedded with them and I'm screwed. But I am my own person. You either take me or leave me, simple as that."

Equally simple is Gross's philosophy of cartooning, which can be distilled to a single sentence: "The highest form of cartooning has no caption." If the evolution of the single-panel gag cartoon can be defined as the gradual elimination of explanatory wordage, Gross's cartooning credo represents the art's democratic magic, an aura manifested most purely, one could argue, in the imagery of Saul Steinberg (who also drew fabulous felines). Lines contain myriad meanings in Steinberg's work. Pictures transform themselves into words, and vice versa. Gross's cartoons, however, are in fact nearly always captioned yet seem especially poignant when they are not. In one of his best "pantomimes," as silent cartoons are known, a man and a pig look down at the ground, where the end of the poor porker's nose rests like a dropped button.

Color is something else Gross doesn't think a cartoon needs. Although artists such as Gahan Wilson have made color work to their advantage to enhance a cartoon's emotional content, Gross eschews it in favor of linear simplicity. He argues that Billy Wilder shot *Some Like It Hot* in black and white in 1958, when color was becoming increasingly prominent in movies. Gross worked in color during his greeting-card days but maintains that, like most cartoonists, he has no particular expertise in its employment.

The New Yorker began experimenting with color cartoons during Tina Brown's editorship. When Mankoff asked Gross to add color to a cartoon, Gross fought back: "Do you want this in color?" Gross asked. Mankoff replied no. "Does Remnick want this in color?" No again. "Then who wants this in color?" Mankoff replied that someone in the makeup department, which coordinates editorial and advertising needs, had requested it. "You mean an *untershtupper* wants it in color?" shot back Gross. Arguing that color would add nothing to his drawing, Gross didn't budge. "Just tell 'em I'm lousy in color," he said.

For three semesters during the nineties, Gross taught cartooning at the Pratt Institute's Manhattan Center. His goal was to break images down to their simplest components, "the way a cartoonist would think." A few dozen students attended his first class, he recalls, but not all stuck around. "Oh, my God, I knew how to get rid of a lot of them! 'Look,' I said to them, 'this is a country of 250 million people and every one of you in this class can probably draw better than me.' Which made them feel very good." Gross explained that his goal as teacher was to move their talent "from their wrist up to their brain." The next week only sixteen people showed up, and Gross was asked to see the director, who asked him not to undersell his expertise to his students.

"These sixteen people knew nothing about cartooning, of course," Gross says. "They drew beautifully, but millions of people can draw and paint beautifully. I was trying to give them a mental advantage I have. I would have them come in with gag ideas, but I had to break the bad news to them gently. 'You're not going to graduate from here and get a job drawing,' I said. 'There are no drawing jobs anymore. But you'll have an advantage over all the other freelancers if you can sell cartoons while waiting for somebody at [advertising agency] J. Walter Thompson to decide whether to give you an assignment or not."

If you wanted to cartoon like Gross, you could start by investing in his basic equipment: Koh-I-Noor Rapidograph pens, in sizes 1 and 2.5, and some "cheap-shit" paper like the twenty-four-pound stock scratch he uses for sketching ideas and roughs. For finishes, he switches to two-ply vellum. And that's it. The simplicity of the cartooning medium is part of its beauty. Gross has never felt inclined to explore painting or any other art form, although he respects the few cartoonists who did, including his old friend Richard Oldden. "I shared a studio with Dick," Gross recalls, "a penthouse on Seventy-Eighth Street. This guy didn't own an eraser, Wite-Out, or even a pencil. He had trained himself to start on the upper left-hand corner, finish on the lower right-hand corner, and just sign his name. I thought everybody was like this."

Oldden, who died in 1995, did a handful of cartoons for *The New Yorker*. Their quality harks back to the era of Peter Arno and Helen E. Hokinson. "It was nice of you to come back for a visit after your enlightenment," a Buddhist priest says to a cigar-smoking man in sunglasses behind the wheel of a flashy sports car in one Oldden panel. A beautifully shaded temple and tree in the background offer a stark contrast to the foreground figures, especially the garishly dressed driver. "Most cartoonists don't go easily from fine art to cartooning, and vice versa," says Gross. "Many years ago at the Whitney, I saw an Edward Hopper exhibit that included a bunch of 1918 cartoons. Oh, God, were they awful! Not funny at all."

Another cartoonist Gross considers underappreciated is Joseph Mirachi, who died at age seventy-one in 1991 after drawing 574 *New Yorker* cartoons about therapeutic drinking establishments, surprising road signs, and acrimonious couples. "He did some really beautiful drawings of New Jersey bars and car-repair places out in the sticks," Gross says. In one of Mirachi's energetically shaded panels, a worn-out husband says to his wife, "For thirty years we've been known as a fun couple. Do you mind if we ease off in the homestretch?"

As the number of magazines that publish cartoons diminishes, it's easy for artists to feel like walking, talking, and drawing anachronisms. "I went into this magazine store in the Greenwich Village of San Diego," Gross says, referring to the city's Hillcrest neighborhood, "and *The New Yorker* was the only thing they had that ran cartoons." And even when magazines run cartoons, it's increasingly rare to see them as part of a regular editorial mixture. Indeed, as far as most

Previously unpublished rough

magazines are concerned, cartoonists lie at the bottom of the editorial food chain.

"When I was president of the Cartoonists Guild," Gross recalls, "I was negotiating a raise at *Cosmopolitan,* where I think they were paying $100 or $150 for a cartoon. The art director said, 'Y'know, cartoons aren't important here. We use 'em as fillers—either them or Red Cross ads. If we end up with a space at the end of an article, we'll put in a cartoon or sometimes a poem. But I'd rather put in a cartoon because it's a pain in the ass to set poetry type.' So I had this fantasy of Emily Dickinson submitting poems to *Cosmopolitan.* She's up there in Amherst, up in the attic, coughing, and she gets this letter back: 'Dear Emily: We've decided to use a cartoon instead of your poem because . . .'" He laughs at his fantasy before continuing. "So I'm busting my chops to match this excellent piece of art with a terrific idea, and this editor's like, 'It's a pain in the ass to set type so we're going to run your cartoon.' It makes you feel really great."

Gross isn't crazy about awards or competitions, either, and refuses to contribute drawings to *The New Yorker*'s popular Caption Contest. "I don't believe in it," says Gross, who believes it insults cartoonists. In 1980, at San Diego's Comic-Con International (the world's largest ongoing comics convention), Gross received the event's Inkpot

Award for his *National Lampoon* work. Gross describes the Inkpot as "a wooden plaque with this metal thing sticking out of it like a little phallus." He brought it home to the Ninety-Second Street penthouse studio he was working in at the time, pounded a nail into the wall, and hung the plaque from it.

"About three or four weeks later," he says, "I hear a clunk! When I go look, the plaque is still on the wall but the metal thing has fallen down. So I put the metal thing back on the board. A day or two later, I hear another clunk! It goes down again. I pick it up and put it back on again. I did this maybe another two or three times. Finally, one day I'm sitting there, it goes clunk, and I take the thing and put it in the garbage. That's my award."

The walls of Gross's current studio remain bare.

3

The Exurban Everymom: Roz Chast

WHERE MOST OF the cartoonists profiled in this book had at least one educator for a parent, Roz Chast had a pair of them: Her father, George Chast, was a French and Spanish teacher at Lafayette High School in Brooklyn, while her mother, Elizabeth, was an assistant principal at various public grade schools in the borough. Her parents' professional interests extended to family life in their Midwood neighborhood. This made Roz, their only child, the beneficiary, willing or not, of her parents' pedagogical expertise. She recalls being tested by them—often—while attending grade school, simply because "they thought it was fun." And the fledgling artist enjoyed sharing the experience with her classmates.

"I would make up math tests for my fellow students on a little Rexograph copying machine we had at home that used purple ink, and give them out to kids in class for fun," Chast recalls with some distress as we chat in her cozy Connecticut home. "They must have thought I was a fucking wacko." Her father would quiz her in French, just to set her on the right path. "Sometimes my friend Gail would say, 'I don't like it! It's too educational,' about stuff I wanted us to do. But everything in my life was educational!"

Once she got to Midwood High School, however, Roz only wanted to draw. She was a diligent student even if school didn't particularly engage her. She describes herself as being "shy, hostile, and paranoid" during that period, i.e., a teenager. Her real rebellion would come later, in the pages of *The New Yorker*, when even doubters and skeptics came to recognize her insurgent talent. She realized early on that the magazine's cartoons were no less powerful than its writing. "I used to think of the cartoons as a magazine within a magazine. First you go through and read all the cartoons, and then you go back and read the articles. It's like I'm reading *The New Yorker Magazine of Cartoons* first."

In a two-page color spread titled "Charles Addams," Chast depicts a primal scene from her childhood. Every summer, her parents, along with other Brooklyn schoolteachers, would spend time near Cornell University, where they would take classes, attend lectures, and acquire what her mother called "a certain degree of intellectualism." Left to fend for herself, Chast discovered a campus library that lacked a children's section but contained numerous cartoon collections by Peter Arno, Helen Hokinson, George Price, Otto Soglow, and other *New Yorker* artists. What really blew Chast's pliant mind, though, were *Monster Rally, Black Maria, Homebodies, Nightcrawlers, Drawn and Quartered,* and other cartoon collections by Charles Addams. In her tribute, she quotes Wolcott Gibbs's introduction to *Addams and Evil,* in which he argues that Addams's work "is essentially a denial of all spiritual and physical evolution in the human race." Addams's work, though, "was the first grown-up humor I really loved," Chast says. "It was dark, and it made fun of stuff you weren't supposed to make fun of. I loved 'sick' jokes when I was a kid." A lightbulb may come on as you gaze upon Chast's depictions of her family at Cornell amid the company of a befuddled academic, a goateed "compulsive punster" of a math teacher, and other aspiring Brooklyn intellectuals.

Addams's sly nihilism informs many of Chast's own characters, camouflaged (or not) by her anxiety-sharpened niceness.

Roz Chast was the first truly subversive *New Yorker* cartoonist. Her 1978 arrival gave the magazine its first real taste of punk sensibility, although she herself was anything but. Young, female, and a less orthodox draftsperson compared with the magazine's older artists, Chast drew a scratchy line more akin to Lynda Barry, Gary Panter, and other mainstays of the era's alternative press. She was part of a new generation of cartoonists inspired by sixties underground comics/comix.

Chast became one of *The New Yorker*'s more versatile artists, at least in terms of formal variation, as well as one of its finer writers. She draws single-panel cartoons, multipage nonfiction narratives, lists, typologies, archaeologies, fake publications, and real children's books. Her work blends urban and suburban sensibilities, with the former point of view usually subtly undermining the latter. Her viewpoint reflects both the Brooklyn Jewish community in which she was raised as well as that of upwardly mobile liberal cosmopolitans who, like Chast, fled to the suburbs (Ridgefield, Connecticut, in her case) during the nineties to nest with their offspring.

Old-fashioned existential anxiety simmers at the core of Chast's art. It's evident in the single-panel "A Note on the Author," in which a nine-year-old Chast is depicted reading *The Big Book of Horrible Rare Diseases* and *Lockjaw Monthly,* among others, in bed. It's very much there in "Millie's Gear Slips," a nine-panel strip in which a woman descends into mild dread over "losing" the four minutes it took her to go back in the house and find a sweater at the beginning of a car trip ("As they were driving, she thought, This is exactly the place I would have been four minutes and eleven seconds ago, but now it's slightly different, and I'll never see what I was *supposed* to see"). It's the anxiety of a man sitting in a chair and realizing that if he doesn't learn how to play golf by age forty-three, he never will. It's "The Party, After You Left," when the hosts break out the good champagne, Benicio Del Toro makes an appearance, and someone shares

a "very, very safe" yet "extremely fantastic" new drug. It's yet another balding man adrift in his oversized armchair contemplating "Birth, bed, bath, beer, bankruptcy, bunions, bifocals, balding, and beyond."

Whether it's the neighborhood of her childhood, the Manhattan of her young adulthood, the Park Slope, Brooklyn, of her young parenthood, or the Connecticut of her prime, Roz Chast's cartoons come out of a specific sense of place. "I have an odd little book Helen Hokinson did about going out to buy a mop," she says, while showing me shelves of *New Yorker* cartoonist collections. "I like that she has this whole world, and I feel like I can go into that world. It's not generic; it's very specific. I don't like cartoons that take place in Nowhereville. I like cartoons where I know where they're happening." One of the enduring pleasures of *New Yorker* cartoons is that they not only take place in New York, but readers can often identify the specific neighborhood in which they're set. "I can't even look at daily comic strips. And I hate sitcoms because they don't seem like real people to me, they're props that often say horrible things to each other, which I don't find funny. I have to feel like they're real people."

What she does find funny are cartoonists as diverse as William Steig and Saul Steinberg, her major influences alongside Addams. Her surprisingly serious introduction to *Cats, Dogs, Men, Women, Ninnies & Clowns: The Lost Art of William Steig* observes how even the darker tones of his later years capture a *"gleeful* darkness, the darkness children feel when they know their most trusted adult is going to tell them a spooky story." It's an effect one might compare to Chast's equally gleeful representation of all the world's anxieties. Other influences include bookish mandarin Edward Gorey, Jules Feiffer, the "kind of creepy" Mary Petty, and working-class autobiographer Harvey Pekar.

The autobiographical spectrum of Chast's work ranges from a sense of place grounded in her experience to stories taken directly from her life. Many street scenes evoke her childhood during the fifties and sixties, when her world was delimited by safe and unsafe blocks. "My father didn't drive but my mother did, and she was a nut. If I asked her, 'Mom, how come we shop on Eighteenth Avenue? Why don't we ever shop on Sixteenth Avenue?,' she'd go, 'You can shop on Sixteenth Avenue when you're grown up!' You'd get screamed at if you left our safe little area." Chast recounts her overbearing mother and fretful father's difficult sunset years in her 2014 memoir *Can't We Talk about Something More Pleasant?*

New Yorker cartoonists rarely indulged in autobiography. But Chast's love of the underground work of R. Crumb and Justin Green led her to put more of herself in her work. A semiregular cast of unnamed characters age at a rate more or less concurrent with her family. (She is married to humor writer Bill Franzen, with whom she has a son, Ian, and daughter, Nina.) It's not exactly Frank King's *Gasoline Alley* or Garry Trudeau's *Doonesbury*, whose characters have been born, matured, and sometimes died in real time over the decades. Chast traffics in stereotypes that satirize her version of domesticity.

The son—often depicted wearing a striped T-shirt, sporting a baseball cap, and exhibiting a chronic acne condition—is usually captured in a state of awkward confusion. His older sister barely tolerates her family with a permanent expression of acute embarrassment. A loving yet diminished father, very much of the James Thurber variety, watches his life pass by. And the concerned, anxious, eternally over-booked mother binds them together through food, guilt, and good intentions. The epitome of this scenario is probably the title cartoon of her collection *Theories of Everything,* in which her ur-family sits on a sofa, each person lost in his or her own thoughts. Father: "Every-thing's gone downhill since 1964." Mother: "Everything is *my fault.*" Sister: "Everything *is* your fault." And brother: "Everything would be perfect if I had a dirt bike."

Her real family comes off slightly better in autobiographical pieces such as "Dog Day Afternoon," in which an overexuberant canine specimen takes its toll on the family unit. "People think that story was an exaggeration," she says. "But it was actually toned down. It was worse. At one point the dog twisted a bone in her hip. We took her to the vet, who had to muzzle her because she was going so crazy. All these horrible things happened over a six-day period. I hardly even mentioned her breeders because I didn't want to get into trouble with them."

Born in Brooklyn in 1954, Rosalind Chast was always younger than her fellow students, particularly after skipping a year of middle school under the auspices of New York's SP ("special progress") program. "I don't know why my parents opted to have me do it in two years, since I was so young anyway," she says, speculating that "in their day it was considered sort of a plus to go through school as fast as you could. And maybe they just really wanted me out of the house. They were a lot older and might have had it with having a kid around."

The Kiwanis Club unwittingly provided Chast's first artistic af-firmation when she won its competition for best poster on the theme of "honor America." Entered as a prank, her submission consisted of "a bunch of people standing on a street with 'honor America' writ-ten above them. I don't think very many people entered." The award ceremony she attended with her "total out-there hippie" friend Claire took place at an Italian restaurant she suspects was a Mafia hangout.

She was "not a mature sixteen" when she entered Kirkland College, an all-girls school across the road from the all-boys Hamilton College. "I had a boyfriend, which was a very good thing because otherwise I probably would have left after one year instead of two. I just did not have the strength of character to stand up to my parents and say, 'I don't want to take any more academic classes. I just want to go to art school.'" Fortunately, the art department's new facilities were going underutilized simply because it wasn't an art school, and Chast took good advantage of them. She learned lithography, silk-screening, etching, developing, and printing.

After transferring to the highly competitive Rhode Island School of Design (RISD), Chast felt out of her league. It was the first time she'd been around so many capable young artists, and she was intimidated. "I didn't feel like I was in the middle of the pack; I felt like I was at the bottom. Everybody there was good, some were extraordinary, and some were extraordinary and knew it. They already knew who they were and how they wanted to dress. I didn't even know how to pick out my own clothes. And, yeah, maybe they were just as lost as I was, but I don't think so."

Neatness counted in graphic design, which Chast studied first at RISD. Her teacher was Malcolm Grear, a legendary designer known for his clean lines and minimalist aesthetic. "That didn't sound like fun to me," Chast says. "I like things to be more interesting to look at." She then switched to illustration, which "was kind of all right," and then to painting, "because I was living with painters and really wanted to be one." She continued to draw cartoons for her own amusement. She showed them to a single teacher, who asked her, "Are you really as bored and angry as all that?" She had no response.

Cartooning turned out to be Chast's main hurdle at RISD. "One of the more terrible things about cartooning is that you're trying to make people laugh, and that was very bad in art school during the mid-seventies," she says. With minimalism and performance art in ascendance, Chast found herself in a downward spiral of frustration and depression when her teachers' attention was not forthcoming. "The quintessential work of that time would be a video monitor with static on it being watched by another video monitor, which would

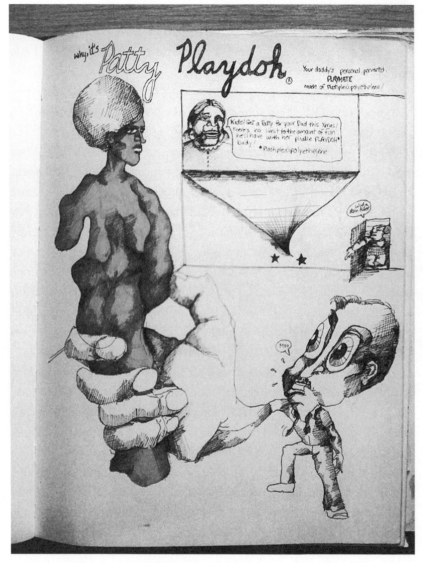

R. Crumb–influenced sketchbook page from early seventies

then go static," she says. "Doing stories or anything 'jokey' made me feel like I was speaking an entirely different language."

There were other cartoonists amid RISD's student body. But when Chast attempted to join them, the experience foreshadowed what would happen when she sold her first work to *The New Yorker*. "This is going to sound horribly bitter," she warns, "but some boys actually started a comics magazine at RISD called *Fred*. And when I submitted some stuff, they rejected me. I cried and cried. I cried like a little girl," she says with a laugh, "which I was! I felt very bad. I was heartbroken. But it makes me very happy now to think that while they may have become good artists, not one of those boys went on to become a cartoonist."

New York City has long been cartoonists' company town. After graduating from RISD in June 1977, Chast moved back to New York. "It's where the work is!" says Chast, quoting friend and colleague Sam Gross. ("I remember what he said about San Francisco, too: 'San Francisco is nice, but there's one job!'") Chast's romance with New York is reflected in a style that overlays a modern sense of humor on top of vintage cityscapes sometimes reminiscent of Ben Katchor's pointedly nostalgic comics. Chast took her portfolio from publication to publication, as one did before the advent of digital imagery, and continued to cartoon while marketing herself as an illustrator—until the day she decided to devote herself to professional cartooning.

Returning home on the subway, she noticed a copy of *Christopher Street*, a gay-oriented magazine that had been left on the seat opposite her. She picked it up and had "one of those weird moments" when her path became clear. After some hesitation regarding the magazine's contents (*What if people think I'm gay? What if it's porn?*), she discovered that "it's not porn at all. It's got short stories and articles and things like that. And cartoons! It looked like three different people were doing the cartoons." She called the magazine, and it turned out that all three artists were actually one guy drawing under different names. *Christopher Street*'s cartoonist was Rick Fiala, who also drew as "Lublin" and "Bertram Dusk." Chast began selling the magazine her own cartoons for ten dollars each, which was "crap pay" even for 1977. The *Village Voice* soon followed.

In April 1978, Chast was still living at home with her parents, "which was not good." She decided to submit her work to *The New Yorker* "even though I didn't think my stuff was right for them." She knew that drop-off day was Tuesday, but the protocol was unclear. "I didn't know how to do it. I had one of those brown envelopes with the rubber band. I left like sixty drawings in this thing. When I went back the next week to pick them up, there was a note inside that said, 'Please see me. —Lee.' At first I couldn't read it because it had this very loopy handwriting." She was buzzed into a small anteroom, where "a very intimidating woman" with red hair named Natasha sat guarding the gates. "She read the note and said, 'You can go in and see him.' It was a really scary feeling. I still didn't think I was going to sell a cartoon. I thought Lee [Lorenz] was going to give me some bullshit talk like 'This is very interesting work, little lady.' But they ended up buying a drawing. I was pretty shocked, but he said to come back every week with stuff."

Her first *New Yorker* cartoon, labeled "Little Things," was a surrealist miniature championing the "chent," "spak," "kellat," and other homely imaginary objects of everyday life. It was an apt introduction for an artist-alchemist who would specialize in transforming ontological absurdity and anxiety into comedy gold. She was paid $250 for the drawing—"real money, grown-up money"—an amount that just happened to be the rent for her first apartment. Chast's acceptance into *The New Yorker*, however, was not as triumphant as one might think. Not only was Chast a woman in what was at the time somewhat of a men's club, but she also had a distinctly different sensibility from the much older and more realistically inclined artists. "I was a lot younger, and I probably didn't want to be there. I wanted to be there, but for me it was just very . . . fraught." She was shy, but she was in.

"I love Roz," says her *New Yorker* colleague Ed Koren. "But I hated her at first, like everybody else; I hated those drawings." Koren is the first artist I've spoken to who admits his initial problems with Chast's art. "Like a lot of people, I thought she couldn't draw, couldn't think, and that she was too simplistic, not developed enough. What you would feel about somebody who was inept." According to Koren, Roz Chast "grew into someone with a complete world vision and a brilliant ability to make it palpable, tangible, and understandable to everybody—and to be funny about it! It's a question of our acculturating ourselves to her, instead of the other way around. It took a while to just understand what a rare talent she was. Ever since then, I've marveled at what she can do. How she can just take so many cultural moments and personal moments and blend them into this great confection of her own mind and imagination. I'm a big fan. She's probably the biggest draw at *The New Yorker* at this point."

Lorenz and William Shawn knew they were taking a chance with the young artist, who displayed less drafting skill than other relatively new cartoonists such as Jack Ziegler and Charles Barsotti. "Lee told me that when my cartoons first started running, one of the older cartoonists asked him if he owed my family money," Chast says. "And at my first *New Yorker* party, Charles Saxon came up to me and had things to say about my drawing style. He even asked me, 'Why do you draw the way you do?' And I said, 'Why do *you* draw the way you do?' Why do you talk the way you do? Why do you dress the way you do? Why is your handwriting the way it is? I don't know. I'm aware that a lot of people probably hate my stuff. But I hate a lot of people's work, too."

Cartoonist Lynda Barry, another fan, identifies deeply with Chast's cool welcome at the magazine. "When Roz started in *The New Yorker*, I noticed it immediately for a couple of reasons. One, because her drawing was so badass. I would imagine there were people who thought she couldn't draw. She's as good as Arno, Hokinson, or Addams, only they couldn't see it. I think it's about being a girl, about being female and having a whole different kind of line. I always wondered what people were talking about when they'd tell me I couldn't draw—or talk about my 'faux-naïf' style, because there's nothing 'faux' about it. And I love the people she drew: these bewildered, flummoxed, pudgy, potato-head people. She's always been inclusive, particularly of middle-aged women. She drew middle-aged women without it having to be: Look, a middle-aged woman! They were just characters."

Despite the criticism (or envy), it didn't take Chast long to get into the *New Yorker* groove. She began delivering her batch of drawings to Lorenz each week, and would wait outside his office until summoned inside after whoever had arrived earlier. "You would hand over your batch to Lee and he would flip through it right in front of you. Horrible! And you'd wonder, 'Is he smiling? Does he find that funny? Do all these cartoons suck? Why isn't he laughing? They suck. I know they suck. Worst batch ever!'" She pauses. "And I still feel that way." Chast dreads passing her sell-by date. "At some point they're just going to say, 'You know what? You're horrible. You're not funny anymore. Just go! This was a big mistake. Out!'" If the magazine had bought anything during the previous weekly art meeting, Lorenz would wordlessly hand it over with any notes, and her audience would conclude.

Amid other projects, Chast tends to concentrate on *New Yorker* cartoons on Mondays and Tuesdays, when she can clear her schedule and "lock myself up with my little ideas and just stay in here and work." She no longer needs to go into the office while current cartoon editor Bob Mankoff appraises her submissions. "I don't put myself through that nauseating experience of looking at someone's face while they go through your stuff. Ugh! It's just horrible! It gives me the cringes to even think about it. I find it disgusting and embarrassing for all concerned. And some of my stuff takes a little while to read. So I feel better that they should look at it in private when they have time, when I'm not sitting there." She faxes her roughs to the office Tuesday evening and works on books and other projects the rest of the week.

Chast used to submit up to a dozen ideas each week but now only sends in about half that number. "It went down when I had kids," she explains. Regarding her whiffs, she notes that "you can find me in the second volume of the Rejection Collection," cartoonist Matthew Diffee's compendia of the best cartoons *The New Yorker* has rejected for reasons of prurience, taste, or downright weirdness. Chast, like most *New Yorker* cartoonists, often resubmits her rejected drawings, sometimes after reworking them. "If I really like a cartoon, I'll just resubmit it and resubmit it until there are like six rejections on the back. At that point it's like forget it."

Rapidograph pens—along with mechanical pencils, brushes, and other pens—are Chast's main instrument. She has always used Bristol paper because of how well it accepts an ink wash. This reminds her of Sam Gross, who prefers inexpensive typing paper. "I remember him looking at me like I was nuts and saying, 'What are you, an heiress?'" Although she works mainly in black, white, and grays, she also uses watercolor and gouache. "I love watercolor because you can really build up the tones."

When accepted, her work is rarely edited. "I remember when I sold this cartoon of a mailbox in the middle of a midwestern landscape. The punch line was something like '1,297,000 West Seventy-Ninth Street.' But I never had a mailbox because I grew up in an apartment house, so I can't draw one. Lee said, 'What's that?' I said, 'That's the handle, to flop open the door.' He said, 'No,' and drew the flag on the rough and said, 'That's what you put up when you have mail in your mailbox.' But I still got it wrong because in the finished version the flag is very tiny, as if it's glued to the side of the box. Another time, I had a guy holding a cane and Lee said, 'It looks like he's holding a bunch of spaghetti.' No, I would not say my drafting skills are in the top ten percent of all cartoonists. But that's not what cartoons are about."

Chast's biggest issue concerns the size of her cartoons. "*The New Yorker* currently prints cartoons in two columns, but they used to occasionally go into the third column. So I've tried to fight the battle of having cartoons sized correctly rather than making them snap to a grid. It's not a battle I'm going to win, but I'm fighting it." Other artists voice the same complaint, and Chast's cartoons, which joyfully display a variety of styles and dimensions, make a better case for a return to the diverse sizes and shapes of the pre–Condé Nast *New Yorker* than most.

Charles Addams once defined a cartoon as "mauling the cliché." Chast also does violence to complacency, but her violence is psychological rather than *unheimlich* (such as Addams's famous ski tracks straddling a tree), creepy, or gory. The headlines in her version of an obituary page, for example, compare the ages of the recently deceased with the reader's; "Assisted Living" on the Upper West Side means giving in guiltily to your child's demands for money and a delivered

Previously unpublished rough

beverage; and the "Schmoozy Reaper" makes small talk before getting down to business. Chast's style of humor blends innocence and anxiety exquisitely. Indeed, she may actually, if sneakily, be the magazine's most aggressive cartooning voice.

"The most wonderful thing about *New Yorker* cartoonists is their different voices, which is what the magazine's known for. Think about the greats: George Booth, Charles Addams, Helen Hokinson, Mary Petty, Gahan Wilson, Sam Gross, Jack Ziegler, and Charles Saxon all have different comic and aesthetic voices. I could name dozens more. Maybe the way they're surrounded by all that type unifies *New Yorker* cartoonists in a funny way. *New Yorker* cartoons can be very timely but also not; yet somehow they reflect their time even if they're not addressing the week's events. Maybe it's because cartoonists can do what they want; they aren't told what to do by an editor who wants all of an issue's cartoons to be on a specific topic. *The New Yorker* has let me explore different formats, whether it's a page or a single panel, and that's very important to me. If I had to do a newspaper strip where it's boom, boom, punch line, I would kill myself. I'm amazed people can do that without feeling like they've just gone to sleep."

Artistic realism is secondary to Chast's genius for mining the big and little unspoken worries and status concerns shared unconsciously by cosmopolitans and suburbanites. And no other cartoonist exploits as many different formats to do so. She blames her constantly changing forms on ADD. Thus Chast creates greeting cards for "under-the-weather appliances," offers a recipe for "low-risk chicken" to "the nervous gourmet," and explores the "archaeology of a sink" from "today's dishes" all the way down to the "Precambrian dishes" awaiting discovery far below.

Imaginary magazines are a favorite medium for her malaise: *Middle Age* is "the magazine for you —yeah, *you!*"; *Bad Mom* reveals "presents you can make in five minutes or so from stuff around the house"; and her cover for the 1999 cartoon issue of *The New Yorker* delivered an entire newsstand's worth of fantasy periodicals, including *Rubber Band Enthusiast, Elderly Abductee, Loser, Winner,* and *Fussy Little Man.* From the "Admissions Test for the Danbury Institute of Philosophy" ("How many minutes a day do you spend thinking?") to the "Required Seventh Grade Reading List" (which includes *The Red Badge of Boredom*), Chast can reduce profound issues to a questionnaire, contract, form letter, quiz, pie chart, greeting card, internal memo, and the countless other ways we visualize information.

Her art is sometimes wordy, but it never wears you down or sends you looking for something easier on the eyes. "Her lettering doesn't make sense to the top of my mind," notes Lynda Barry, "but it's so satisfying to the back of my mind. Her lettering's a little unstable, thin, and she uses a mixture of lowercase and caps. It looks like the kind of writing you'd find on a grocery list." And it probably is exactly that, on certain days.

Chast fishes for ideas the old-fashioned way. "I jot things down on pieces of paper," she says, "and I have a little box of ideas. I'm not organized enough to have a notebook, so it has to be little pieces of paper, evidently. I pull them out when I sit down to do my weekly batch. Sometimes I do cartoons from those ideas, and sometimes they lead to other ideas. I get ideas from all kinds of places, like something my kid said, an advertisement, or a phrase I've heard. It really varies. It might be something someone did that really annoyed me but actually made me laugh after I thought about it."

The New Yorker intermittently puts artists on hiatus when it over-buys their work. When this happened to Chast in fall 2010, she used the break to stretch other comedy muscles. She wrote and illustrated a Shouts & Murmurs piece about eating bananas in public, noting how "disgusting" the fruit's browning, smelly peel is. She wrote a piece for the magazine's online News Desk about a friend's father, who for the last fifteen years of his life typed out the details of every meal he prepared on alphabetized three-by-five cards. And she began her own alphabetical project, a book about her personal phobias called *What I Hate: From A to Z.*

A book of adult fears disguised, almost, as a children's book, *What I Hate* mines Chast's most effective material: the personal. More than a list of wacky phobias such as fear of air (anemophobia) or music (melophobia), these are all hers. Among fears Freud would probably categorize more as "reality anxieties"—such as alien abduction, rabies, and water bugs—the greatest, she says, involves balloons. "I've hated them since I was a kid but I don't think it's a common phobia. I'm afraid of someone popping them. I hate that. I don't worry about Mylar balloons at all, but if I see latex balloons I don't want to be in the room with them. So now people are going to send me balloons! 'Hello, Roz. I know you like balloons sooooo much!'" If you suspect she probably wasn't much fun at kids' birthday parties, you'd be correct. "No, I wasn't—for so many reasons."

We spoke mostly in Chast's studio, on the second floor of her family's 1940s colonial home. A carpenter was repairing a leaky bathroom ceiling down the hall (the downstairs bathroom also serves as a gallery of original cartoon art by *New Yorker* colleagues and others), and

Chast was preparing to depart that evening for a pair of West Coast lectures. A TV was on in the kitchen, which may be how Marco and Eli, the pair of African gray parrots in the adjacent room, learned to speak. The *kusudama*-style origami and *pysanky* (Ukrainian Easter eggs) on display reminded me of how much Chast's own cartoons resemble handcrafted folk art that functions both as decoration, sociology, and, of course, old-fashioned comedy.

Chast has never felt completely at home in Connecticut and doesn't pretend otherwise. "I don't belong here!" she maintains. Yet she has mined her suburban milieu for hilarious accounts of learning to drive, the aforementioned family dog, and even a napkin-folding class she

Wall-mounted original

once took. "Oh, God, that was just fucking incredible," she recalls. "And real. I'm glad I live here. I feel very lucky, and I'm not ungrateful for many things. I love Ridgefield. My kids got a great education here—I think—and seemed more or less happy. But, yeah, suburbia is . . . kind of weird."

Her spouse used to celebrate that weirdness annually. Bill Franzen's elaborate Halloween displays, which he would begin assembling months ahead of the holiday, drew up to a thousand spectators to the Chast-Franzen abode to enjoy tableaux with names like Death in the Desert or Alien Lunatic Asylum. Chast took it with resigned annoyance. "I don't like holidays," she told the *New York Times*. "And I don't like crowds of people. I don't like noise. There is a lot of noise. I don't like amusement parks, and it's sort of like an amusement park."

Her own obsessions run more toward the sort of thing one might do late at night if one suffered from insomnia, as Chast sometimes does. Her *pysanky*—decorated with colorful cartoon images of fictional family members—are unmistakably Chast-ian. And like so much else in Chast's world, the process includes the potential for high anxiety. "It's a wax-resist kind of thing, like batik," she explains. "You melt a little wax in something called a *kistka* and draw on the egg with the melted wax. Then you dip it into different dyes, which don't color the part you've drawn on. You start with the lightest colors and build up to the darker, like batik. At the end, after you've worked on it for hours and hours, you sickeningly punch a hole in the egg and use the *kistka* to blow out the yolk and stuff. Then you carefully melt all the wax off the egg, so only the colors remain. I've had them break at every stage of the game."

Chast also makes brilliantly colorful *kusudama,* a style of origami thought to have evolved from when real flowers and herbs were formed into "medicine balls." Another recent craft obsession, which has been displayed at the Julie Saul Gallery in New York City, consists of beautiful, labor-intensive hooked rugs. One celebrates the four seasons with appropriate cartoonlike figures. Another features Eli and Marco, the latter of whom Chast has also cast as the protagonist in a pair of books for young children (*Too Busy Marco* and *Marco Goes to School*). Whether through a deficit of attention or simple curiosity, Roz Chast explores diverse forms of artistic expression both on and off the page.

There's one type of gag she hasn't gotten around to yet, however. "I'd love to do a desert-island gag, which I've never done. I love the end-of-the-world sign guys and tombstone gags. Anything to do with death is funny."

Sam Gross was wrong. Roz Chast is indeed something of an heiress, if only to Charles Addams's dark wit. But Addams never opened the door for as many unorthodox cartoonists as Chast has with her shaky, anxious lines. So if any one artist could be said to epitomize the current *New Yorker* cartoon aesthetic, she is it.

4

King of the Scrapyard: George Booth

"Better bring me another cookie. The last one fell in the water."

T HE FIRST TIME George Booth visited *New Yorker* art editor
James Geraghty, in 1969, he was surprised to find cartoons by
another George—George Price, the artist Booth has been most frequently compared with—lying around Geraghty's office. The meeting was a tad awkward: "Jim Geraghty was looking at my batch and I
was looking at the George Price stuff," Booth recalls. "I couldn't help
it, it was right in my face. He said, 'That's George Price's work.' And
I said, 'Yes, I know.' And Geraghty said, 'It's too bad he can't draw.'
Yeah, he didn't know whether I knew anything. And I said, 'Yes,
it is. But he knows enough tricks to get by.'" Booth guffaws loudly
at the memory as we eat lunch along with his wife, Dione (rhymes

with "eon"), in the Three Village Inn a few blocks away from the couple's saltbox house in Stony Brook, Long Island.

George Price imported memories of his New Jersey hometown, which he described as "inordinately loaded with oafs, nimble jacks, and weirdos," into *The New Yorker*'s cartoon pages. Booth concedes that Price broke the ground from which the younger cartoonist later mined cartoon gold. Price didn't come up with a single gag of his own for the magazine, however, while Booth combines images with language to create a world irrefutably his own. It extends from the front-porch shenanigans of his midwestern upbringing to the tenement-apartment confines of New York City. It's populated with versions of his Missouri family and neighbors as well as a rotating cast of cranky urban and suburban yokels.

In addition to his infinitely particularized cats and dogs, Booth's world includes the crew at Bohaty's Garage and their regular customer, Mr. Ferguson; the hapless Leon and a philosophically inclined older female companion Booth calls "Youbetcha"; the man in the bathtub; the man in the armchair under the hanging plant; the man alone in an apartment with his dog(s); the woman alone in an apartment with *her* dog(s); and, most famously, Mrs. Ritterhouse, a knock-kneed elderly musician depicted furiously pounding out a fusillade of piano notes on the magazine's cover as recently as January 2012.

"The great George," pronounces Ed Koren. "You look at the drawing, and you just laugh, even if you've seen one iteration or another of the same drawing over and over again. At the beginning, I thought he was way too close to George Price, but he established his own turf as time went on. You can use a class as subject matter in different ways; and there are different people in different classes, so it's not the same." Regardless, Booth is simply a great artist no matter what he's depicting.

"One of my favorite Booth cartoons is the one with the guitar string breaking and the dog up in the air," says his *New Yorker* colleague Arnie Levin. "There's just a little dot of white where the string breaks, which to me is creative cartooning: working with a sound — not a line, not a gag, but just the *sound* of an object."

For a time, Booth and fellow cartoonist Henry Martin competed to see who could get the longest cartoon caption into *The New Yorker*. Booth eventually won with a caption to a truncated image of a middle-aged couple in bed. The wife, eyes shut, recounts to her wide-eyed husband that "Mrs. Van Lewis-Smythe, third wife of your chairman of the board, said to me this evening at the corporate hoodingy, and twenty people within earshot, 'We all know what *Mr.* Parmalee does. He is a very important vice-president of the Hi Lee Lolly Corporation. What we are all wondering, Mrs. Parmalee, is . . . just what is it that *you* do? . . .' I said, 'Mrs. Van Lewis-Smythe, Your Grace, I fix dropping faucets around our house. I prop up sagging bookshelves. I glue broken china. I clean windows, mirrors, floors, walls, pots and pans, and dishes.'" The caption concluded with "'I mow the lawn, clean the basement, feed the birds, the cats, a dog, and a chicken, *and* I chauffeur a very important vice-president of the Hi Lee Lolly Corporation to and from the bar car every blessed day'"—for a total of 205 words. The personal, as they say, is very much the political.

To my knowledge, George Booth is the only *New Yorker* artist ever to earn a profile in the magazine itself. When David Owen considered Booth's life and work in 1998, Booth was working out of a multi-room studio that used to be a plumbing business. Owen describes the studio as housing vertiginous piles of paper containing potential ideas, drawings, clippings, books, a proposal of marriage ("I know you're no spring chicken, by your shaky line"), and much, much more. Booth no longer rents that studio and works at home. Dione was unwilling to let me see his work area, which, she claimed, was barely large enough for the artist himself. Booth's memories, like his studio (presumably), are a fascinating collection of mental bric-a-brac, mental odds and ends from which true treasures emerge seemingly at random.

In 2003, the State University of New York at Stony Brook awarded Booth an honorary doctorate in fine arts. While discussing his work there, Booth illustrated his "chalk talk," producing dust every time he turned a page. A woman in the audience, which included the univer-

sity president and his wife, became enthusiastic to the point of mania and wouldn't quiet down. "I kept looking around to see if I was going to be thrown out," he recalls. A chalk talk at the 2010 New Yorker Festival was augmented by David Owen egging Booth on while cartoonist Matthew Diffee provided sound and visual effects from the other side of his easel. Booth once again worried that he might possibly be causing a disturbance.

The illustrated monologue known as a "chalk talk" originated in the Methodist church during the last years of the nineteenth century. Booth was nine years old when he delivered his first chalk talk to a group of Methodist women in his hometown of Fairfax, Missouri (pop. 800). He had been drawing since he was three years old, when he made his mother laugh with a picture of a race car stuck in the mud. But that day he refused to talk as he drew, and Mawmaw, as everyone called her, was not pleased.

"She got disgusted and said, 'All right, you do the drawing and I'll do the talking.'" As his mother spoke, Booth drew punning images from a 1930s book of drawings based on numbers. "In one, you draw two wheels like a Model T Ford and you put fenders on, the axles and spokes, and a little bit of road underneath, and that changes into a face with a guy holding a steering wheel. The wheels are his eyes, the road is his mustache, and the mountain is his cap." Booth knew what he was doing and his audience applauded politely. "I didn't bow or anything. I just shot for the nearest tin chair to get outside. Maw Maw came over, gathered my shirt in one hand, yanked me up, and said, 'You stand up there and act like you know something, whether you do or not!' That's been a good lesson in life."

George William Booth was born June 28, 1926, in Cainsville, Missouri, eighty-five miles east of Fairfax and about a third its size. His mother, Irma Norene Swindle, met his father, William Earl Booth, at Stephens College in Columbia, Missouri. George's father, who went by Earl, was attending the University of Missouri and worked at the all-female college as a dishwasher. During their marriage, she called him Billy and he called her Bill. Like George's friend Roz Chast, both of his parents became schoolteachers. Irma taught all eight grades—alternating between even and odd ones each year—in a one-room schoolhouse located in a town called Lonesome. Earl was a teacher, coach, and, eventually, administrator. He once tamed an unruly group of students by becoming their boxing instructor. When the school board was unable to pay his wages, the family moved into a one-room schoolhouse with a kitchen.

Pap, Maw Maw, and their three boys—Gaylord was two years older than George, Jim four years younger—lived on five acres in Fairfax along with some hogs and a big vegetable garden. Raised by parents who possessed a healthy sense of humor, George enjoyed a frugal yet loving Depression-era childhood.

He recalls hanging on to his mother's finger in town one day as a six-year-old. A "stuffy" local woman approached the pair and asked, "How is the superintendent, Mrs. Booth?"

"He's just fine," replied Irma.

"And which one of the three boys is this, Mrs. Booth?"

"This is George W. Booth."

"And what does the 'W' stand for, Mrs. Booth?"

"Wiltonpoot," replied his mother.

George laughs heartily at the memory. Cartoonist Charles Barsotti once folded the six-foot-three-inch Booth into his Volkswagen Karmann Ghia for a road trip from Kansas City, where Barsotti lived, to visit Maw Maw (who died in 1989). "She called me when Nixon left office to say that 'the sun has broken through, the drought has lifted . . . ,' and on, and on, and on," Barsotti recalls.

After retiring as a teacher, Irma drew a regular weekly cartoon called *Erfie and Ophie* for the *Princeton (MO) Post-Telegraph Gazette* and signed it "Maw Maw." She painted portraits in oil and pastel. And she and George lettered state-mandated identification information on truck doors for a dollar each.

Pap's sense of humor was somewhat edgier than Maw Maw's. Once, while returning from a wrestling tournament in his '35 Chevy, Earl was accompanied by a few of the gentlemen who regularly haunted the town post office. "He called them the Barbershop Quartet," says George. "They would spread rumors that weren't true, talked too much, and didn't have much of a life. And this one ol' country guy with whiskey breath was sitting right behind my dad, who was a very good driver and taught driver training. There was a highway where the turn was ninety degrees, one way or the other, with a boulder in the middle. My dad was driving maybe forty-five or fifty miles per  hour, and he knew he had good brakes. He was talking to the guy in the passenger seat, and the guy behind him got up behind his ear and said, 'Watch out, you gotta turn left or right up here, so slow down a little bit.' My dad got a kick out of that and didn't slow down. And this guy panicked right in his ear until the last second, when Dad slowed down and made a safe turn. He got a real kick out of torturing that guy." Fairfax, George adds, was the sort of town where tying the axle of the sheriff's car to a fire hydrant was considered good fun.

In grade school, George drew a comic strip called *Cherokee Cherky* (he is part Cherokee on his mother's side). In high school, he drew for the school newspaper and a pair of local weeklies. At age sixteen, his father facilitated George's employment as a printer's devil, where he learned to operate a linotype machine for the local paper. "I didn't really learn spelling in school," Booth says. "I learned it with a dictionary in my lap when I sat at the linotype. The copy I got was country writing from housewives, mostly in pencil on brown paper sacks: 'Mr. and Mrs. Morris Graves visited Mr. and Mrs. Raymond Kincaid on Saturday afternoon. A good time was had by all.' My boss said, 'You're going to run into wrong spelling and grammar. But these ladies are giving us free copy, so don't be too rough on them.'"

Dione Booth's mother used to say that her friends thought the couple lived like the characters in George Booth's cartoons — with rooms full of cats, dogs laying on porches, and shiftless country folk sipping moonshine. But over time, George's midwestern roots were transformed into a warm, comforting vision of a resilient Middle America. As difficult as his childhood must have been, it was normal to him; and by translating it into satirical imagery, he humanized it for the rest of the world.

Booth left Fairfax to join the Marines, where he pulled two hitches over eight years. The service gave Booth the opportunity to become not only a great cartoonist, but also a journeyman art director. Booth worked at *Leatherneck* magazine in Washington, DC, during both of his tours. "My folks stood with me in June of '44 when I enlisted. I'm signing the contract, and Staff Sergeant Harry K. Bottom asked, 'What do you want to do in the Marine Corps?' I said, 'I want to draw cartoons.' And he wrote it down because he had to."

Two years later, having avoided combat, Booth was in Pearl Harbor waiting to return to the mainland after V-J Day. "I'm sitting in the Quonset hut, and a telegram came to headquarters saying that PFC Booth can come to *Leatherneck* magazine as staff cartoonist," he recalls. "They were losing all of their staff, and they'd looked in the file and saw that I wanted to draw cartoons." A second telegram stipulated that he would need to reenlist at the end of the war in order to do so. He decided to take his chances with the Ma- rines rather than return to Fairfax, where a future in linotype operation awaited him. "The Marines would bring their buddies back to look at the geek who was going to reenlist. They stared at me like they couldn't believe anybody would do that. They were so sick of the war."

Arriving at *Leatherneck* in 1946, Booth was given a corner office he shared with the illustrator John DeGrasse. "I found paradise there," Booth says wistfully. "I just sat and worked. They told me to do cartoons, so I started doin' my best. Staff Sergeant DeGrasse helped me. They had a little bit of experience." Booth's first cartoons were captionless pantomime efforts. "I didn't know how to write, or thought I didn't. That probably helped me, too, because I still place a big importance on the picture with or without words."

At *Leatherneck*, Booth began honing his style with regular cartoons and spot illustrations. In one drawing, three scowling and snappily dressed officers confront a slovenly G.I. sitting on his bed surrounded by a meticulously rendered assortment of possessions: "Knocked myself out for yesterday's inspection . . . you didn't even show up. Today I decided to hell with it . . . and here you are bigger'n sin!" In another, the landing of a butterfly on a grunt's overburdened pack leads to his violent collapse. And the first appearance of a signature Booth cat could be discerned in an intricate *Leatherneck* cover depicting a gunswinging Marine scattering a crowd of Korean and Chinese soldiers. "Some guy wrote in and said, 'You've got everything in there but the kitchen sink,'" Booth told Lee Lorenz in *The Essential George Booth*. "The editors wrote back and said, 'Look closely, the kitchen sink is in there.'"

Recalled for the Korean War in 1950, Booth repeated basic training at Camp Pendleton before returning to Washington and *Leatherneck*, where he remained until 1952, when he moved to New York to study at the School of Visual Arts (SVA) with the help of the G.I. Bill. He also attended the Corcoran School of Art, the Chicago Academy of Fine Arts (now the Art Institute of Chicago), and Adelphi College at various times, all without graduating. At SVA, Booth studied with

Burne Hogarth, the master renderer of the human physique, known for his daily *Tarzan* strip.

When he moved to New York, Booth shared a house in White-stone, Queens, with two other "country boys," as Dione calls them, whom he met at the Academy of Fine Arts: Harold LeDoux, from Texas, drew *Judge Parker* for more than fifty years beginning in 1953, while Virgil Arnett, from Tennessee, became a longtime art director at *Billboard*, sold occasional cartoons to *The New Yorker*, and was the namesake of Virgil's Real Barbecue in Times Square. "We were barely getting by," says Booth, whose monthly rent was $37.50.

Booth's father occasionally taught Sunday school, and Booth followed in his footsteps for a short while in Whitestone. He began attending a Methodist church a few blocks away from his apartment, sitting in the back to avoid being noticed. One Sunday, the preacher zeroed in on him, asked if he'd be interested in teaching, and followed up with a house visit. "He said, 'We've got a back room behind the pulpit, with about twelve thirteen-year-old boys. And they've run one teacher after another out of here. I've heard you were a sergeant in the Marine Corps.' I said, 'Yes.' And he said, 'We need you!'"

Putting his father's example into practice wasn't easy for Booth, Queens kids being notably less compliant than midwesterners. One Sunday, Booth lost his temper and went outside to cool down. When he returned, he asked them, "Do any of you have the guts to come back next Sunday? We will make an effort to be nice to one another, be polite, and try to learn something. I know you've run one teacher after another out of this classroom, but starting next Sunday that won't happen, because I'm going to run *you* out of here, one and two at a time until you're all gone. And then I'm going to close the door and go home." Booth laughs at the memory, adding drily that it was the "best thing I ever did for those kids," especially insofar as he wasn't being paid.

Many Booth cartoons contain a silent man often on the verge of exploding in anger as he listens to his nagging wife. "I've seen a lot of that in the American home," says Booth. "Women just talk, talk, talk, while the man's sitting there in another world. I don't know what you call that, but it exists." There's also the caveman perched on a rocky outcropping, who notes of his simmering female companion, "You seem depressed."

During the early fifties, Booth hit the streets with his cartoons and was soon "moving batches all over town." *Collier's*, the *Saturday Evening Post*, and *Look*, he recalls, paid close to $60 per cartoon, but he also sold gags for as little as $7.50. After winning a contest, he was awarded a daily United Features Syndicate strip. In 1954 and 1955, he drew *Spot*, which featured a dog who thought he was human. The endless routine of a daily strip wasn't for Booth, however. "I didn't want to be pinned down to a cartoon every day, forever. Some guys go after that, and it's fine, but I preferred the variety, sophistication, and humor in *The New Yorker*." DeGrasse had already suggested that Booth zero in on *The New Yorker*, which he was unacquainted with in 1946. "The more I looked at it, the more I wanted it," he says.

In 1956, George met nineteen-year-old Dione Rankin, whom he first saw performing in a production of *Twelve Angry Women* (an all-female version of the famous play *Twelve Angry Men*) in Northport, Long Island. Seeing her onstage, Booth feared she'd be too old for him; backstage, however, he thought she was too young. "But we got through all of that, somehow," he says. He did have some difficulty with her name, which she'd changed from Diane five years earlier. "Her family continued to call her Di. I wasn't sure what her name was, so I started calling her 'Die-on,' and nobody corrected me. After I'd been dating her for about a year, and knew I was going to marry her, a good friend said, 'George, if you're gonna marry that girl, learn how to pronounce her name!'"

Once they were married, in 1958, it took Booth only two weeks to decide that a freelance cartoonist's salary wasn't going to cut it. He worked for a year on the advertising industry's *Tide* magazine before it "washed up," he says with a chuckle. He then went to work for Bill Communications and became a one-man central-ized art department for nine magazines, including *Floor Covering, Fast Food, Rubber World, Modern Tire Dealer*, and the largest, *Sales and Marketing Management*. He

did whatever cartooning was needed for all the magazines
and marketing materials. He enjoyed the work, but the
"one-man" part quickly lost its appeal. Deciding to leave
"wasn't hard for me to do," he says. "I just walked across the
hall and put one guy in charge and told them I'd be back to clean my
desk out." The time had come for Booth to pursue cartooning single-
mindedly.

During the subsequent salad days, the Booths resided on West
Twenty-Second Street in Chelsea, across the street from Rip Torn
and Geraldine Page. "George was happy doing his own thing, submitting to different magazines, and it was just an interesting time,"
Dione says. "I remember saying to my mother, 'I don't want to marry
somebody who gets on the train and goes to work for a living.' Her reply was 'Where did I go wrong?'" The couple was broke much of the
time, and Dione recalls reshelving Cadbury chocolates and mayon-
naise they couldn't afford to pay for.

Booth almost got his big break at the *Saturday Evening Post,*
where Charles Barsotti was cartoon editor. Booth wrote Barsotti a
note — "My wife Dione and I like your work, and we think you'll like
mine"—and dropped by one Wednesday afternoon. Barsotti, Booth
recalls, looked at his drawings and simply said, "Jesus Christ." Unfortunately, the magazine ceased publication with the issue prior to the
one containing a Booth-designed four-page spread that was going to
reintroduce his work to the *Post*'s readers. "George came in and said,
'I know it's never going to see daylight, but I just wanted you to see,'
and he had the layout," recalls Barsotti. "Three grown men burst into
fucking tears."

When William Shawn asked William Emerson, his *Post* equivalent, what he could do to help, Emerson's response, according to
Booth, was "take a look at these two guys," i.e., Barsotti and Booth.
Dione suspects that the *New Yorker* editors were afraid that Booth,
because of what he drew, might be elderly himself. Barsotti earned
a meeting with Shawn, while forty-three-year-old Booth was rele-
gated to James Geraghty and his assistant, cartoonist Frank Modell.

"I never met William Shawn," Booth says of the famously low-key editor. "As I started selling to *The New Yorker* over the years, I saw him once going upstairs, once going downstairs, and once getting off the elevator. That was his personality. He didn't babysit everybody, I guess."

Booth's midwestern manners have never left him, either. "I'd walk into Mr. Geraghty's office and greet him the way I was taught to greet people. I said, 'Good morning, Mr. Geraghty.' And he'd say, 'Good morning, Mr. Booth.' I didn't think anything about that. Except one time he commented that everybody else called him Jim." Booth didn't get buddy-buddy with his editors, but he and Shawn nonetheless maintained an excellent relationship via Geraghty.

Few cartoonists lay claim to creating masterpieces, and most consider all their "children" to be equals, but Booth has a definite favorite among everything he has drawn. Published as a two-page spread in the issue of January 20, 1975, "Ip Gissa Gul" is nearly as much poem as comic strip. In it, the hirsute hominid Ip looks for a mate ("Hom wompa gul") as a crusty chorus hovers nearby. After rejecting a "hig" (pig), "izzard" (lizard), and "durb" (pterodactyl), Ip finally runs across the desperately reluctant rock-throwing girl—or "krokton gul"—of his dreams. The idea for the strip came to Booth during a New Hampshire vacation with Dione and her mother. "I should've been relaxing up there, but I couldn't quit cartooning. I don't know why I was pushing so hard; I guess I needed the money. I wanted an idea for a spread, and Dione's mother prayed for it. Ip's probably the best thing I've ever done. Yeah, I lay responsibility on Dione's mother for praying about it." When Booth proposed a sequel to his brilliant "Ip Gissa Gul" spread, Shawn relayed through Geraghty that he didn't want him to try to improve on a classic. "I just dropped it," says Booth. Shawn was right, of course, and diplomatic as well.

"People used to write and call George on the phone and say things in Ip language," adds Dione. "You just never know how you touch people. It's a continual surprise." She mentions a woman who survived a long illness with the help of Booth cartoons taped around her hospital room. Another fan offered herself to him via a letter, adding that "he better make up his mind, because she didn't have an awful lot of time left." As he appears in the magazine less frequently, his fan mail tends to be more along the lines of "I haven't seen you in *The New Yorker* for a long time. Are you well?"

George's creativity hasn't flagged. "George works morning, noon, and night," Dione says. "He'll stop whatever is going on in order to create something. When I married George, I didn't really know what cartooning was. But I grew with it and came to understand that *anything* can be turned into a cartoon: tragedy, frustration, anything else." He's a lucky man, too. "He's known what he wanted to do since age three and has been able to do it." She is proud to have inspired some of his punch lines. "I was stretched out on the couch one day and said, 'Talk to me; say something meaning-ful.' And instead of saying, 'Gee, honey, I'm sorry I've ignored you all of these years,' he said, 'Wait a minute, let me get a pen!'" Another of Dione's contributions illustrates George's flair for capturing the countless mini-monologues of which domestic life consists. "Edgar, please run down to the shopping center right away, and get some milk and cat food. Don't get canned tuna, or chicken, or liver, or any of those awful combinations. Shop around and get a surprise. The pussies like surprises."

So does Booth, whose art depends on serendipity to a larger extent than usual for his medium. Inspired by Picasso—who "would draw a profile of a face looking one way but also have another eye out here in space looking at you; the painting is looking at you but over there, too"—Booth strives to access the pre-educated, natural artistic talent of the child. "It's a matter of relaxing, letting go, and drawing some-thing that has a lot of feeling as opposed to drawing consciously. And it isn't easy," he says. Over the decades he has developed a technique for capturing and tweaking spontaneous moments of creativity. He calls it "retaining controlled accidents," which is to say, "controlling things usually thrown in the wastebasket."

"Sometimes I'll draw a thing, look at it, and see that it needs a little something. So I'll make a copy of it, enlarge it a little bit, cut it out, and put it on the drawing. Or I use a pen that's not very good on paper that's not very good, and then take it out in the backyard and spray part of the line so that it spreads across that not-good paper, and cut that out." Sometimes the enlarged copies give effects he can't achieve with his pen. Lee Lorenz characterizes Booth as "a virtuoso of the cut-and-paste." But he doesn't use paste so much as Scotch tape. His drawings are almost three-dimensional objects, with dogs, cats, noses, hands, and other objects attached with glue or tape.

In recent decades, the Booths have taken keener interest in maintaining the archival quality of George's work. Frustration can be sensed in regard to the sheer quantity of images he has amassed over the years, relatively few of which begin in the many Moleskin notebooks their daughter, Sarah, has given him. "I've faced the fact that everybody works differently, and maybe some people never really get organized," concedes Dione. George's personal archive remains a work in progress, as it were, with stacks of papers and fragments of uncompleted cartoons everywhere.

As he has since art school, Booth uses packs of India ink pen points delivering a range of lines from very thin to very thick. He began drawing with pencil at *Leatherneck*. "I would get my accidents with a 4B pencil," he says. "Sometimes I'd spit on it, smear it, and take it down the hallway to the photo shop to get what I wanted. But I kind of gave that up when I left the art department."

Celebrity portraitist Al Hirschfeld was known for teasing readers by hiding variations on his daughter's name — Nina — in his drawings, then adding the number of Ninas to his signature. Booth's fans, however, do his work for him. A woman in Chicago, for example, wrote him regular letters informing him how many cats he'd crammed into a picture. "I hid a lot of them, of course, with just a little bit sticking out." He reckons the most cats he ever drew in a single cartoon was eighty-six.

George and Dione have owned several cats in their day. But the dog he is best known for? The iconic canine barking the thistles off a pussy willow on the cover of his 2009 book *About Dogs*? "He's all in my head."

Another of Booth's stock ensemble members is a gentleman opining about a variety of matters while taking a bath. We view him through the door from his living room, where his wife is sometimes doing laundry, often with a dog or cat—or several dogs and cats—lying about. Booth doesn't recall how he got on the guy-in-the-bathtub thing. "I decided just to leave him there," he says. "You'll be sorry you made that crack if I win the lottery," warns the man in one cartoon (twelve cats). "I'm working on Plan B," he says in another (twelve more cats). And "How times flies! It was just thirty years ago tonight that you first ran me a hot bath—right here in this very tub" (seven cats).

Yet another series of drawings depicts a man in an old-fashioned pump-driven diving suit sitting at a table in a kitchen with one or two people. Dogs, cats, and odd and sundry objects litter the floor. Booth got this idea from a newspaper article about a New Jersey man who spent his time diving into the Hudson River in search of antiques. "In the paper, he came up with what he thought was an antique or some wonderful prize. He washed the mud off, and it was just some common monkey wrench or something. Another disappointment in the life." In one, the diver sits in this familiar tableau with a man and woman. "No doubt about it," reads Booth's caption. "Scientifically speaking, knowledge of the river will expand in direct proportion to the length of Mr. Van Gundy's new air hose."

Booth points out the provenance of various objects scattered about these cartoons. There's a blowtorch he bought because it fascinated him. And a tire pump, an old typewriter, and something he can't recall the name of. Hundreds of found objects litter the yards, porches, and rooms of Booth's characters. "Broken stuff" appeals to him, too. He vaguely recalls a pulley wheel he hung on to. He doesn't know where it is today, but it's around somewhere.

One of George Booth's more cherished memories is a drawing of his mother, who holds a special place in the history of *New Yorker* cartooning. The week of September 11, 2001, the magazine announced that cartoonists were welcome to submit material but nothing would be purchased. Booth offered a drawing of his mother, "sitting like I've seen her sit." The only cartoon image the magazine ran in the issue of September 24, 2001, depicts Maw Maw on the contributors' page. She perches on a stool facing away from her music, praying with closed eyes. Her glasses lie on the floor near her fiddle, the bow parallel to it as she was taught at Stevens College. A cat covers its head with its paws.

The Beastly Beatitudes of Edward Koren

"Your father and I want to explain why we've decided to live apart."

THE FIRST THING that happens when I visit Edward Koren at his home in the town of Brookfield, Vermont (pop. 1,310), is that the squawk box he keeps near him most of the time comes to life and he gets called to a fire. A car is burning on a nearby highway, and Koren is a volunteer fireman of some three decades. He dons his turnout gear—heavy heat-resistant jacket, pants, and helmet—and we hop into his gray Saab. The SUV is only smoking, fortunately. Koren and the rest of the rather younger crew position safety cones, force open the car's hood, and spray it down. Mission accomplished.

It's just another day in the life of the former New Yorker, but it reflects the satisfaction Koren takes in contributing to the community that has been his full-time home since the mid-eighties. Since selling his first cartoon to *The New Yorker* in 1962, Koren has mined a rich vein of humor that at first reflected the values and vanities of Manhattan's Upper West Side. He bought his Brookfield house in 1978 and "oozed" up there permanently in 1987. His subsequent cartoons often zero in on the permanent and weekend inhabitants of what Koren calls the "Vermont *profonde.*"

His work reveals a split yet ultimately resolved geographic personality. In one cartoon, a young trick-or-treater wearing a scowling mask—who replies, "Can't you tell? I'm a depressed and angry white working-class male," to the perennial identity question as he waits for his candy on a pumpkin-decorated porch—could be either a displaced Manhattanite or a Vermonter. And Koren's most popular *New Yorker* cover in recent years (published July 2, 2012) depicts an oblivious fellow atop a lawnmower, grooming an impeccably square patch of lawn, as beasts peer at him balefully from the surrounding forest. But is he a local or a weekender? Hard to tell. Koren is a keen observer of man's usually skewed relationship to nature, and "the issue of the giant lawn" and "this absurd desire to hurry home and organize nature" troubles him.

"Maybe this is the world we live in, and it crystallized in a way I had thought about but didn't know would come out the way it did until I started to draw it," he says as we speak in his warm art- and book-lined living room. "But I think about this all the time because I live in an area where gradual suburbanization has exalted all these huge expanses of lawn that have no point and no purpose, other than passing time. I read something online like 'Those who really desire eternal life the most are those who don't quite know what to do with their Sundays.'" He laughs. "And I keep thinking that these guys out on their lawnmowers don't know what to do with themselves, and this is their solution. Then I came across this Michael Pollan quote I realized I should've used for the cover title: 'A lawn is nature under totalitarian rule.'"

The New Yorker's finest social critic of his generation works in the tradition of Honoré Daumier as much as Saul Steinberg. In addition to being a prolific cartoonist and cover artist, Koren has produced a substantial amount of "serious" art since graduating from Columbia

University in 1957. Writer Calvin Trillin, a longtime friend and *New Yorker* colleague, refers to it as Koren's "Uptown Stuff." But as Koren explained in an essay included in the catalog for his 2010 show *The Capricious Line,* "I always thought that my comic work was fundamentally serious, and what might be called 'serious work' had its basis in my generally comic disposition."

Koren has been contributing to *The New Yorker* for more than a half century without becoming either jaded or complacent. A thousand and fifty OKed cartoons into the game, he still sends in batches occasionally but currently concentrates on cover ideas. For all his success and admirable track record, Koren realizes that selling a drawing is more of a lottery than ever. "Any time something appears there, it feels like a triumph of sorts," he says. "It never becomes routine. Certain covers are triumphs in the sense that there's some response, because most of the time there's none. Zero." He compares the process of submitting cartoons to Bob Mankoff to fishing: "You bait the hook with your wonderful drawings, throw it in, and you have no idea what's going to happen to it. It might get nibbled away and you come up with an empty hook," he laments. "Or it comes back with the worm, or drawing, still on it, and you have no idea what's going on down there."

Young Edward Benjamin Koren was more devoted to the comics pages of the *New York World-Telegram and Sun,* which his dentist father brought back from Manhattan to his family's Mount Vernon home, than to *The New Yorker,* which also arrived at the Koren household. The local *Mount Vernon Daily Voice* had a cartoon page as well, and *Dick Tracy* and *Alley Oop* strips led eventually to Captain Marvel, Superman, and Batman comic books. An early aficionado of monopanel gag cartoons such as Fontaine Fox's *Toonerville Folks* and Jimmy Hatlo's *They'll Do It Every Time,* Koren relished "that single moment" where image and idea come together. He also acknowledges the subliminal influence that V. T. Hamlin's *Alley Oop,* with its "fuzzy, hairy creatures," may have had on his own furry creations, which rarely extend beyond a single panel. "The funny thing is I never was attracted to sequential strip drawing," he says. "I could never tell a story."

Koren was born December 13, 1935, in Woman's Hospital on Manhattan's Upper West Side (the facility merged with St. Luke's Hospital and moved; the site is currently a Con Edison plant). His mother taught school and his father was an electrical engineer. Koren wonders whether there might be a connection between teaching and cartooning, "which is, in some way, pedagogical." This tradition extends back to the eighteenth century, when British caricaturists like William Hogarth and Thomas Rowlandson were satirizing politics and society. The barbs became even more pointed during the nineteenth century in the work of French satirists Honoré Daumier and Gustave Doré. "They're all storytellers," Koren says. "Some of their work's funny; some of it's not so funny. Some of it's political; a lot of it is social. Some uses animals; some doesn't. We don't understand all of Daumier's drawings because they're so specific to the time. What's most attractive to me is how he saw the social world of lawyers and doctors, for example, and how his drawings told stories about them." Like the earlier generations of *New Yorker* artists, Daumier supplied the exquisite art for captions — or "legends" — written by his editor, Charles Philipon, with whom he was once arrested for depicting King Louis Philippe as a gluttonous pear.

While the *New Yorker* tradition of lightly lampooning its audience extends back to its earliest issues, it may have reached its apex in the seventies and eighties in the work of Koren, William Hamilton, and Charles Saxon, among others. The odd thing, according to Koren, was how much the audience enjoyed the attention. "The East Side group Hamilton satirized so well evidently loved seeing themselves. It's almost like publicity for them," he says, laughing. "And just as there's no such thing as bad publicity, there's no such thing as a bad satire." Saxon had an equally sharp eye for the tribe he lived and commuted among. Koren characterizes "the self-satisfied Fairfield County country clubbers" as more hapless and less interesting than their city equivalents, arguing that Saxon raised their profile by targeting them. "Sometimes it was almost *too* gentle. You almost wanted to say, 'Go at 'em, Saxon!' I sometimes feel like I should be a little bit more sledgehammer than feather myself," he adds, "but that's me, I can't change it."

Koren may have inherited his integrated-outsider outlook from his parents. Elizabeth and Harold Koren met as students on Staten Island. She was born in Belorussia and Harold came from Warsaw, Poland. "They both worked like one can hardly imagine now," Koren says. His father was a bricklayer who earned a degree in engineering but couldn't find a job because of anti-Semitism. "How did they know?" he asks rhetorically. "They always asked for a recommendation from your priest or pastor."

Seeking financial independence, Harold returned to college. He attended the Columbia University School of Dental and Oral Surgery, and established a practice on East Fortieth Street, where he worked for some forty years. Ed often helped out in his father's lab, "a favorite place of mine."

Molars and cuspids figure prominently in Koren's drawings and etchings from the sixties. But they didn't haunt so much as amuse him. "There were all these plaster casts of teeth in my father's office, and I always thought, 'This is hilarious.' There's something really funny about teeth lined up without anything around them. No skull, no smile, no expression, just teeth." Teeth have played a progressively smaller role in his work, although fangs still pop out on occasion: "I detect a little laxity in your flossing," a dentist informs his bestial patient in a 1991 cartoon. "Over time, not by any decision, I seem to have withdrawn the teeth into the lip," says Koren.

A solitary kind of kid while attending the Horace Mann School, Koren accrued status and confidence by dedicating himself to the school's literary magazine and yearbook. Encouraged by his parents to become a dentist ("or even a *doctor*"), Koren enrolled in Columbia as a premed student and registered for a full load of physics, chemistry, and math. Unfortunately, he was terrible at all of it. The futility of medicine as a career became readily apparent within a week. Following a film depicting a thyroid operation, "I got sick—literally—and the next day I was no longer premed," he says.

SHORT HAPPY LIFE
(Continued from page 13)

He dropped the cigareet.
"Why not?" (Pianissimo)
"Why not?" (Mezzoforte)
"WHY THE HELL NOT?" (FORTISSIMO)

thought . . . I thought . . . I must have been out of my mind."
"No, I won't shoot you."
"No, not in the stomach."
"No, not in the stomach, even if you take off your . . ."
"Just get out of here."

TO HIS DEPARTED
MISTRESS

We went together very well,
As well as eggs and ham:
You worshipped me as woman should.

Published originally in the Jester

Switching to the humanities, Koren immersed himself in art and writing. He became editor of the school humor magazine, the *Jester.* One issue lampooned the administration's aim to establish a "citizenship program" of mandatory volunteerism, which much of the student body and faculty opposed. Critic Lionel Trilling, a professor at Columbia, congratulated him for the takedown. Koren explored the city during his spare time, walking from the Upper West Side to Battery Park. He haunted the Metropolitan Museum of Art and the Frick Collection; he dug jazz at Birdland and the Five Spot Café.

Although he'd been accepted into the graphic design program at the Yale School of Fine Arts, Koren took a year off and accepted an "awful" position with a city-planning firm involved in razing neighborhoods for Title I housing projects. Disillusioned and at loose ends, he consulted Columbia art professor Dustin Rice, who suggested that his former student move to Paris and study at Atelier 17 with Stanley William Hayter, the great British printmaker and engraver. As Koren was being initiated into the chemical mysteries of printmaking, he also became immersed in French life and culture. He won a Wooley fellowship, which earned him a second year in the city of Daumier and de Gaulle.

Koren returned to the United States in 1959 and joined the army reserve. He was assigned to the public information office at Fort Dix, New Jersey, where he wrote press releases. Mainly, though, he "just sat around, drew, and did what people did in the army, which was goldbrick." He met another soldier, Calvin Trillin, who would become a lifelong friend and colleague, on the day Elvis Presley was discharged from the army at Fort Dix. Trillin, like Koren, recalls little about the mustering out "except that Nancy Sinatra was there."

Back in New York, Koren wrote press releases for *Bottling Industry* magazine, produced catalogs for the Associated American Artists gallery (noted for its affordable prints), and worked for the Abelard-Schuman publishing company before being offered a job at Columbia University Press as assistant advertising manager. In 1961, he married Mimi Siegmeister, daughter of composer Elie Siegmeister. The couple had two children, Nathan and Sasha, and divorced in 1971.

Soon thereafter, Koren decided he wanted to become a cartoon-ist, an artist. "I didn't want to go nine-to-five. It was not fulfilling." Cartoonist-playwright Jules Feiffer's memoir is titled *Backing Into Forward*, and Koren can relate. "What a great title, because that's my life. I've backed into everything I've done. I never really went all-out for it—although I kind of did, and Feiffer did, too." Backing into cartooning for Koren meant making the weekly rounds of publica-tions in a "desultory" way. He began selling to *Dude, Gent*, and other testosterone-oriented magazines, as well as *True, Collier's, Saturday Evening Post*, and *Look*.

He also submitted work to *The New Yorker*, which he cracked in 1962 thanks to the help of a fellow Columbia alum whose parents were Connecticut neighbors of James Geraghty. His first sale to the magazine depicted a paunchy, frustrated writer sitting at a desk clut-tered with a typewriter, crumpled paper, a pack of cigarettes, and an ashtray. His sweatshirt reads SHAKESPEARE.

Taking the advice of artistic and academic friends, Koren began attending the Pratt Institute part-time and graduated with an MFA in 1964. He immediately found a job at Brown University, where he taught drawing, printmaking, and other standard art courses. "I felt that I could do anything creative now without having to scrabble around. I'm a child of the prosperous middle class, and I was uncom-fortable. I could drive a taxi just as well as anybody, and I could be a bartender, but I didn't want to." Koren resigned from Brown in 1977, but he continued to teach there as an adjunct. "I made some good friends there, and some good enemies," he says with a laugh. "There's nothing like a university department to make you think about survival of the fittest and the struggle in the jungle. It was comical. Those for whom the stakes were the lowest would fight the hardest."

Cartooning wasn't part of Koren's curriculum, however. "I have this sense that you can't teach it. I mean, you can teach the nuts and bolts of it, for sure, how to set up a situation and tell a story. But you can't teach that bedrock of humor and alienation, whatever the engine of satire, resistance, and subversion might be. And without that, there's nothing." Moreover, he firmly believes that a comic's art should be as funny as the gag it illustrates. "With a lot of newer people, like [Bruce Eric] Kaplan, the drawing doesn't make you laugh. If the caption weren't there, nothing in the drawing would make you realize that this is supposed to be funny."

Previously unpublished rough

Even the most prolix of Koren's cartoons work as art. Drawn in 1963 for the *Outsider's Newsletter*, a publication of political satire helmed by future *Nation* editor Victor Navasky, *Introducing Super-kahn: Government Contractor* would be Koren's sole attempt at sequential comics. His word-heavy strip parodied the career of Hudson Institute political strategist Herman Kahn, who believed that nuclear war was both possible and winnable. Koren's Superkahn ("the only superhero under contract to the U.S. government") goes undercover disguised as peace activist Hermes Batson but is mistaken for a Cosa Nostra member. And so on. It's as narrative driven, and as left leaning, as Koren ever got.

"I've always been a semi-lefty," he says. "I've always been uncomfortable about the really wild, crazy progressive stuff. I did Superkahn because the Hudson Institute was doing these terrible stupid things about nuclear disaster. Maybe I was more lefty then than I am now. I think I've given up hope for politics altogether," he says with a rueful laugh. Koren considers himself a "very conservative, traditional guy." He never took LSD but once suffered a bad trip from an overdose of pot brownies. He worships R. Crumb's work but admits that he's very square by comparison. "In a way, I regret that I didn't go way out there and have a wilder life."

After his divorce, Koren found himself torn between Providence, Rhode Island, and New York City, where his ex-wife and children lived. With the illustration work being procured for him by Ted Reilly, his agent, and the forty to fifty drawings he was doing for *The New Yorker* each year, he found teaching increasingly difficult. "I was killing myself with all the commuting, and I had no place in New York. I was hanging around my friends' apartments, cobbling together places to bring my kids; it was getting very unhappy." He moved to New York and tried to reduce his teaching schedule, but his work life became increasingly intense. So, "with great trepidation and sadness," he quit his tenured position at Brown.

Koren purchased a house in Brookfield "almost on a whim" in 1978 partly because his neighbors were friends who had children the same age as his own. "It was in pretty shabby condition for quite a while, but the village was appealing. There was no construction around it at the time. It was like an English or French village, insular and iso-lated. It's become a bit more of a suburb than I would care for it to be, but here I am." There's no way he'll ever be a real Vermonter, he says. "They're very proprietary, especially in this part of Vermont, which is exceptionally rural." In his art, he often mocks other New Yorkers' urge to be accepted by Vermonters. In one drawing a wife, referring to her bearded, overall-sporting husband, says to a friend, "We're only here summers, but Roger likes to be taken for a local." When play-wright David Mamet asked him what kind of car he should buy for his Vermont vacation home, Koren suggested a practical Saab. "So he got one," Koren says. "But he felt uncomfortable because it wasn't enough of a regular guy's car and he wanted to be a regular guy. So he sold it and got some beast of a thing."

Down the road from Brookfield lies the even smaller village of Randolph Center. There Koren likes to hang out on the front porch of the local general store with owner Al Floyd and his cronies and bloviate, as he has depicted in several cartoons. THIS IS NOT A

GALLERY, reads the sign in the window of "Floyd's Store" as a city woman approaches some locals in one of them. In a related, more idealized drawing, the Pond Village Store rebrands itself as "Generalists," with locals and weekenders sharing space on the front porch.

Vermonters have been more forgiving of Koren's attention than a certain group that objected to a cartoon he drew for *Esquire* in the early sixties. While living near Little Italy, he switched out the Italian airline Alitalia's big airplane model with an old lady cooking pasta in a cartoon. One day his doorbell rang. He answered it to find two gentlemen with Italian accents.

"Are you Mr. Koren?" one asked him.

"Yes," he replied.

"You do this?" They pulled out the cartoon.

"Yeah, I did," Koren answered. "You like it?"

"This doesn't look good for the Italians," one informed him. "I wouldn't do any more of this, know what I mean?"

Koren was taken aback. "Are you kidding me?" he asked them.

"Nah, we don't joke around. See ya."

Koren was stunned. "What possible slur on the Italians could that have been?"

Koren says he has always felt like an outsider gazing upon the human condition with affectionate skepticism. "I often put cats in as observers," he says, "and I think that's who I am. I'm the narrator, an observer talking about the main action. And when I have people around, I sometimes put myself in, like Hitchcock did, sitting in the back, observing."

Great cartoonists cast their own productions with memorable characters. "I always admire artists who make a world of their own people," says Calvin Trillin. George Price, Peter Arno, and Charles Addams each populated his particular realm with immediately identifiable characters. "Ed did that in New York and once again in Vermont. You look at the cartoon and you know a little about the people in it before you even register the cartoon because you've seen them before and they look roughly the same. It's the same as somebody like August Wilson making a world of black people who've moved up from the South, or Pete [A. R.] Gurney's world of upper-class Buffalonians. It seems to give all their work an extra charge."

Saul Steinberg was another great observer Koren considers an artistic mentor and model worker. In addition to admiring the unique genius of his *New Yorker* colleague's literary and visual blends, Koren also appreciated the older artist simply because "he was nice to me." Steinberg occasionally invited Koren over to his studio just to schmooze. Open and encouraging, Steinberg once told Koren, "I like what you are doing. You have a very interesting notion of America. America's a strange place." Referring to Koren's rural life, Steinberg observed that "there are no girls," and Koren knew exactly what he meant. "America's rural women tend to be not terribly attractive—not particularly pretty, charming, worldly, or anything. You look around and there are these large, overweight, helmet-haired creatures, who do everything they can to make themselves unattractive." As for Steinberg, "He was a bit remote, and he was also very predatory with women. He liked his young, pretty ladies around."

During the seventies, Koren and Trillin worked together on an irregular feature called *The Inquiring Demographer*, a delightful take on a newspaper staple that even the *Onion* preserves with its cast of recurring American Voices respondents. In December 1975, five fictitious Americans answered a typical week's question: "How Has New York's Financial Emergency Affected You?" The made-up respondents included Max Gold, proprietor of Max's Super Sandwiches in Manhattan ("If you think this is an emergency, buddy, you must be from out of town. You want *emergencies*, we got emergencies"), and Jimmy Bushmill, mayor and duck hunter in Martin's Crossing, Kentucky. Koren portrayed them all in large panels full of rich, emotional detail.

Trillin is an aficionado of *New Yorker* cartooning as well as a frustrated caption creator. "My view of *New Yorker* cartooning is colored by the fact that I have a one hundred percent turndown record on suggesting things," he says. "When I first arrived at *The New Yorker*, they routinely accepted ideas and then had cartoonists draw them. I don't know when they stopped that. I would buttonhole cartoonists

YOU'LL FIND THERE'S NO 'RIGHT' OR 'WRONG' HERE,
JUST WHAT WORKS FOR YOU!

Previously unpublished rough

in the elevator and force my ideas on them. Sometimes, to be nice to me, artists such as Ed would draw a rough of my idea and turn it in. But they always got turned down.

"Once, however, Ed and I were talking in the hall about a story I'd just done in Charleston. I often got lost in strange towns, which was about every three weeks, and while lost one day in Charleston, where I'd seen all these beautifully restored brick houses, I came upon what I thought was a pile of bricks. A sign on it said, 'Another beautiful Charleston house awaiting restoration.' When I told this to Ed, he said, 'Aha!,' and went back to his office and drew a cartoon that got in the magazine, minus Charleston. But that didn't exactly count, because I didn't *mean* to give him an idea."

In 1978, Koren and Trillin were in East Los Angeles documenting Chicano lowriders for a feature headlined "Low and Slow, Mean and Clean." The reporters became friendly with some local "car clubbers" and were invited to a memorably sketchy party. "Things got very strange," Koren recalls. "At one point, one of the guys said, 'Hey, man, I think we gotta get you out of here, fast.' There were guns, people were getting angry at each other, and there was a lot of drinking. They took us out of the house some serpentine way and he said, 'Now get out of here.'" Koren's gently humorous drawings captured a car-hopping contest, the "cholo" look, and a show-car interior, complete with TV set. "They were so meshed in this little subculture. And God knows you could go to the tractor pull at the Tunbridge Fair here in Vermont and see the same thing."

Trillin, it turns out, had established a relationship with a former gang member gone straight, and he arranged for Koren to ride around with one of the more dangerous gangs, whose members "were trying to be nice but were sort of volatile." After returning to New York, Trillin revealed the meaning behind Koren's driver's nickname, Muerte (Death). "I told him I had just talked to our guide," Trillin says. "I asked him, 'Guess how Muerte got his name.' Ed said, 'I don't know.' And I said, 'He's a professional assassin.' Ed sort of turned into one of his characters and looked kind of shaky-lined."

Many artists rue the gap separating commercial illustration work from the galleries they'd prefer to be associated with. Likewise, Saul Steinberg always struggled with reconciling his gallery work with his copious illustration assignments and cartooning. James Geraghty once wrote to Steinberg that "the Magazine Steinberg and the Gallery Steinberg can't be the same person and you shouldn't ask that they be." Koren, on the other hand, sees little difference between a certain type of painting and cartooning.

"It's about telling a story in the simplest means possible," says Koren, who has described cartooning as "a lightning-fast one-act play that takes place in a frozen moment in time, with a specific goal: laughter." Koren argues that an effective cartoon is essentially no different structurally from, say, a Paolo Veronese painting like *Allegory of the Battle of Lepanto,* which unfolds an entire narrative in a single rectangle, depicting the battle's events frozen in time. "It's like that great Arno cartoon of a plane that just crashed: An ambulance is rushing in and a guy is returning to his office with his plans, saying, 'Well, back to the old drawing board.' I wouldn't compare him to Veronese—but I will. Some of Arno's elements are exactly the same as Veronese's, and Arno's drawing is equally as refined, individual, and inspired. You can tell a Veronese because of the brushwork, line work, and structure of the palette, and the same thing with an Arno. So where is the value system of high and low? Is it the ambition that one is a religious painting and the other is just a—well, that's old hat since the French Academy. The first time caricature and satire in this kind of drawing was ever considered, as it should be—in my opinion, of course, because I'd like to be important—was by Baudelaire, who wrote about Daumier in the same way he was writing about other painters."

Modern cartooning has tended to strip away detail and ornamentation, leaving nothing but the bare essentials. Charles Barsotti in particular has taken this reductionism to a transcendent extreme. Addams, Arno, and Hokinson, on the other hand, filled their often page-sized drawings with detail, atmosphere, and decor. Koren considers himself to be another cartooning maximalist.

"I love to elaborate," he says, "because that's part of the story being told. Nuances and things in the background relate to or illuminate the action I want to focus on. It adds to it. If it's too fussy or busy, then the drawing loses focus. I think of myself as a theater director or a playwright because I'm unfolding a drama. I cast these people as who I want them to be. I have a costumer come in to dress them, a designer, a lighting director, and I put it all together. I don't think of it that way consciously, but it's how I operate. I want the action, the emotion of the moment, to be clear and profound—and also funny. It's like a juggling act." One challenge, he finds, is deciding where to stage his mini-dramas, which take place in restaurants, bars, living rooms, offices, kitchens, cars, streets, and beds—anywhere people come together to converse.

"A big problem with a lot of the younger, newer artists is that there's no eye contact," he complains. "There's no facial or emotional interaction. They're like stick figures, ideas, and lines. They aren't humans. Every time I hear actors talk about their craft, I'm impressed by how much they get into it and add emotional depth to a character

Previously unpublished rough

and how that connects to the ensemble. And this is what cartoons, at their best, should be."

Koren draws his roughs quickly, in small bursts of inspiration. "I try to keep the fresh, dynamic part of it." He admires Lee Lorenz's "incredibly vivid and lively" drawing style. His finished drawings are substantially larger than his roughs and more about drawing than concept. Koren appreciates the minimalism of R. O. Blechman, who may sketch a figure using only two or three lines, but "each one is as considered as carefully as one would consider a major military move." Blechman once looked at one of Koren's drawings, kind of shuddered, and said, "All those lines," the memory of which makes Koren laugh. "I keep thinking about that because, yeah, there *are* a lot of lines."

Lacking strong outlines, Koren's figures seem to shimmy and shiver into existence with a sort of beautiful indeterminacy that echoes his fuzzy and furry human menagerie. "I'm *always* uncertain," he explains. "Part of it is almost a fear of commitment. I'm a little bit off-the-wall about it. I'm not happy unless things are really bouncing around and coming into collision with each other, and not quite clear." Koren says that style of indecisiveness can sometimes be discerned in his characters' characters as well. "Maybe there's a bit of malevolent bemusement in them, a bit of camouflage for harsher feelings I have about things—a nicer way to put what's really mean-spirited."

Koren is, of course, famous for his anthropomorphized animals. But even he never always knows quite why he's drawing an animal rather than a person. Of course he knows that cartoon animals are never *simply* animals. "And that's the point," he says. "They are and they aren't. An animal is very much a surrogate." When we spoke, *The New Yorker* had just published a Koren cover (October 22, 2012) depicting a group of older animals at the starting line of a race. "If I'd done it with humans, it wouldn't be funny to begin with, at least to me. If it were humans with the same emotions, expressions, or intensity as they were starting a race, you'd look at it and say, 'So what? That's the way people are. What's new?' But using animals turns it upside down somehow." Yet it's never quite clear why this should be the case. "I'm satisfied with it in an unclear, almost unconscious way," he says.

"I like his animal cartoons particularly," says Trillin, "the ones with those Koren beasts. I have some of his Uptown Stuff"—meaning his paintings. "My theory is that in the cartoons it's difficult to say what kind of animal it is, and in the Uptown Stuff it's hard to say whether or not it's an animal."

In the end, whether Koren draws humans or beasts comes down to intuition. Some ideas are funny one way but not the other, and Koren just knows "in my bones" the way it ought to be. Sometimes he tests ideas to see if they work better with humans or animals. "I just had an OK [i.e., sold] one that uses birds. It has to do with all this turmoil about where our food comes from. It makes perfect sense with birds." In the cartoon, a mother bird says, "Wait—did you procure that worm humanely?" as her mate prepares to drop a fat worm into a nest of hungry chicks. "If it were a father who'd brought something home from the market, and she's questioning whether it came from the food co-op or the supermarket, it wouldn't work! It wouldn't be as pointed and sharp and driven as with the bird with a giant worm." Clearly there would be no joke if a human were making the same comment. "It's the little smile they give each other, too," he adds, sealing his argument.

Few cultural productions are more artisanal than a *New Yorker* cartoon, of course. I have yet to hear of any artist who draws on a computer exclusively, although some occasionally do. Even the way Koren describes his work schedule has something of seasonal temporality to it. "If I'm working on roughs, I'll do it for a day if I'm actually firing on all cylinders, or two or three days if it's bumping along and I'm not quite getting it. Sometimes it requires just sitting there, and then it happens; and sometimes one sits there for hours and nothing happens, no good ideas. Sometimes ideas come one right after the other in a process of free association or mental disassociation. Arno once said something to a woman like 'Madam, these ideas don't just happen. They come from long hard hours spent sitting and working.'"

For roughs, Koren uses Eberhard Faber's soft 3B drawing pencils with eighty-pound bond paper. "It's a nice, kind of stiff bond that reacts well to a pencil," he says. He used to use nonarchival bond for his finishes, but he says his work from the sixties and seventies is threatening to deteriorate from acids in the paper. Now he uses Arches archival watercolor paper or, more frequently, 270 gsm BFK Rives. "It has a wonderful pebbly surface that pencil and pen react to brilliantly. It gives back. There's a feeling of resistance I relish when I draw." He also uses the Arches and Rives for prints. "I do a lot of etching in the summer, and lately I've been doing stone lithography using BFK Rives. It's such a hearty, responsive paper." He prefers Speedball nib pens with oval points dipped into Pelikan India ink. "It's very sensitive to changes of pressure and direction," he says, "and it flows beautifully. I just love the way the pen and paper shake hands all the time; they're like a partnership. I love using my hands and playing on the paper. It feels good, and it kind of gets moving like a rhythm. Bliss."

After he gets his OKs, Koren jumps right in without much futzing. "If I'm in it, I'll just stay in it. Basically, I'm there from morning until night, with interruptions along the way to take a bicycle ride or go for a run. In the winter, I'll put on the old cross-country skis and go off into the woods. That's very much part of my day."

His batches of *New Yorker* submissions have diminished over the

GOOD NIGHT, SWEETIE —
SLEEP TIGHT, AND DON'T LET THE BED BUGS BITE.

Previously unpublished rough

years, and Koren now sends in five to seven ideas at a time. "It's a great achievement for me to get six sharp, viable, funny ideas. I send them off hoping they'll seem that way to Remnick and Mankoff, too. And then I sit back and wait to see what happens with them because there's not much that can be done at that point. Off you go! Have a nice trip! Come back safe!" He frequently changes rejected roughs — re-captioning, reparsing, rewording, or changing the situation's dynamics.

Not everything is funny to everybody, of course, and Koren has suffered his share of humor heartbreak. One of his favorite rejected ideas is a Mayor Bloomberg–ian notion involving a New York City police car with a bumper sticker — alongside CALL 911 and WE'RE HERE TO SERVE — that reads EAT MORE KALE.

Rejection never gets easier, he says. "It's not hard to get bummed out. Part of it is the silence. You just never know why something wasn't accepted." Like writing or acting, cartooning is a profession in which you tend to be perceived as being only as good as your last gig — or, in this case, gag. "There's neither dignity nor respect for what cartoonists do," Koren concludes with a sigh. "That's dwindling everywhere. But it's tough to take after a long career, even a short career. You want a little feedback; that's all one really requires."

6

The Kansas City Curmudgeon:
Charles Barsotti

"Your love gives me strength."

IN 1990, CHARLES Barsotti received a piece of fan mail from another Charles, who wrote, "I think the little dogs you draw are the funniest cartoons that anyone has been doing in recent years"—signed "Sparky." Having the creator of *Peanuts*, Charles Schulz, tell you he thinks you draw cartooning's funniest dogs is not unlike having Tiger Woods express envy at your follow-through. Snoopy and Barsotti's "little dogs" actually bear some resemblance, though Barsotti uses fewer lines than Schulz did to sketch even more psychologically fraught canines. Barsotti's cute little mutts always work under the radar.

Barsotti (who, sadly, died on June 16, 2014, during production of the book you're reading) didn't collect his favorite dog cartoons into the book Schulz also suggested in his letter until 2007. Titled after a drawing of a couched canine patient complaining to his shrink, *They Moved My Bowl* is one of the purest distillations of unaffected style in all cartooning. The dog-therapy cartoons are particularly, uh, fetching: "Oh, God, am I housebroken," says the patient in one; "They *think* they're accidents," claims another; and, in a typical Barsotti flip-flop, the floppy-eared therapist tells a tearfully grateful human patient, "Well, *I* think you're wonderful." One is tempted to quote virtually every caption in the book.

They Moved My Bowl is dedicated to Jiggs, the half-Dachshund pet Barsotti owned as a child in San Antonio, Texas. "He was a great dog," he says, "and he was run over by a car; broke my little heart." Jiggs's spirit endures, however, in hundreds of cartoons depicting variations on the same nameless dogs in myriad emotional manifestations. Lee Lorenz's former assistant, the photographer Anne Hall, "used to deny that it was a dog at all." She was right, of course. Those aren't dogs; they're *us.*

Charles Barsotti—or "Charley," as nearly everyone refers to him—was born September 28, 1933, in his grandmother's house in San Marcos, Texas, halfway between Austin and San Antonio on Interstate 35. "Everything down there either had thorns on it or bit," he says, "and that includes the adults." His father, Howard, sold furniture in San Antonio, where Charley was raised. His mother, the delightfully named Dicey Belle Branum, was a schoolteacher. Charley credits his hardworking parents with inspiring his determined work ethic. "That, and fear," he adds.

Forced from Tennessee during the Civil War for some forgotten reason, the Branums were among the "gone to Texas" breed of Southern Baptist. Barsotti recalls tales of wagon trains and Indians and "probably exaggerated" accounts of prewar poverty. His father, on the other hand, was "this Italian harsh guy" who brought his big-city ways with him down South. Nicknamed "the Yankee," Charley's father "was a bit of a dude" who swept a Southern Baptist schoolteacher off her feet. The Branums were hostile to Howard until the intervention of Dicey Belle's mother, the family matriarch, who "set everybody straight."

San Antonio, for Charley (who, not wanting to be confused with Edgar Bergen's dummy sidekick Charlie McCarthy, was never

"Charlie"), was a "really nifty place." His family resided on the south side of town. "We'd call it 'semirural,' but it was more lower-middle class." His mother taught in a two-room schoolhouse outside of town. She eventually transferred to Hot Wells, named after some local sulfur depositories, where Charley attended school from first grade through his senior year of high school. He entered school at age five. "Mom pulled some strings, which I'm still upset about. Charles Schulz and I discovered that we shared this: Being the youngest boy in class was not really ideal. I was skinny, underweight, and untalented," he says, and laughs.

Charley frequently rode the bus into downtown San Antonio to take swimming classes at the YMCA and read Sherlock Holmes stories at the library. At home, he enjoyed the cartoons in *Look, Collier's,* and the *Saturday Evening Post*. Comics were also a passion, although "I don't remember a great generosity in purchasing them." His parents read as many as three newspapers a day, which meant a bounty of comic strips. "One of the great pleasures was when Dad would come home Saturday night with the big Sunday paper and a jar of pickled pigs' feet he got at the delicatessen. I was very heavily into that."

Charley accompanied his mother to her Baptist church and was later "dragged" into Catholicism, following his parents' conversion, just as he hit puberty.

A McCarthy-era chill was in the air when Barsotti began attending the conservative Southwest Texas State College (STSC, now Texas State University) in San Marcos. His mentor was a music teacher named Ira Bowles, who introduced him to such non-Texas media as *The New Yorker* and the Sunday *New York Times*. "He sort of insisted that these things be on my reading list, and paid attention to, in order to know what was going on."

When Texas's governor ousted a popular STSC professor who wrote a poem parodying state politics, Barsotti responded with an editorial cartoon. Every comic Barsotti drew for the campus newspaper, the *Star*, was subsequently scrutinized and sometimes censored by STSC's president, the lauded education advocate John Garland Flowers, who would paste pieces of white paper over images as inoffensive as a can of beer.

After graduating in 1955 with a degree in social science, Barsotti married Jo Ann Zibberman, with whom he would have four children: Kerry, Mike, Sue, and Wendy. He was then drafted into the army. "I hated basic training," he says. "Worst time of my life." He served as a unit clerk at Fort Sam Houston's Brooke Army Medical Center in San Antonio, where his pregnant wife was living. "I did what I was supposed to do and was glad to be there," he says.

Following his discharge, Barsotti returned to STSC in San Marcos, where he studied for a master's degree in education. He was employed part-time at the Brown School Treatment Center (now the San Marcos Treatment Center), a residential facility for mentally disabled adolescents and adults where he'd worked as an undergraduate. "The guy running the place was doing something underhanded, and they suddenly said to me, '*You* run the place.'" Barsotti found the Brown School both challenging and rewarding. As its sympathetic director, Barsotti did his best to humanize the facility, such as by creating a special Boy Scout troop. As the Brown School's community representative, Barsotti joined the San Marcos Rotary Club and ac-

quired a reputation as a liberal, or worse. He gently mocked its members in the club newsletter while endearing himself to them through
his caricatures.

Barsotti still yearned to draw for *The New Yorker*, though, and his
opportunity to do so arrived unexpectedly thanks to a beneficent, encouraging gesture from Brown Schools founder Bert Brown. "We
didn't agree on anything politically," Barsotti says of their relationship, "but we were good friends. One day when I was at work, he
called and said, 'I want you to go home and just draw some cartoons,
because you're going on a trip with me.' So I went home. It was the
first time I ever did any single-panel stuff and it was really exciting."
Brown took Barsotti on the artist's first trip to New York City, where
he visited every magazine in town that ran cartoons. "*Esquire* was not
nice," Barsotti recalls, "but everybody else was wonderful, including
The New Yorker. They bought." It was a time when a twentysome-
thing kid from Texas could fly into New York, cold-call magazines
with his art, and lucky things might happen. "I was walking down
a street and saw a little plaque that read '*Pageant Magazine.*' It was a
small, pocket-sized magazine like *Reader's Digest*. But I walked in
and they bought a couple of spreads right away."

The New Yorker bought a gag from Barsotti, who eventually sold
ideas that were drawn by Chon Day, John O'Brien, and Otto Soglow.
"I remember that one in particular because this stuff was all fresh and
new and exciting. Well, it still *is* exciting. But that one had to do with
Sargent Shriver, something about all the traveling he did and a native village." When Shriver later turned up in Austin for a speech, the
local papers referred to "Soglow's *New Yorker* cartoon," though it was
Barsotti's idea. He snorts. "I got no credit in my almost-hometown
paper."

Barsotti's first *New Yorker* cartoon appeared in the magazine's August
25, 1962, issue. A young man carrying a sign reading BAN THE BOMB
says to a young woman carrying a STOP THE TESTS sign: "Just think!
If it weren't for nuclear fission, we might never have met!" He wouldn't
become a regular for another decade, however.

While working at the Brown School, Barsotti replied to a job ad placed by Hallmark Cards in *Advertising Age* magazine. He received writing and psychology tests in reply. His desire to leave Texas mounted following President Kennedy's assassination in November 1963, when Barsotti realized that most San Marcosans didn't consider a Democratic Catholic president's murder a tragic occurrence. With the help of William H. Whyte's bestseller *The Organization Man,* Barsotti came up with appropriate answers to Hallmark's psych test (including: "I love my father and my mother both, but I love my father a little bit more") and was hired. "I used your book to cheat," he told Whyte when he met the writer years later, "and he gave me a hug." Barsotti moved his family to Kansas City, Missouri, in 1964. He worked in Hallmark's humor-oriented editorial department before being reassigned to the edgier realm of "contemporary" design.

While at Hallmark, Barsotti continued to submit "frecklebelly" cartoons to William Emerson at the *Saturday Evening Post.* The term, which Barsotti believes Emerson coined, refers to cartoons whose humor "is broader even than slapstick." He experienced a technical epiphany when he discovered Rapidograph pens. He splurged on a set of the then new implements and learned (as he told Lee Lorenz in 1998's *The Essential Charles Barsotti*) that unlike fountain pens, "with the Rapidographs, you never have to stop—and I didn't." He has long preferred a 0.70 mm point, approximately in the middle of the fine to

"WELL, IF YOU DON'T RESPECT ME, RESPECT THE OFFICE."

Previously unpublished

broad spectrum. They last him a long while, and he doesn't mind if one breaks and gives him an excuse to visit an art-supplies store to see what's new.

Accustomed to hearing back quickly from the *Saturday Evening Post,* Barsotti was surprised once when his latest batch elicited a longer response time than usual. So he did another batch, and the following week he received a call from Mike Mooney, the *Post*'s cartoon editor. "Mike said he had turned the big hallway at the *Post* into a gallery. 'I've got your cartoons up and down it.' I thought it was a joke." After meeting *Post* editor William Emerson (who once characterized the cartoonist as a "supersophisticated yokel"), Barsotti began drawing spreads for the magazine. These led to *My Kind of People,* a regular feature that often showcased several cartoons linked thematically to topics; for example, one *People* page involved bricks, another bombs.

Early in 1968, Emerson asked Barsotti to move to New York to become the magazine's cartoon editor and Barsotti accepted the position without hesitation. "It took me about three months before I felt like I had a handle on it," he says. "And then I thought, 'This is what I wanna do, forever.' I loved it." The Barsottis moved to Westchester County, first to Larchmont and later to Mamaroneck, a neighborhood Barsotti describes as "a rip in the silk-stocking district."

Unfortunately, Barsotti's time at the *Post* turned out to be all too short. The magazine folded in January 1969 before he could implement most of his ideas. He published broadly funny "frecklebelly" cartoons, "suburban" cartoons about the middle class, and a third category of somewhat edgier images. The *Post*'s "America, America" page contained the sort of politically slanted cartoons *The New Yorker* had not yet begun to print, even as writers like Jonathan Schell were reporting extensively on the Vietnam War and civil rights issues in its pages.

To this day, Barsotti still seems devastated by the *Post*'s demise at the moment of its highest circulation. (A $760,000 combined award to Georgia Bulldogs football coach Wally Butts and Alabama Crimson Tide head coach Bear Bryant, who filed a defamation suit against the magazine and its parent company in 1967, contributed to its failure.) Barsotti loved editing, relished being able to treat cartoonists as respected artists, and publishing the work of friends at Hallmark and elsewhere. He bought work by George Booth before *The New Yorker* did and was about to "introduce" him to the *Post*'s readership with a substantial spread when the magazine ceased publication. To add insult to injury, Barsotti's first *Post* cover was slated to appear the week after the magazine folded. Bill Emerson held up the cover for television cameras covering the magazine's closure.

Barsotti's unpublished cover featured Emma June, a love-struck — or perhaps *life*-struck—character he had been drawing in *Look* and the *Post* since 1967. It's not unusual for male artists to create significant female characters. But Emma June was atypically vibrant, a cartoon version, say, of Liza Minnelli's Pookie in *The Sterile Cuckoo*. Barsotti's "silly" character was the flower child obverse of the existentially tortured dancers and beatniks Jules Feiffer was drawing for the *Village Voice*. Published in 1969, Barsotti's first book was an expanded collection of his charming strips titled *A Girl Needs a Little Action*. It recounts the modern fairy tale of how this "warm and freckled girl" finds her man and settles down happily in—surprise!—suburbia.

At Hallmark, Barsotti had started to develop another female character, an Emma June variation named Sally Bananas, as a syndicated daily strip, which *Newsday*'s comics syndicate picked up in October 1969. Barsotti describes Sally as a "whimsical" barefoot girl who gamboled around a park with a few friends. The failure of the strip to catch on, Barsotti believes, was due to the Times-Mirror Company purchasing *Newsday* in 1970 and the departure of publisher Bill Moyers three days later.

The week after the *Post* folded, Barsotti met with William Shawn at *The New Yorker*. Their meeting occurred thanks to Bill Emerson, who'd asked Shawn to speak with both Barsotti and Booth. The tête-à-tête, he recalls, "really made me feel good. But I can't remember a word Mr. Shawn said except for 'We hope you stay in cartooning.' He was very formal yet very vague at the same time. I didn't understand that *The New Yorker* was more magical than logical." The following

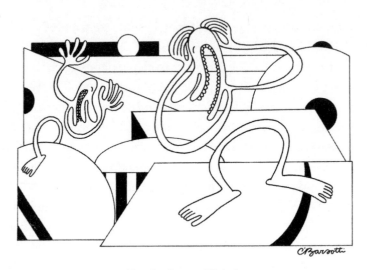

Previously unpublished

week, Barsotti had lunch with cartoon editor James Geraghty and artist Frank Modell. "I thought it would be like a corporate lunch but I don't know what the hell it was. It was extremely awkward but nice." Nevertheless, Barsotti returned to *The New Yorker* in 1969.

While visiting the magazine's office one day, Barsotti learned that the head of the Newsday syndicate had been fired. "It was close to the holidays, and Geraghty, in his mystical Irish way, said something like 'By the way, we would like to have legal recognition'—some phrase like that—'between the two of us. You might take this to your lawyer, look at it, see what you think.' I went to lunch with a *Newsweek* writer and said, 'I don't know for sure, but I think I might have just been offered a *New Yorker* contract.' And that's what it was. But there was no hint of it ahead of time. If there had been, I would never have gone down the painful path of the comic strip." With contract in hand, Barsotti moved his family back to Kansas City.

Barsotti's late-sixties lifestyle tended toward the conservative, but his politics were decidedly left of center for a Texan, especially when it came to the war in Vietnam. "That just ripped things apart," he says. "A Texas friend called me after I got to New York. He claimed to work in the Johnson White House, but I think he was lying. He said,

'We want to invite you to the White House, but sometimes people change about the war when they move from the Midwest to New York.' I said, 'I changed *before* I fucking moved to New York.'"

Passionate opposition to the war roused the staid corridors of *The New Yorker*, too. Visiting Manhattan the day of the first Nixon-authorized incursion into Cambodia, Barsotti recalls an electrifying scene. "Even Shawn was out in the hallway talking with a group of us: 'Somebody do something, do something besides the magazine.'" In Missouri, the Barsottis found liberal fellow travelers through the Unitarian church, but the readjustment was "jarring" for the artist and his family.

In 1972, Barsotti threw his hat into the ring as a Democratic candidate for Congress. "It was awful," he says, adding that only his New York friends appreciated his activism. He ran in the Third Congressional District in Johnson County, a Republican stronghold, and would come to regret not following his initial disinclination to participate. "We'd been involved in getting the right people to the state Democratic convention, and this just kind of happened without any planning at all. Before I ran, a friend of mine said, 'You have never shown a propensity for suffering fools gladly.' And I thought, 'Nonsense.' But it was a terrible experience. I must have been out of my mind. But I thought the Vietnam War was a horrible, horrible mistake." Barsotti eventually withdrew from the race because, he says, "they were making deals with people I didn't want to talk with."

The collapse of the *Post*, failure of his daily strip, move back to Kansas City, and campaign all took a toll on Barsotti's marriage. Charley and Jo Ann divorced in 1973. "Things just kind of fell apart. I'm not gonna say moving back here was a mistake, because I wouldn't have met Ramoth," he says, referring to his second and presumably final wife. "The kids are all doing OK, although they did get a little antsy once in a while and ask, 'Why in the hell did you move us back here?!'"

In Kansas City, Barsotti transformed himself into the freelancing dynamo he remains today. He illustrated for the opinion pages of the *New York Times* and *Kansas City Star* ("I must have done a hundred Nixons"); did some of his best work, including cover illustrations and experimental collages, for the venerable British humor magazine *Punch;* and began drawing for *National Lampoon,* to which he contributed perhaps his most widely appreciated cartoon: A hot dog stands at the mailbox holding a postcard that reads "You may already be a wiener."

Like every *New Yorker* contract artist, Barsotti is theoretically obliged to at least give the magazine a first look at every cartoon he creates. Barsotti did so ("at least when I took it seriously"), although Lee Lorenz told him that "if it's obviously for *Playboy,* I don't need to see it." *The New Yorker* "still gets a lot of stuff from me," even if its editors don't see every image.

Not long after he began drawing for *Playboy,* Barsotti found himself embroiled in an unexpected legal kerfuffle. *Playboy* cartoon editor Michelle Urry had said to him, "We like your cartoons, but our readers really like sexy stuff. Could you give that a shot?" So he did. In the September 1975 issue, a Barsotti drawing depicted a smiling girl sitting in a chair with a man under her skirt. An older woman in the background pronounces the caption: "Really, Clarice, if you had simply assured Lord Cowdray that the hors d'oeuvres were to be served presently." But there was art to it as well! "I wanted the setting to be kind of formal," Barsotti says. "I was using a different drawing style that was a little more ornate, more fanciful." Unfortunately, he used the wrong lord's name to make his jest. "It turns out that if you name somebody Lord Something, and there's somebody by that name, there's only one in the world. Who knew?" Barsotti had unfortunately neglected to consult *Burke's Peerage* before choosing this particular surname. "Only years later did it occur to me that I'd heard this name through Monty Python, but I didn't associate it with a title." As it happened, the real Lord Cowdray was not amused. "This particular Lord Cowdray's now dead," Barsotti says, "but he has a son who I believe called it to his father's attention."

Barsotti was at his drawing board one day and heard a knock at the door. "I guess you were expecting this," said the summons server. "No," Barsotti replied. "Are you the Internal Revenue Service?" *Play-*

"HE'S GOT A POINT."

Previously unpublished

boy's lawyers were on the case immediately. "We don't want any Kansas City lawyers involved in this," they told Barsotti, who enjoyed repeating the caution to local lawyer friends. "But I don't repeat it anymore, because Ramoth's family is *full* of Kansas City lawyers." The November 1975 *Playboy* contained a correction: "*PLAYBOY* regrets . . . any embarrassment it may have inadvertently caused Lord Cowdray." *Playboy* also removed all the pages containing the cartoon from its British edition. "*Playboy* was really behind me," says Barsotti. "I was just starting with them and they could have asked me not to send them any more cartoons because 'We don't want any more trouble.' But they bought more cartoons."

Barsotti married tireless supporter and enthusiast Ramoth Millin in 1978, and the two work closely enough together to have earned the nickname "Barsotti Incorporated." During the eighties, Barsotti became a regular cartoonist for *Punch*, to which his aesthetic translated easily. In the drawing captioned "Business lunch," for example, one businessman chews the arm of another, who is stabbing him with a fork. In 1992, the British stationery chain Niceday (now owned by Office Depot) licensed Barsotti's iconic canine, which became known as the "Niceday pup." The dog's ability to master any number of different European leisure activities made it a ubiquitous presence in the company's advertising campaigns and company Christmas cards. The United Kingdom even issued a postage stamp featuring the dog.

His relationship with Niceday has allowed the Barsottis to maintain a pleasant middle-class life even as his appearances in *The New Yorker*—"I'm always happy to be in it, and I'm really pissed when I'm not"—have fluctuated. A table in Barsotti's office supports a pair of precarious stacks of drawings on his standard two-ply Strathmore paper cut to 7.5 by 9.5 inches. (Lorenz once accused Barsotti of sending in his work on "index cards.") I ask him what the stacks contain. "They are just what they are," he replies with a hint of testiness. "They're cartoons *The New Yorker* didn't buy—or things they haven't bought *yet* is the way I'd like to look at it." In the past, Barsotti might have been able to sell his *New Yorker* rejects elsewhere, but now, he says, "It's like [they're] the last deal in town, which can be just frustrating as hell when I give them something I really like and they don't see the wisdom or share my enthusiasm. And what do I do with it? Maybe I can change a caption or something."

Barsotti does not view *The New Yorker* as currently representing a golden age of single-panel cartooning. "I would rather go out in a blaze of glory now, speaking for *The New Yorker*, in a blaze of good cartoons." (He mentions a couple of cartoonists whose work he dislikes intensely, but Ramoth requests they go unnamed.) He finds many current cartoons hard on the eyes. "I don't think a cartoon needs to be ugly. It can be mean, it can be pointed, it can be satirical, it can do a lot of things, but it doesn't have to be ugly. This is, after all, *The New Yorker*. David Remnick has said, 'We're a magazine, not a museum.' There is such a strong, wonderful history behind all of this, and I don't think you'll find too many cartoons from that tradition that are just out-and-out ugly." Does he admire *any* of the magazine's younger cartoonists? "I'm trying to think," he deadpans. "I'm thinking! I'm thinking!" Pause. "No."

"Oh, Charley," says Ramoth soothingly, as Charley works himself up.

"Stop it, Ramoth! Don't be Midwest nice." Charley calms down as Ramoth leaves the room to fetch a glass of water and the medicine her husband has taken since the quadruple bypass he underwent in 1997.

Returning, Ramoth notes that "Charley's a tough editor. He would be like William Shawn. But his sense of humor isn't always like everyone else's." How would she characterize it? "He has a good sense of humor. He's kind of somber, though, more on the quiet side. In a group you wouldn't say, 'Oh, there's the cartoonist.' No, he's not that way." I suggest that there's a gentleness to Charley's cartoons even when he's critiquing the harshest social conditions, and that maybe it's a southern thing. "Charley is very sensitive," Ramoth adds. "He's a sweet person, really, even though he comes off as a curmudgeon sometimes."

"Yeah," Barsotti says, laughing. "My kids seem to use that word excessively."

Barsotti continues to cartoon as he always has: doodling until an idea comes to him and then sketching it out in pencil. The Strathmore paper lets him get away with a lot of erasing until he applies a Rapidograph to a sketch over a light box. Bottles of Wite-Out sit on his drawing table. "I just work until I'm happy with it," he says. Unlike most other cartoonists, Barsotti never draws rough drafts; his roughs and finished product are the same. His minimalist drawings seem to leap off the page energized by their own simplicity. There's nothing superfluous in his lines and no need for ink-wash halftones to flesh out backgrounds or hint at perspective. A Barsotti cartoon has the brisk immediacy of a mentholated cough drop.

It's the clean joy of Barsotti's lines that sells his anthropomorphic wit. Chickens, cutlery, fruit, corkscrews, magazines, and toothpaste tubes display easily recognizable human emotions. "Fusilli, you crazy bastard! How are you?" asks a piece of rigatoni over the phone. In Barsotti's world, objects are as familiar as our friends and neighbors;

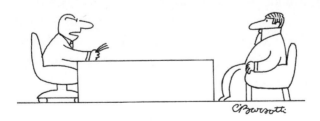

"NOW ABOUT THAT NECK TATTOO..."

Previously unpublished

they're displaced stand-ins for our own desires, fears, and hierarchies. In one series of cartoons, a businessman's sock puppet says what he himself cannot.

Anger and angst lurk in Barsotti's work as well. In *The Essential Charles Barsotti,* Lorenz described the cartoonist's King character as "devious and sentimental, ruthless yet subject to deep self-doubt, serene in his sovereignty but not above sharing a pizza with the palace guard." In other words: Isn't he a bit like you and me? This regal figure ominously informs a crowned colleague, "My loyal opposition wasn't loyal enough." The King is the pup's egotistic counterpart: The monarch is tough yet sympathetic, the pooch infinitely sympathetic yet subtly entitled.

Beneath the lightness and whiteness of his drawings, Barsotti has a tough, deep sense of the power and status relationships that define New Yorkers' lives especially. Sometimes he combines dogs and businessmen in scenarios. In one, a boss points to a pup sitting behind his desk and tells an underling, "Go ahead, Albertson. Ask Toby for a raise. It'll be cute."

Although he taught cartooning briefly, if "really stupidly," at the Kansas City Art Institute one summer, Barsotti claims to have no theories regarding the subject. His drawings seem to have become increasingly clean over the years to the extent that some are realized with less than a couple of dozen lines. If Barsotti did have a theory of cartooning, his current work suggests it would probably revolve around a sort of two-dimensional Zen.

"I distilled both the caption *and* the cartoon," he explains. "You want the caption to be conversational, boiled down. And, yeah, I like to simplify very much." He recalls a relatively recent cartoon by Nick Downes. "It was set in a doctor's office with a sign that said 'Thank you for not mentioning Dr. Oz,' which I thought was wonderful. But if I'd thought of it, I'd just show the doctor in a white coat, with the stethoscope, and he's talking to somebody. You've seen a doctor's office, so I don't need to show what they look like. It pleases me a lot that I can distill it to that point and it still works. The same goes for the aggressive or evil businessman. The less important characters in medieval paintings were always smaller. So when I have somebody picking on somebody economically, I just draw the picked-on person small. I like that kind of shorthand. It allows for a more abstract situation."

In the eighties, Barsotti consciously tried to appeal to *New Yorker* editor Robert Gottlieb with puns, collages, and more ornate cartoons than usual. "I don't think Gottlieb liked my stuff particularly," Barsotti says. "I changed the style and did some running puns—but I thought I was just amusing Lee [Lorenz]." One, for example, depicted an anthropomorphic bean wearing a sombrero. The caption, which Barsotti admits was "just terrible," reads: "El L. Bean." He explains that "it was only meant to be an inside joke, 'cause I thought it was so extreme and awful." He waits a beat. "But I didn't tell him not to buy it!"

Although Barsotti admits to shamelessly attempting to please Gottlieb, he found the collages "a lot of fun but Glen Baxter–ish in the extreme," referring to the British collage cartoonist Gottlieb brought into the magazine. Barsotti describes the process of repurposing intriguing images from old comics as another kind of "doodling." "The men from the pasta squad know their stuff," reads the inset caption to a faux-vintage image of a pair of '40s-style heroes dealing with a hot-water crisis. "Remember, *al dente*," says one. "Hey, this isn't my first rodeo, pal," replies his teammate. In a cartoon mocking product plugs in classic movies, Miss Cheeses of the World 1940 asks Humphrey Bogart (with a photograph for a head) if he remem-

"OF ALL MY CLIENTS YOU'RE THE MOST FUN."

Previously unpublished

bers Paris. "I remember every detail," he replies. "The Germans wore gray. You wore bleu."

"That was the kind of stuff they were buying," says Barsotti, adding that both Lorenz and Gottlieb were enthusiastic about his work. Today, however, he couldn't get away with it.

According to Barsotti, Gottlieb once asked Lorenz to find another Peter Arno. "That'd be interesting," Barsotti says as though he were the cartoon editor. "I'll see if I can find one for you." His relationship with Tina Brown was easier. "She was very nice and knew my work. Tina loved and responded to cartoons about power. I did one of two businessmen with lion heads: 'I'm taking you to the Four Seasons. You'll enjoy the fear.' There are differences you pick up on with these guys. The guy from Simon & Schuster [Gottlieb], though, was full of crap."

7

The Beatnik Biker: Arnie Levin

"Relax. I've come for your toaster."

THE LATE FRANK Modell once related a party conversation:
"What do you do?"
"I'm a cartoonist."
"I love cartoons. Where do you publish?"
"*The New Yorker.*"
"I love *The New Yorker*. What's your name?"
"Frank Modell."
"Yes? [*Pause.*] I've never heard of you."

Arnie Levin is one of the many *New Yorker* cartoonists and cover artists whose style may not be immediately identifiable to readers, but whose constant presence since 1974 has contributed incalculably to the magazine's identity. "Howard, I think the dog wants to go out," says an aproned woman to her pipe-smoking husband in Levin's most popular Cartoon Bank image. Their pet, dressed to the nines under a top hat and cape, waits patiently in the living room. In another popular Levin panel, a matron returns an item to a department store, explaining, "It's fancy-schmantzy. I just wanted fancy."

In person, Levin turns out to be neither fancy nor schmantzy but rather a remarkable study in cognitive dissonance. Born on February 11, 1938, the diminutive Long Islander sports the shaved head, goatee, and slightly rolling gait of a badass biker. An artist renowned in yakuza circles for having tattooed much of his upper body with ornate Japanese imagery, Levin has lived as an outsider among artistic outsiders and has the stories to back it up. With the possible exception of certain members of the original San Francisco underground crew, cartoonists are not a defiantly wild bunch. Levin, on the other hand, had lived the hipster, smoke-a-reefer beatnik life to a hilt before he ever walked in *The New Yorker*'s front door—with a dash of *Mad Men* on the side.

His attic studio in Sea Cliff, Long Island, is filled to the rafters with books, posters, and other nostalgia-laden cultural collectibles. It has the air of an antique store, and it's somehow unsurprising to learn that Levin used to own one of those as well: a long-ago Brooklyn operation called the Elusive Spondulla.

Levin served in the Marines before winding up as an aspiring painter in New York City's late-fifties bohemian heyday. "Swept up in the glamour of the beatnik era," as he puts it, Levin co-operated an espresso house that hosted readings by the likes of Allen Ginsberg and Jack Kerouac. He worked parties as a rent-a-beatnik, encountering another new kid in town—Bob Dylan—at one such event. At Push Pin Studios, then at the height of its influence in the design world, he was plucked out of the messenger pool by cofounder Milton Glaser, who recommended him to Lee Savage's Elektra Films, noted for forward-looking trailers and commercials. After leaving Elektra, Levin was recruited for *The New Yorker* by Lee Lorenz in 1974.

Many an underground cartoonist has lived a quieter life than Levin, whose love affair with motorcycles struck him suddenly at age fifty-nine. "I realized I was in the best shape I was ever in." He'd ridden a couple of times earlier in his life, and the kids he hung around with in high school had motorcycles, so he decided to get a license. His first bike was a black-and-white version of Yamaha's popular Virago 750 cruiser. He describes it as "heavy, but nice." He didn't want to bash up a Harley, and he did drop the bike a number of times. "I'd made a pact with myself that the minute I saw myself slipping, I would stop, no arguments," he says. "There's no second chance on a bike." He's had some close calls during almost two decades of riding and, with the exception of a minor incident that "wasn't my fault," he feels very lucky.

He celebrated his new hobby with a torrent of tattoos, beginning with some small skeletons borrowed from Mexican illustrator José Guadalupe Posada's etchings. "Everybody thinks they're from the Grateful Dead," he says with a laugh. Levin took the image to one of the oldest tattooists in the city, when tattooing was still illegal (the practice was banned in New York until 1997). The tattoo artist's son, who worked there as well, was doing Japanese tattoos. Levin looked through his sample books and found his work magnificent. "Where do you start? I wanted the carp, which was traditional; and Pam wanted the chrysanthemums, which are also traditional. I said to him, 'Look, just do it, this is your arm; it's your portfolio.' He took

particular care because he knew that if there were one wrong line, I would obsess about it.

"I just love my tattoos," says Levin. "I could look at them in the mirror for hours. People get caught up in it. If I had more money, I'd probably get more tattoos. I like them, and other people like them because they're so extensive. I'm approachable, so people can enjoy looking at them and I can explain it. People always go, 'You don't want a tattoo. That's still gonna be on you when you're ninety-five!'" Levin can't wait to find out.

Arnold Levin began buying *The New Yorker* while still a kid. His mother, Dorothy Elfenbein, was an accountant who aspired to become a writer, as did his father, Ernest Levin. "They both wanted to be fuckin' writers," Arnie says, "so it was fine for me to be an artist." The couple separated, and Dorothy raised Arnie as a single mother. She started out as a bookkeeper in a Greenwich Village speakeasy and later worked for a Rockefeller Center accounting firm next door to the William Morris Agency, which supplied her with clients like actor James Mason. On Saturdays, Dorothy would take Arnie into Manhattan from their home in Brooklyn's Flatbush neighborhood. He would draw for hours on a yellow pad in a small room beside her office, "just looking out at the street." His reward was dinner at Tad's Steak House on Forty-Second Street, near a bookstore where he could buy ten used *New Yorker*s for a dollar, though he doesn't recall why he chose them as a treat. Perhaps he just found their covers appealing.

Ernest Levin went missing from Arnie's life early on, although, like his ex-wife and son, he eventually moved to Miami, where he changed his name to Pike. "He didn't want it to be so Jewish," Arnie says. "But it's Miami!" he adds with a note of incredulity. Arnie subsequently met his father only once, while in the Marines. Hoping to reconnect, Arnie called his father, who invited him to meet at Miami International Airport, where Arnie's grandfather was due to arrive. "So we're in the terminal, the plane comes in, and nobody sees my grandfather. My dad has them page Mr. Levin. A half hour goes by. He has him paged again. We start walking around and see this older gentleman flirting with a flight attendant. 'Dad! I've been paging you!' 'I didn't hear my name,' says my grandfather. 'Mr. Levin!' my dad says. 'No,' says my grandfather, 'my name's Mr. *Pike.*'" Arnie chuckles at the memory of this dig at his dad. "I didn't say good-bye and I never saw my father again."

Enrolled at Miami's Technical Senior High School during the early fifties, Arnie skipped ninth grade. He flourished in a commercial-art class that took three hours of the school day for two years. Artists taught even his academic courses. "But they didn't teach anything," he recalls fondly. "Everybody just drew all the time." One of Arnie's favorite teachers employed Kimon Nicolaïdes's classic text *The Natural Way to Draw,* which he augmented with reading suggestions. Prior to graduation, Levin was offered a scholarship to the University of Miami—either for art or dancing.

"I was dancing *bop.*" Levin chuckles when recalling the televised citywide dance contest he won in Miami. "My partner and I were up against this brother-and-sister team. We weren't romantic, but we'd travel to different venues and compete against our archenemies, this brother-sister team. There was this whole thing between the northerners and southerners, like the mods and rockers, because I was from New York. We had these big rumbles in the park. It was like a movie!"

He decided to decline the scholarship following a visit to the University of Miami's primary art teacher. "I looked at his paintings and thought, 'Naw . . .' He was the head of the department and his work made me think of decorators' paintings. I feared it would be a course in learning to paint something to go with the drapes." By then, Levin was fired up by the work of Jackson Pollock, who inspired the young expressionist to dribble some paint himself.

Duty called, however. While still in high school, Levin joined the Marine Reserve, believing it would assure him seniority down the line. Identified as an artist, he silk-screened for the corps even before basic training. At seventeen years old, Levin barely fulfilled the height requirement and needed to bulk up to make his weight. On his way to Parris Island, South Carolina, he arrived in Beaufort, which "looked like a set from *Once Upon a Time in the West.*" Levin looked quite the young dude with his black T-shirt, powder-blue pegged suede pants, and ducktail haircut, "an outfit reflecting my dance prime." The impression was confirmed when a large boot swept his feet out from under him. "Welcome to the Marines!" said the sergeant. "Wow!" Levin recalls. "So we went to Parris Island and I thought it was just wonderful. Everyone played the parts they were supposed to play. And, of course, I ran afoul." The Marine Corps' policy of allowing recruits to purchase their own tailored uniforms appealed to the dandy in Levin, who coveted a gabardine version with "forever" pleats. "When I first got to Parris Island, this blond, blue-eyed guy with a buzz cut, Smokey the Bear cap, and swagger stick came into the office and I thought, 'Oh, God! I want to look like him!'"

Asked what function he'd like to perform as a Marine, Levin answered "photography" and was transferred to Jacksonville, Florida. Intimidated by the prospect of being sent to paratrooper training in New Jersey, Levin "worked like a son of a bitch" and came out third in his class. He chose assignment to the auxiliary air station eighty-five miles north of Los Angeles in the Mojave Desert's Antelope Valley, across the road from Edwards Air Force Base—simply because it seemed like a good place to lose oneself. Unlike Parris Island, Mojave "looked like a scene from *M*A*S*H*," Levin says of his first morning there. "One guy's got half a uniform and his underwear on. They're all lined up and I hear, 'Twelve missing and unaccounted for, sir!' 'Fourteen present, eight missing, sir!' This was getting better and better. One of the commanders stole an airplane, crashed it, and got killed," he notes sardonically.

Levin quickly made an impression on his fellow jarheads. Assigned to KP duty in the salad room, he decided to embellish an unappetizing tray of cottage cheese by sculpting a reclining nude out of the curds and whey. A side benefit was that "instead of mauling it, people ate around the edges, so we could just fill it in and use it for another meal." Receiving rave reviews for his creation, Levin followed it up with a cottage cheese White House, using parsley for trees. "Nothing really spectacular," he says humbly, "but everybody loved it."

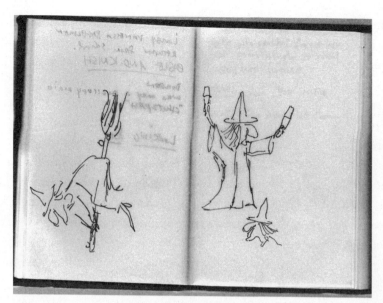

Sketchbook pages

Seeing that the Marines were testing the Vought F-8 Crusader, Levin proceeded to sculpt and serve the fighter jet . . . and was told to visit Internal Affairs. "Internal Affairs asked, 'Did you sculpt the F-8 Crusader in cottage cheese?' I replied, 'Yes, sir!' They said, 'This is a top secret plane!' The funny part was that you could see it from the road; it was just sitting out there."

Removed from the kitchen, Levin found himself driving far into the desert at sunrise, where he helped coordinate target practice for pilots dropping dud bombs. In his spare time, he would play his bongos and paint. His fellow soldiers called Levin "the Tourist" because of his trips into the desert with his watercolors and sketch pad. He hitchhiked to Los Angeles and San Francisco on his days off, and hung out in Tehachapi with Chicano friends, who nicknamed him "Que Paso?" because of his inquisitive nature. If the military had a bohemian unit, Levin would have been its captain.

Following his discharge, Levin returned to Florida but soon moved north to study at the Art Students League of New York. Expressionism was at its apex, and he studied with Julian E. Levi and modernist forerunner Vaclav Vytlacil while doing action painting on the side. One day, Vytlacil said to him, "Look, you're wasting your time. Just go out and paint. You don't need any of this stuff. Just work, work, work, and you'll be OK." Levin was sharing a room on West Ninety-First Street and hanging out at the Seven Arts Coffee Gallery in Hell's Kitchen, where he soon ended up living and working.

Seven Arts was owned by John Rapanick, a burly former longshoreman, circus roustabout, and Trappist monk from Jersey City whose military service ended with dozens of electroconvulsive shock treatments. Seven Arts opened at eight p.m. Its Saturday-night poetry readings began at midnight, to ward off tourists, and featured Allen Ginsberg, Gregory Corso, Peter Orlovsky, Hugh "Wavy Gravy" Romney, Bob Kaufman, Barbara Moraff, and Jack Kerouac, who memorialized Rapanick as the character Stanley Popovich in *Big Sur*.

Levin became Rapanick's partner in the arts space and crashed in a sleeping bag on its tables. He also shared a loft inside the Hoboken, New Jersey, longshoremen's meeting hall seen in *On the Waterfront*, and then an apartment on Third Street, off the Bowery. Rapanick found Levin a painting studio in an abandoned apartment on Ninth Avenue near Forty-Second Street. One day while working there, Levin heard a sudden crash and saw a hole appear in the wall. Rapanick knew that the building was going to come down, just not when. "This is not going to work," Levin recalls thinking as he ran down the avenue with his canvases. "I am not going to be a painter."

While living at 7 Bleecker Street in the East Village, Levin could hear trumpeter Don Cherry rehearsing nearby. He caught Sun Ra and other jazz greats at the nearby Five Spot Café and befriended a teenage Pharoah Sanders, then known as "Little Rock." For three weeks, he spent most afternoons observing John Coltrane practicing onstage at 80 St. Marks Place. He also picked up a drug habit, another aspect of the "bohemian way." For three years, he sometimes hung out with Herbert Huncke, the poet-hustler who introduced William Burroughs to morphine in *Junkie* and who allegedly coined the term "Beat" in a conversation with Jack Kerouac.

One night, a prostitute who lived in Levin's Avenue B building asked him if he wanted to work one of photographer Fred McDarrah's rent-a-beatnik parties. "You'll just walk around, eat as much as you want, drink as much beer as you want, and you get twenty bucks," she told him. "So I go there, and I'm walking around, eating, and being obnoxious and surly like I'm supposed to be. There was a folk singer at this party. I was sitting on the floor and couldn't see him because there was a big crowd. Somebody yelled, 'Play "Goodnight, Irene"!' This guy's good! Later, I leave just as the folk singer leaves, and we wait for this big industrial elevator together. 'I hear a lot of Woody Guthrie and Charley Pride in you,' I say to him, 'but you got something of your own in there. You're gonna be great!'" Levin declined the singer's offer to visit friends in Greenwich Village. It wasn't until a couple of years later, upon seeing his debut album in a store, that Levin realized, with a chill, that he'd been chatting with Bob Dylan.

Feeling he didn't have it "together" enough to manage a studio and earn a living, Levin gave up painting. He bought a black notebook and a Rapidograph pen. Two nights later, while walking past Greenwich Village's famed Eighth Street Bookshop, a volume in the window by the celebrated French caricaturist André François caught his eye and a lightbulb lit up.

Enamored as he was of a select few cartoonists, including Virgil "VIP" Partch, Levin regarded the form as mostly kind of corny. He found European-style gag cartoons beautiful, however, and was struck especially by François's use of either a bamboo pen or a brush, which he adopted himself. The day after his Eighth Street epiphany, Levin went to the Donnell Library on Fifty-Third Street, staked out a table, gathered some books, and started drawing. He began going there almost daily, gathering ideas from pictures and photos and filling notebooks.

Levin drew his first cartoons for *Playboy* as he recovered in bed from a broken hip and two dislocated shoulders, which he suffered during a car crash with some musician friends while visiting his mother in Florida. Inspired by a copy of *Writer's Digest*, Levin whipped out twenty drawings on typewriter paper with a bamboo pen ("the clumsiest instrument known to man") and sent them to Chicago. Following an argument with his mother, Levin, confined to a wheelchair, undertook an epic journey back to New York involving a burned-out engine, another car crash, rides hitched with Jim Beam–drinking rednecks, and the belated discovery that wheelchair-bound lodgers were unwelcome at the Fourteenth Street YMCA. Several months later, Levin's mother informed him that *Playboy* had bought a drawing and would like him to "finish" it.

"She sends it up, I look at it and think, 'What finish? There's more?' So I looked in the magazine and noticed the grays in 'em. There were two other roughs they wanted to buy in the envelope, too. So I finished the first drawing and sent it back. Six months later they sent me a check for $80. OK! So I finished the next two drawings and six months later got checks for $85 and $90. It took me a year to make about $200. This was not a profession for me—or anyone, for that matter!"

As he improved, Levin would sometimes squat at outdoor art shows in Greenwich Village. With the help of Rapanick, he would mat some drawings and throw up his stuff when a space along the fences became available. They'd always sell a couple of things, and "as soon as we had enough money for a really nice dinner, that was it! We'd pack up everything and off we'd go to Il Bocconcino on Sullivan Street." Levin sold his first real drawing, of a musician, out of the window of Patria art supplies. The purchaser, who paid twenty-five dollars for it, was Shel Silverstein, Levin's idol. "I thought he was the funniest cartoonist around, along with VIP."

Boho life began to catch up with Levin during the mid-sixties. A Houston Street rental turned out to be an amphetamine den. "They were kind of crazy and so was I." Levin was in such bad shape that he simply walked out and slept rough on the streets for a couple of months. He believes he was slipped LSD at a West Side party, on which he overdosed, and awoke the following day in an abandoned store on Third Avenue. After experiencing a mental breakdown, he slept in the bushes beside Bellevue Hospital for three days before go-

Sketchbook pages

ing inside. Two weeks later, he was institutionalized in the Columbia Presbyterian Psychiatric Institute for several more weeks. ("I'm with you in Rockland," as Allen Ginsberg called the facility in *Howl*.)

"When I got out," he says, "I decided it would be best if I didn't go below Fourteenth Street for a while." He joined a therapy group and took messenger jobs while staying at Rapanick's Third Street abode, "but I didn't go to any of my hangouts and kept away from everybody." He continued to draw, too. "While hanging around with Herbert Huncke, I realized that a lot of people were on the street because they didn't have any other choice. One reason I decided to quit the drug thing was that I considered myself lucky: I had talent."

After completing an illustration night course taught by R. O. Blechman and Charles Slackman at the School of Visual Arts, Blechman sent Levin to trendsetting Push Pin Studios, where he was hired as a messenger. One of his tasks was to pick up research photos for Milton Glaser, Seymour Chwast, and their colleagues. "They'd gobble the stuff up," Levin recalls, "and watching them at work was a complete blast." Not too many years ago, Levin ran into Chwast at a *New Yorker* party. "I'd been drinking, so I told him how I'd sit in the back of the bus and open up all their envelopes. I wanted to look at their original artwork and see how it was done. He almost had a heart attack!" At Push Pin, Levin learned about Celtec colored plastic, which he would later combine with silk-screening techniques for *New Yorker* covers.

In Blechman and Slackman's class, Levin constructed a large film storyboard involving several dozen unfolding panels, collaged imagery, and a sound track. Shortly after, Blechman asked Levin if he was still a Push Pin messenger. He was. A week later, Glaser called Levin in and asked him if he'd like to work in animated film. "Oh, no! I'd rather be a messenger!" Levin laughs at the memory.

Glaser sent Levin to Elektra Films to meet co-owner Lee Savage, who explained Levin's duties with the help of a copy of *Advertising Age* magazine. On its cover was a man putting laundry into a washing machine. Savage took a grease pencil, made a few marks, and said, "OK, that's a full shot"; he drew a box around the hands: close-up; and he drew some arrows: truck in, truck out. "You got it?" Savage asked Levin, who did. "Go in the back and ask for Hal Silvermoth," concluded Savage. "He'll give you a desk. You're a film director."

At Elektra, Levin worked on television and movie trailers that combined graphics, his specialty, with animation. At the initial meeting for his first project, *The Unsinkable Molly Brown*, a large man in a blue suit, stiff white shirt, and tie belted out, "*Molly Brown* is a darling, / Biggest movie in town. / Step right out and go on up, / *The Unsinkable Molly Brown!*" Levin found it all delightfully absurd. He also worked on *The Night of the Iguana* ("One man, one woman, one night. Never before! *The Night of the Iguana!*") and others alongside future *New Yorker* colleagues Charles Saxon and Gahan Wilson.

The trailer business was a form of advertising, and Levin considered advertising to be pure surrealism. In his first captioned cartoon, a dapper ad man presents a storyboard to a group of sour-faced executives, saying, "At this point, the product smiles and says, 'Good day, Mr. Froggie.'" As a matter of fact, Levin actually pitched a "Mr. Froggie" animation, and it stirred up a bit of controversy. His version was called "Toad Talks about Warts" and it starred a Dr. Toad image that was a product of Levin's prankster nature. "I was waiting for someone in the ad agency, and I see a painting of one of the agency partners. We have our meeting, I go home, and I do a picture of the frog sitting in exactly the same position as this agency guy. When I showed it to them, they kept saying, 'There's something familiar about the frog . . .' I didn't say a word." Many of the advertising jokes in Levin's future cartoons were gleaned from personal experience.

By the time he left Elektra, Levin was married and living in Brooklyn with his first wife and their daughter. After freelancing for a while, he was hired by Pablo Ferro, with whom he created trailers for *Kaleidoscope, The Russians Are Coming, the Russians Are Coming*, and other movies. Until the city's independent producers were pushed out by larger companies, Levin worked on projects for *Sesame Street, The Electric Company*, and on a series of movie takeoffs. By 1974, the year Bob Blechman referred him to Lee Lorenz at *The New Yorker*, Levin had gotten a divorce and had married his current wife, Pam.

"I always felt like Forrest Gump," says Levin. "I just keep stumbling and bumping into things." Levin's arrival at *The New Yorker* was not overly auspicious. He first approached Lorenz with a batch of cover ideas. Lorenz liked a couple but nothing came of them until, one day, Lorenz saw the "big, wild, goofy drawings" in Levin's portfolio. Lorenz phoned and asked Levin to redo one of them in black and white.

"He hopped on the subway and ran right into the office with it," says Lorenz, who told Levin, "You didn't have to finish it *today*."

More art drawing than gag, Levin's first *New Yorker* cartoon was a romantic, William Steig–like image in which three musicians—in the form of musical instruments—perform on plants. This was his comfort zone: Levin had spent a lot more time *looking* at cartoons than *drawing* them. But he soon kicked his training into the gutter and took off. "As I was drawing my third cartoon for *The New Yorker*, I got to the hands but I couldn't draw them. I finally thought, 'Fuck it, maybe they won't notice.' I worried they'd immediately look at the drawing and go, 'Look at those hands!' But they didn't say anything and I thought, 'Maybe this is not set in stone.'"

Another part of the anatomy evolved in Levin's cartoons as well. For about a year, all the noses in his cartoons came to a point, not unlike Saul Steinberg's drawings. But suddenly, a guy sitting in a room had a big bulbous snoot, as did his fish, and nearly every subsequent Levin character would display a pronounced proboscis of one form or another. "When I was in the animation business, I made a vow: 'I will not draw a big nose just for a laugh!'" Levin says. In his cartoon world, no nose is precisely the same as another. "But there's a method to my honkers: If you look closely, I have several variations." Having gone from painting to illustration to animation to cartooning, Levin has more than the usual respect for the medium's form. "It's like a key signature in music. For instance, if I wanted to do something outrageous or stupid—Lee used to say, 'Make it more dumb'—I would make a stupid nose in the key signature of dumb. But if I want to make a point in a political gag, I draw something with a little more resonance or focus. How goofy or serious a guy sitting in front of a television set looks depends on what's on the TV."

Whitney Darrow Jr., Charles E. Martin, Robert Weber, Ed Fisher, and Charles Saxon number among Levin's primary *New Yorker* inspirations, all of whom, he says, produced beautifully drawn work. "Do you know they dropped Saxon without even telling him?" he asks. "They just stopped printing him. I understood that Bob Gottlieb didn't like Saxon's work and remarked, 'What's with all the white space?' And *I* worked with white space! You'll notice that from then on there's a lot more grays in my stuff. I would have preferred a lot of them not to be so gray, but he couldn't understand white space."

Like other longtime *New Yorker* contributors, Levin regrets many of the changes that occurred with the departure of William Shawn. "Mr. Shawn wouldn't let the artists use their *New Yorker* art commercially outside the magazine; he was very tight about where the art went. He also believed that stories should run as long as they needed to. The business department was unhappy about that, because they didn't want readers to get bored." Levin learned this during one of the annual off-site meetings where artists, writers, editors, and members of the business side of the magazine would get together and discuss

At home in Sea Cliff, Long Island

their mutual concerns. "One year, I was chosen to go as the artist along with [writer Lawrence] Ren Weschler and [editor Charles] Chip McGrath. Peter Fleischmann, who owned the magazine, was also there. And one of the guys from the business department said, 'Chip, don't you think you could make the stories shorter?' McGrath explained to them what Mr. Shawn said about stories running as long as they should. But the business department is persistent, and they say, 'Yeah, but people tell us that blah blah blah . . .' Fleischmann said, 'I can answer that.' And everybody in the room turns to Fleischmann, who simply says, 'No.'" The magazine's extensive reads continued as before.

Since arriving at *The New Yorker*, Levin has published more than seven hundred cartoons and around twenty covers. Most contemporary *New Yorker* covers are commissioned. During the Shawn years, however, covers were chosen from a large bank of previously purchased art. Levin was particularly tickled by how the magazine would publish both a Christmas cover and a *pre*-Christmas cover. Likewise, many of Levin's cartoons are subtly attuned to the season. "If you did a drawing of somebody in a topcoat, they might buy it during the summer, but it wouldn't appear until fall. So it had to be pretty funny for them to buy it in the summer." For Levin, this reflected the magazine's preference for artists with a personal outlook who took an active interest in the world around them; its readership demanded it.

"I just kind of fell in the front door and suddenly realized where I was playing," he says. "I was working with guys who were really up there, with editors who really pushed for intelligent, thoughtful, beautifully drawn work." He acknowledges that not all cartoons are meant to be home runs. "Some are just meant to be singles. Pete Rose made a living out of it."

When he first pitched ideas to the magazine, Levin would come in with large batches of around thirty cartoons. He once submitted fifty, saw Lorenz make a face, and decided to back off. "I was not a cartoonist, right? So I never had the opportunity to do all the bad ones: the guys dueling with swordfish, the garage sales. I never got that out of my system, or even tried." As a filmmaker, Levin was interested in how an idea might be improved by reframing, so he would sometimes submit three versions of the same concept and let Lorenz pick the best. The only editorial fix he recalls is an editor changing two words in a single image among hundreds: Set in a campaign headquarters, it depicts two men carrying out a queasy-looking senator. "It was either the knish in Coney Island, the cannoli in Little Italy, or the divinity fudge in Westchester," one says, with the last local taste sensation being his editor's replacement for something even the artist no longer recalls.

When it comes to standard *New Yorker* setups, like the desert island or end-of-the-world signs, Levin takes credit for reviving the Grim Reaper in the modern era. "Relax, I've come for your toaster," says Death in one of the panels that inspired new interest in the setup. "What I love most about the Grim Reaper is applying the black watercolor; playing with this black is just so luscious," Levin says. His toaster Reaper was inspired partly by the short films he worked on for *Sesame Street* and *The Electric Company,* studios "where objects came to life" and bumping into a chair might elicit a mental apology. The joke itself is a takeoff on a Woody Allen nightclub routine about murdering an appliance, and the visual's in keeping with Allen's style.

Gillette steel pens are Levin's tool of choice for cartoons, though he doesn't use them for everything he does. "I bought a box of a hundred Esterbrook pen points in a Planned Parenthood thrift store; they turned out to be perfect for the *New Yorker* drawings I did the first number of years. I love lines so much that I would work with a magnifying glass. I had to see *exactly* what that one would do. *Excess* pen made me happy." His early work consisted simply of pen, ink, and a little bit of Dr. Ph. Martin's dyes, grays, and watercolors. He uses different media for illustrations and "would buy a kid's painting set if it had a color I liked," he says.

Whether it's one of his many drawings involving birdbaths, or a sight gag of a guy pushing over a circle of giant dominos to commit suicide, Levin's cartoons always involve some form of ocular choreography.

"I try to avoid talking-head ideas as much as possible," he says. "A cartoon is structured and you have to start someplace. If it's a gag cartoon, you look at *this* and then *this* in a certain order, and after you get the impression you go down to the caption. That's the cartoon's choreography, the path your eye takes. The timing has to be correct. The situation you set up is a wonderful place to play in, and clichés are fine, because you want people to think they know what they're looking at." Sometimes an "inverse cartoon choreography" comes into play, and the payoff is somewhere off the page entirely. "Ed Frascino had a wonderful gag, very simple. A guy is sitting on a chair, looking really smug. His wife, leaning over him, asks, 'When did you have your ear pierced?' Well, the gag is right there in front of your eyes, but you don't see it. It's a sleight of hand."

Other Levin cartoons involve playfully twisted words and phrases. The inner caption reading "Nasdaq, Meshach & Abed-nego" jumps out at you even before you take in a man in a business suit with a briefcase leading a pair of biblical nobles through a temple. "I went around with that in my head for a long time before I got the guts to draw it," he says. "Words set me off." So do objects. One of Levin's favorite cartoons depicts an upside-down bat whose keys lie on the floor. "That came out of throwing my pants over the couch one time too many." Snagging his gags where he can, Arnie Levin's art remains rigorously crafted yet strangely innocent, the everyday nature of the content belying the intensity of both his earlier *and* later years.

8

The Coupled Cosmos of Victoria Roberts

"What gear are we in, biscuit?"

W HILE NEW YORK City's population continues to rise, the number of actual *characters* it contains seems to have diminished over the decades. The pages of *The New Yorker* are no longer filled with artists and other eccentrics profiled charmingly and sympathetically by the magazine's own stable of sometimes equally eccentric journalists. The abyss separating the very wealthy from everyone else in New York has swallowed up many of the artists who made the city so fascinating in the first place. And that, frankly, sucks. Because at least until Detroit—or wherever—becomes a robust petri dish for the next generation of creative geniuses, New York will devolve into the place where America's analog arts slowly, barely perceptibly entered hiatus.

Fortunately, Victoria Roberts remains one of the self-created old-guard New York characters one fears no longer exist. With her red hair, neo-Victorian fashion sense, Australian accent, and theatrical demeanor, Roberts epitomizes a certain type of cultural crusader. "New York is one of the loves of my life," says Roberts, who, although born in New York, was raised in Mexico City, where she attended elementary school, and Sydney, where she spent her high school and art-education years. But like most great love affairs, New York has been both a source of great joy and occasional disappointment to the artist, who began cartooning for *The New Yorker* in 1988. In 2012, Roberts published her first novel, the charmingly illustrated *After the Fall*, which explores an Upper East Side family forced to relocate to Central Park, with attitudes and class aspirations intact, when the economic bottom drops out.

"I always wanted to come here," says Roberts. "I used to watch the TV show *Taxi*, which I loved. At the same time, I was *afraid* to come here because I thought, 'How will I survive?'"

I meet Roberts in her small one-bedroom apartment on the Upper East Side, not far from New York–Presbyterian Hospital, where she was born on April 8, 1957. And while Roberts comes off more as a SoHo spirit than an Upper East Sider in person, there are no cartoon characters more intrinsically UES (not to mention *New Yorker*-esque) than the long-married pair—call them the Couple—Roberts has depicted in the magazine hundreds of times. "They were a New York couple," she says. "They always were. I drew them in Australia but they were still New Yorkers." (She to he: "Our life is sort of like a bad play, but somehow we've managed to get good reviews.")

Her other keynote creation is Nona Appleby, a flamboyant, often nude personage she began drawing in her teens while working as a geriatric nurse in Sydney's Mosman Nursing Home. Roberts channels Nona at odd moments in an absolutely disconcerting fashion, as though this Depression-raised matron were always lurking within her, near the surface, ready to emerge.

"That's right, dea-uh," Roberts says, uncannily channeling Nona, who subsequently refers to Roberts in the third person. "It's lovely to meet you. I didn't know she was doing interviews today. She didn't tell me or I would have been ready for it. But I suppose I'm right out

At home in Manhattan

of it because it's always about *her*. But it should be about me, really. The superstar within."

"She's really something," Roberts adds in her own voice.

"I *am* something," she replies as Nona, blowing my mind somewhat. "Would you like a piece of fruit instead of a biscuit?"

A tri-national creation, Roberts has been inventing and reinventing herself her entire life. She came to New York, she says, to either work on *Sesame Street,* join the Wooster Group, or cartoon for *The New Yorker.* She has fulfilled only one of those goals to date, but one suspects she's an artist with superb, if undeveloped, late-life skills. During our most recent contact, she was immersed in an intense video-editing course. "It's the first thing I've loved to distraction since I started drawing," she tells me.

Roberts began submitting her work to *The New Yorker* regularly after moving to New York at age twenty-nine. "I used to send things from Australia but never sold anything," she says. Upon her arrival, she submitted for about two years before selling anything. "I stopped for a while because I would just get rejection slips." But then she received a rejection slip with "Please try us again" written on it. In her *New Yorker* debut, an ATM machine informs a surprised matron that "Your financial institution no longer exists"—which, Roberts notes, "would be funnier now, actually." Cartoon editor Lee Lorenz added an editorial note to her rough: "Less crazy eyes," he wrote, circling the orbs in question. "I didn't really change anything when I redrew it," she confesses.

The New Yorker looms large in Roberts's back pages. Her stepfather, a Manhattan ad man, subscribed to the magazine in Mexico City, where her family lived amid a small community of temporary and permanent expatriate New Yorkers. Magazine and city conflated for Roberts, who imagined the publication to be almost a *place*. "It seemed like a very *respectful* place when Mr. Shawn was editor," she says. "It came through in the type, or something. It was like a refuge. If my parents fought, or anything like that, my stepfather had a library with a little bathroom off of it that had *New Yorkers* in it. I didn't read it or anything, but I wanted to *live* there. It was a place where there was respect because rationality would prevail. I remember the *feel* of the whole thing."

Although she was hired by Lorenz and Robert Gottlieb, Roberts idealizes the magazine under Shawn's editorship. "Honestly, I always felt that the cartoonists who were chosen by Mr. Shawn were the 'real' people," she says with a self-deprecating laugh. George Booth and the artists of his generation are the magazine's authentic artistic voices for her to this day. "I hope I'm the real deal, too," she adds, "but I always had an inferiority complex." She was nonetheless awarded a contract in 1989 by Gottlieb. Coincidentally, the September 28, 1992, Cinderella-on-Halloween cover she did for the magazine happened to be Gottlieb's final issue as editor. It had been scheduled "ages" earlier, she says, but that didn't stop it from being misinterpreted, she feels, as a commentary on the ballet lover's relatively brief editorship.

James Thurber's art opened the door to a world of cartooning possibilities for Roberts. Observe the genetic material of the Couple in Thurber's famous image of a woman crouching malevolently on a bookcase as a man below says to an alarmed visitor, "That's my first wife up there, and this is the *present* Mrs. Harris." Roberts compares her exposure to Thurber to an artistic door swinging open. She took Booth and Ed Koren as models for the type of work she'd like to do for *The New Yorker*, and she puts Roz Chast in a category by herself: "I don't think of her work as an influence because it's so out there. And when somebody's *that* good, they break ground for the whole profession.

"The whole *New Yorker* thing," she says, "was that everybody did what they did very, very well. They had their own worlds, which was magnificent. I remember looking in the drawer at what people had brought in once, peeking into Mick Stevens's folder for the week, and thinking, 'Every one's a home run. How do they choose just one?'"

Her taste also runs to artists from the United Kingdom, such as Glen Baxter, the *Private Eye* magazine cartoonist John Glashan, and Roald Dahl illustrator Quentin Blake. Roberts suspects there was a certain amount of Anglophobia in the cartoonists' negative response to Baxter's work, yet she sees a strong connection linking Baxter's absurdist themes and inside-panel captioning with those of Jack Ziegler.

Many of *The New Yorker*'s best cartoonists—such as Thurber, Chast, Booth, and Koren—have also been some of its best writers. Roberts also numbers among them, as demonstrated by *After the Fall* as well as the handful of books she published before relocating to New York. As a teenager, Roberts submitted a strip about Gertrude Stein's Sunday activities to the *Nation Review*, an influential left-of-center paper published every Sunday in Australia from 1970 to 1981. The paper bought it immediately and asked her to do something similar weekly. The job involved digesting biographies about Margaret Thatcher ("I try not to repeat myself," Roberts has the prime minister say. "The shortest currency in the world, you know, is the currency of new ideas"), Sigmund Freud ("Finally I retire. One dreams so as not to wake because one wants to sleep. *Tant de bruit*"), Truman Capote ("Lunch with one of my back-up girls. I won't say which one, but her name rhymes with

My Day by James Thurber

8 A.M. THE CLOCK SAYS' IT'S MORNING. I FEEL LIKE A SLIGHTLY ILL PROFESSOR OF BOTANY WHO IS ALSO LOST.

SO DOES MY ROOM. I'LL HAVE TO CHANGE HOTELS. I'M ALSO OUT OF CLEAN CLOTHES. I'LL HAVE TO BUY A NEW SUIT.

9 A.M. AT THE NEW YORKER, IN THE OFFICE WHERE E.B. WHITE AND I ALMOST FIT.

DOROTHY PARKER COMES BY, LOOKING FOR A PENCIL, BUT SHE CANNOT GET IN, NOR WILL SHE FIND A PENCIL. THEY WERE ALL GIVEN OUT LAST MONTH, THE WHOLE YEAR'S SUPPLY.

From My Day

oil well"), and other cultural celebs on a weekly basis. Her "Sunday" strips, often redrawn, were collected, retitled *My Day,* and published as the first of a three-book deal with London's Chatto & Windus press in 1984. She later drew similar strips depicting contemporary figures such as Hillary Clinton for the *Huffington Post.*

Published in 1986, Roberts's *Biographees* contains a handful of surrealistically illustrated, fancifully reconceived memoirs concerning Pablo Picasso, Howard Hughes, and a Bloomsbury hound, among others. Her most fascinating book, however, at least until *After the Fall,* is *Australia Felix,* which the Australian Bicentennial Authority commissioned as part of the country's 1988 bicentenary festivities. It's the illustrated story of a poor Irish family—"When other Irish persons had one potato, the Boyles had none"—whose teenage daughter Agnes is transported to Australia for the crime of poaching a rabbit. Two hundred years later, Roberts depicts the family's motley multigenerational history as a work still in progress. The book is dedicated to Roberts's Sydney landlady, Ethel O'Brien, who sustained the artist's spirit with copious amounts of tea and sympathy and became a primary source for Nona Appleby.

Roberts's path to Australia began when her Argentine mother, Inés Roth, the product of Welsh and Hungarian parentage in Buenos Aires, married Charles Sumner Roberts III, from Texas. Her parents met in Las Vegas, where Inés was getting a divorce from an earlier husband. "It was a bit of a rebound," surmises Victoria, whose parents separated prior to her birth. "She realized it wouldn't be a happy life with him." Victoria's grandmother, meanwhile, had been transferred to Mexico City from Buenos Aires by her employer, *Selecciones*, the Latin American version of *Reader's Digest;* Inés and Victoria followed. There Inés met and married Bob Benjamin, the ad man whom four-year-old Victoria would come to view as her authentic father.

She recalls a sixties Mexico City before the smog arrived. "You could see the two volcanoes, Popocatepetl and Ixtacihuatl. You could drive around and get from point A to point B. Now it's a nightmare to get anywhere." She misses the rubber wheels of the Metro, silent but not so swift. Bob Benjamin's PR career entailed lots of socializing, as when the Goldwaters came to dinner, yet she felt the family's domestic help always led more interesting lives. "We had no religion, but they had solutions and superstitions. They'd say things like 'Nothing's going to happen, it's OK.' I've always thought of Mexicans, even uneducated persons, as being very sophisticated people. Even though I was in an American household, I grew up quite anti-American because Mexicans were more . . . I want to say 'sophisticated,' but it's not really that. Where Americans had solutions and idées fixes, they had more *stories.*"

Roberts's artistic talent was confirmed in 1968 when she drew some stunning flames for the faux Olympic torch her stepsiblings and friends were using as part of the mini–Olympic Games they played on their dead-end street. Her unconscious precedent was Abel Quezada, the great Mexican cartoonist who had created the Olympic poster hanging in her bedroom. She was enthralled by Mexico's rich tradition of black-and-white drawing. The skeleton woodcuts made famous by José Guadalupe Posada were everywhere, as were the *calaveras* (skulls), cartoons, and poetry associated with Mexico's Day of the Dead ceremonies. Victoria could also buy American comics at the supermarket, and she adored *Richie Rich, Little Lotta,* and *Archie.* Her favorite newspaper strip was *Bringing Up Father,* even if she found the Spanish translations strange.

She attended Tres Picos kindergarten and then Greengates, the British international school. One day, on a whim, Inés transferred young Victoria and stepbrother Alan to the Lycée Franco-Mexicain, an institution that sounds as though it could inspire a career's worth of material. ("Sometimes I wonder if English really is my native tongue," the Woman will say to the Man many years later in *The New Yorker.*) Students were sent home for wearing unacceptable fabric. Ink mishaps were rewarded with the word "*tâche*" (stain) inscribed accusingly beside the offending spot, thereby adding insult to humiliation. Victoria was tossed out of the *lycée* at age nine after a dramatic intervention by her mother concerning an inappropriate pair of stockings.

"Terrific and generous" Inés Roth could also be "a bit roller-coaster-y." Inés and Bob were together only eight years, although both mother and daughter remained in touch with their Mexican family over the ensuing decades. Inés and Bob even lived in the Mexican expat haven of San Miguel de Allende at the same time. The couple divorced when Victoria was about eleven years old. Inés became a copywriter and then a creative director at an ad agency. Among her accounts was Qantas airline, which flew her to Australia. There, with what Victoria calls a "view to the future," her mother saw the potential to raise her daughter, with socialized health care and education, and away from increasingly polluted Mexico City. "She thought it was a bit like Argentina because the Brits had lived there," Victoria surmises of their new beginning in 1970.

Australia does sound idyllic if only by current US standards. Roberts received a commonwealth scholarship at North Sydney Girls High School, which she hated. Fortunately, she was able to transfer to the national art school at East Sydney Technical College at age sixteen, where she received an independent living allowance. "I worked weekends, there were no fees, and so I was actually kind of paid to go to school." She worked for David Denneen's Filmgraphics Entertainment production company and was later awarded funds by the Australian Film Commission to produce her own animated film, *Goodbye Sally Goldstein.* The Australian film scene was flourishing, with directors such as Phillip Noyce, Peter Weir, and Bruce Beresford; cartoon-

Conrad Boyle set to work with three new mates. For four weeks they were bitten by marchflies, sandflies, blowflies and devil flies. They found four grains of gold (one each). Hooray, hooray, hooray, hooray.

From Australia Felix

ists Michael Leunig and Bruce Petty were exploding the form; and Victoria was intoxicated by the possibilities of writing, theater, film, and art.

By the mid-eighties, Inés had moved back to Mexico and Victoria was traveling back and forth between San Miguel and Sydney. She received a grant to create *Biographees* in Venice and returned home via New York. Her stage-designer boyfriend was hired to work with the composer Philip Glass at the Adelaide Festival in 1986. Prior to the festival, Wooster Group performance artist Spalding Gray came to Sydney to perform his self-descriptive *Interviewing the Audience*—and Roberts was one of his subjects. While enjoying the Adelaide Festival thanks to her boyfriend, she saw the Wooster Group's controversial *L.S.D. (. . . Just the High Points . . .)*. "I'd already gone kind of bananas seeing Spalding Gray, whose acting was so seamless that it wasn't acting. And I was just crazy about *L.S.D.* Steve Buscemi was filling in while Willem Dafoe was filming *Platoon*. I went to every performance. I just wanted to run away with the Wooster Group." Roberts was performing occasionally, too.

With the help of her mother and an unexpected insurance settlement—her original *My Day* manuscript, destroyed in a truck accident in Scotland, had been insured for £5,000— Roberts packed her bags and moved to New York City. Her grandmother had snagged a sublet for her, and Roberts had a contract for *Australia Felix* to keep her afloat.

Viewed together as a group on Condé Nast's Cartoon Bank website, Roberts's cartoons suggest a single lifelong theme with infinite variations. The Man and Woman who star in the vast majority of her cartoons exist in different settings from image to image. But the most striking visual distinction in each of Roberts's drawings is usually a remarkable fabric pattern, always different, on her dress or his shirt. Textiles and other surfaces have always fascinated Roberts. "When I drew trees as a kid," she says, "I used to draw every line of bark. It has to do with the way I saw things. If I were looking at the newspaper, I wouldn't see a headline but I might see the phrase 'Jewish women and girls, sunset at 5:30 p.m.' Detail and patterns are meditative for me. I'm not great at perspective. I prefer a figure in a ground; I'm not very interested in background."

The Man, usually referred to as either Howard or Harold, resembles her former stepfather, Bob Benjamin. The Woman—very occasionally called Martha—may not physically resemble Victoria's mother, but she still gets all the best lines. It's hard not to imagine echoes of Inés in observations like "We're getting more vulgar with age, something I had not foreseen," spoken by the Woman, who is wearing a sexy dress and holding a sparkly drink, as her husband reads the newspaper. Or when, strolling together under an umbrella, she says to him, "The problem with you is that you try to be a lot nicer than you really are."

Roberts didn't notice the resemblance between the balding man and her stepfather until a nephew pointed it out. "Bob was a real New

Yorker. He was always dry, and he read everything. But he kind of had the personality of a fish." Likewise, the Woman in the Couple seems constantly ready to flee from the confines of their hell-is-other-people life. "They both are, in different ways," says Roberts. In one cartoon she had the Woman threatening to run off with the Wooster Group (Roberts's own early escape fantasy) but her editor requested she change it to something less obscure: the Women's National Basketball Association.

Although her cartoons provide a periscope view into the socio-sexual mores of the Upper East Side (and elsewhere), Roberts claims she is no reporter or Stan Mack stealthily recording her neighbors' remarks. "I do a distillation, a kind of blinker work," she says. "The Couple just does stuff on their own—like Nona Appleby does her own thing—in their own world. But they're real New Yorkers and always have been." Her cartoons are theatrical vignettes, extremely short plays for precisely two people, a G-rated *Who's Afraid of Virginia Woolf?* condensed to its essence.

Roberts's theatrical career focuses on internal dialogues. Her research for *The Life of Truman Capote*, which she also performed, involved a visit to a Baltimore gender clinic. For *Fridalogue,* based on Mexican artist Frida Kahlo, she wore a very large revolving skirt, "like one of those Puerto Rican cakes." She describes *Forty Winks,* about a woman who refuses to leave her bed, as her first autobiographical work; during the performance, Roberts drew onstage while an actor spoke her lines.

Nona Appleby remains Roberts's strongest voice. "I *always* drew her," Roberts explains, "and I could always speak"—Nona again—"*in this voice.* I've been drawing her since I was a teen, when I worked as a geriatric nurse in a nursing home on weekends. She has the voice of older Australians, who don't sound like that anymore. It's the strongest voice I have." Roberts was reluctant to put Nona onstage, however, "even after seeing John Leguizamo's *Freak* eight times!" Director Linda Mancini helped Roberts shape her first rendering of Nona. "Unfortunately, she decided that I had to drop my top when

Nona changes her outfit, which I thought was unnecessary and very embarrassing. I realized later that she was somewhat obsessed with nudity and people sitting on toilets and such."

Wearing heavy makeup and large black spectacles, Roberts channeled the crotchety Australian in a series of video shorts shot in Manhattan and on Long Island. In one, Roberts pranks a Canadian news crew staking out former International Monetary Fund director Dominique Strauss-Kahn's temporary residence in Tribeca. (Cartoon images of a nude Nona frying eggs, setting fire to the *Encyclopedia Britannica*, and pursuing other escapades appear, as do her videos, at victoriaroberts.net.)

Past and present coexist in all Roberts's work. She drew an updated version of *Little Women* for *Ms.* in 1988. In her version of the March sisters, "shrilled up to their worst," Amy yearns for a nose job, Jo experiences ADD, and Beth lashes out over not owning a Bösendorfer piano. The episodes usually end with their mother providing a "through pain to peace" lecture about behaving themselves. There's something a little old world about Roberts herself, too, a sense of propriety and respect enhanced by her Australian accent and exemplary manners. Still only in her fifties, she recalls both the adventurous spirit of the pre–Rudy Giuliani avant-garde and the Shawn- and Lorenz-era *New Yorker*.

New Yorker cartoons used to feature many more recurring characters, from Peter Arno's aristocrats and Helen Hokinson's matrons to Charles Addams's fearsome family. Today's *New Yorker* cartoons, though, are more about jokes than relationships. As a cartoonist who traffics almost *solely* in characters and relationships, Roberts feels understandably estranged. "They'll tell you: 'We don't want character-based work.' Which is like telling me I might as well shoot myself, because that's what I *do*," she complains.

"There's no longer the same sense of wonder there once was; no longer the world I thought was the respectful world. I love gags, but now it's *completely* gaggy, and that isn't enough. When you first look

"WE'VE ALWAYS BEEN PLUMBERS, EXCEPT FOR MY BROTHER EDWARD WHO DEFECTED TO THE VACUUM CLEANING BUSINESS," SAID MRS. S.

From Biographees

at the cartoons, you don't get the same good feeling you used to get. Now it's 'Gee, aren't they clever but . . .'"

Although she was never comfortable with Tina Brown's attempt to "buzz" up *The New Yorker,* Roberts was often pleasantly surprised by Brown's artistic choices. "She took chances and was off-the-charts bright." Roberts never experienced discrimination as one of the art staff's few women; indeed, she felt herself to be in "a sort of privileged position of being admired and treated well by the guys. Think of the kind of minds that were looking at your world," she says. "It was fantastic and a real education, to take fifteen to twenty roughs in and see what they chose." Now, she says, it's more "blokey." She believes her gender has even allowed her to speak up more, "often foolishly," because she's not a man challenging the male editor.

Roberts's work accrues credibility by repetition. Seen once or twice, her Man and Woman seem like random vestiges of a bygone sensibility. Over time, however, they assume a sort of Everycouple stature unique to the magazine. Cartoonists such as Bruce Eric Kaplan and William Haefeli nail certain *types* of New Yorkers, but Roberts's Couple soars in a sort of mutual romance-affirming fantasy nearly as often as they knowingly rattle the bars of their cage. ("Wow—I didn't know you could put that much guilt into one sentence," he says to her, delightedly, over dinner.)

The Couple's mutual fantasies appear less frequently than in the past, however. As a decidedly interested party, Roberts can't help but notice how the magazine's cartoon department has changed under David Remnick's editorship. She sees fewer cartoons being published and more cartoonists. "There's a different commitment to people's work," she says. "It's a smaller book with more artists. In order for you to have a world that makes any sense, it has to be seen. That's how people became fond of the Couple, I hope, not because there's one cartoon a year, y'know?"

Asked to choose the cartoon she feels best represents her *New Yorker* work, Roberts cites one in which the Couple sits together happily in a car that's escaping Earth's gravitational pull and entering the solar system. "What gear are we in, biscuit?" he asks her. The image of the Couple alone in their vehicle in space sums up this ultimately joined-at-the-heart duo. Runners-up for her aesthetic affection include the Woman announcing to the Man, "I had a bit of a quiet day, so I sculpted you in butter." In another favorite, the Woman festoons her partner with garlands of flowers, lights candles on his armchair, and announces, "I'm treating you like a living deity for one day." Each of these cartoons suggests the tip of a much larger emotional world.

"I've been told to get them out of the living room," Roberts says. "But the fact is it *works* in the living room. You know they've been together for years and years and years, so we also know what every little comment *means*."

"Guilt is my chauffeur," the Man says with a smile to a friend in the wood-paneled confines of an old-fashioned businessman's club, and Roberts admits to working in a state of mild panic: "Blank page, deadline, fear. I have a deadline, and that's what I work to, usually at

the last minute. I really do sit there with a blank page. I always have a notebook, so I write things down. I sometimes draw first, but usually the caption comes first." She has no weekly routine but rather assembles batches as the mood strikes her.

In the past, Roberts found cartooning for *The New Yorker* to be a very open brief. "I remember being embarrassed because a lot of my cartoons were not home runs, not good. And Lee would say, 'Don't ever edit yourself. Just bring them in. Don't worry about it.' That was a real gift, because I've had things that didn't work until three months down the line."

Roberts's roughs—which she draws with a Brause 66 calligraphy nib and India ink on Arches paper—tend to be *very* rough: "I'm more interested in the writing, really, and in fact I've gotten into trouble for that. I've been told I have to show more in the rough. But I do them very fast, which provides a lot of information about the drawing's energy and focal point. It's better than a tidied-up rough."

When Roberts started working for *The New Yorker*, the magazine's contractual artists were asked to submit their drawings over the course of two days per week, followed by a group lunch. One group delivered its roughs on Tuesday, another, including Roberts, on Wednesday. "That meant I made friends with Ed Fisher, Dana

Fradon, and Al Ross—the older group." Roberts's lunch group also included best friend Huguette Martel and cover artist Heidi Goennel. These days, Bob Mankoff invites all the magazine's cartoonists, even prospective cartoonists, to see him in his office on Wednesday afternoons. Various cartoonists still go out to lunch together, but it's no longer as tight-knit a group, and Victoria Roberts is rarely there.

9

Auteur d'Horreur: Gahan Wilson

"Gee, I'm sorry this had to happen on our first date!"

A GAHAN WILSON CARTOON is a tiny ghost story for adults. A puff of fright—*boo!*—leavened by laughter. Haunting the pages of *The New Yorker* since 1980 and *Playboy* since 1957, his characters tend to be either frumpy misfits, whose swollen features and baggy clothing almost manage to disguise the vampires, aliens, and miscellaneous monsters lurking inside each of us—or actual vampires, aliens, and monsters. We're all a bit monstrous, Wilson implies, each and every one of us whether we know it or not. It's probably the human condition.

In his most terrifying *New Yorker* cartoon, a fortune teller peers into her crystal ball and informs a young woman that "you will make the same foolish mistakes you have made before, not only once but many, many times again." For Wilson, horror is the rule rather than the exception. When aliens and other monstrosities do appear, they usually find their dark missions already accomplished. Nothing threatens the human race more than its own membership. As one squat tween-age troublemaker says to another, "You know you've got it right when your parents can't look at you without wincing!"

The successor to the legacy of elegant spook-meister Charles Addams, if in a less urbane mode, Wilson frets about Earth while looking at the stars, casting his gaze upon sublime spacescapes through the Hubble telescope's digital dazzle. "The Hubble pictures are some of the most gorgeous things I've ever seen in my life," says this earthly master of form and color. "It so expanded the wonderfulness of the cosmos. Our idea about it was so limited, so confined, but these glimpses are staggering." And yet Wilson dreads what might be lurking among all that dark matter. "I think Stephen Hawking is right: *Don't be so fast about advertising that we've got this planet inhabited. Remember the Indians.* We may be under very close examination even as we speak." Unless, of course, we simply haven't recognized the enemy because he is us. "God knows what we're turning into," continues Wilson, "but it's obvious we're going to transform ourselves into something spectacular. Those Hubble photos just changed everything for me."

The entryway of the modest picket-fenced cottage in Sag Harbor, Long Island, that Gahan Wilson shares with his wife, Nancy Winters, is filled with vintage toy theaters, cardboard replicas of popular plays produced during the eighteenth and nineteenth centuries. The circus atmosphere befits a grandnephew of P. T. Barnum, which he happens to be. Wilson uses cartoons to stage direct macabre miniature mise-en-scènes. Inspired by the pulp fantasies and B movies of his midwestern youth, Wilson aims a powerful shrinking ray at atrocities perpetrated upon small, fearful, and confused ordinary people by more rapacious individual and institutional entities. He distills encounters with the weird into beautifully rendered panels that disturb, comfort, and amuse us at the same time. It's a terrifying world out there, his art seems to say, and this is how I've learned to cope with it. Inside his abode, Wilson can usually be located in his living-room

At home in Sag Harbor

studio surrounded by internationally sourced figurines, or perhaps in his kitchen, where I tracked him down one rainy winter day sipping milky coffee out of a Pyrex measuring cup.

Although he had been a successful cartoonist for many years, Wilson was already fifty when he sold his first piece to *The New Yorker*. In that panel, an older Buddhist monk answers a younger adherent's implied question about sitting zazen: "Nothing happens next. This is it." The funniest thing about the cartoon is that it's actually not that funny. That really *is* the essence of Zen practice. Wilson became interested in Buddhism when D. T. Suzuki's works began filtering into the public consciousness during the fifties, and he characterizes himself as a "half-assed Buddhist" to this day.

"I was pretty far ahead of the pack," he says. "I did the thing where you go to the little zazendo and sit around and do the whole number." He's not so enamored of the Buddhist concept of rebirth, though. "Reincarnation strikes me as absolutely ridiculous. It supposedly makes you respect animals more on account of it being somebody human. What's really wonderful about squirrels is that a squirrel's a squirrel. So that kind of makes me a bad Buddhist right there." At the end of the day, however, Buddhism's existential insights center his artistic flights. "It inspires gorgeous art. It's human. A fisherman looks like a fisherman, the fish look like fish, and water looks like water. It's the message about being alive and it makes you think, 'Thank God, what a lucky break.' Just *be*, you know?" Wilson also subscribes to the Buddhist notion of *dukkha*. The Sanskrit word is usually translated as "suffering," but Gahan believes it more accurately signifies the always already "askew" nature of existence.

And when it comes to existence, Allen Gahan Wilson almost missed the boat. Born October 18, 1930, in Evanston, Illinois, Gahan emerged from his mother's womb blue, breathless, and apparently dead because of the anesthetic his mother had received. He appeared *so* dead, in fact, that a nurse put his tiny body into a sink in preparation for its disposal. Fortunately, the Wilsons' family doctor was on the scene, observing the birth through a window. He burst into the room, grabbed the comatose infant, doused him alternately in hot and cold pans of water, and applied a few slaps to his posterior. "He got me coughing and puking and breathing, and I was alive," says Wilson. He notes that John Steinbeck had a similarly traumatic birth, adding, a little wistfully, "I could have spent some time in the afterlife. I was indeed born dead."

Aside from the potentially dire circumstances surrounding his birth, Wilson's affinity for the macabre extends back to his earliest cartoons: ghostly, eerie figures his mother celebrated and nurtured with loving comments such as "Terrible Monster." His taste for the grotesque was sated by the work of Chester Gould, whose "horrible" *Dick Tracy* adventures were gory pulp masterpieces in which villains, as Wilson once recalled for a journalist, were "beaten and bruised and burned." He was also enthralled by Harold Gray, whose Little Orphan Annie was raised by that "merciless son of a bitch" Daddy Warbucks, and by the violent, squishy sound designs of creepy thirties and forties radio dramas such as *The Shadow* (voiced by Orson Welles), *Inner Sanctum Mysteries*, and Arch Oboler's *Lights Out*, which included proto-Wilsonian episodes like "Spider," wherein a pair of men violate a giant arachnid's lair.

At the age of eight or nine, Gahan was browsing in a second-hand bookstore when he stumbled across a set of bound volumes of *Punch*. "I bought one volume for fifteen cents and took it home. After pleading with my father, he very sweetly drove me back to the place and plopped down for the entire set, bless his heart." The purchase changed Gahan's life. "I can't say how important that was." His new collection introduced him to talented painter-caricaturists such as Honoré Daumier, Isaac Robert Cruikshank, and Sir John Tenniel.

"Some of them were wonderfully political," he says, launching into a brief description of cartooning's defining mutation from fine art. "They'd have a drawing with a caption underneath, but it wasn't necessarily a joke. They eventually hit on the idea of the one-liner and it became more than an illustration. The form was established, and it could work with or without a caption depending on what sort of joke you were creating. I later realized that those were the artists who got me into cross-hatching. I'd begun to think, 'What the hell, let's make a really interesting drawing while we're at it.'" Wilson's childhood graphics diet also included *The New Yorker*, newspaper cartoons, and his favorite pulp fantasy magazine, *Weird Tales*.

Most parents might have been alarmed by their child's esoteric tastes, but Wilson's encouraged his. "My mother was rebelling against a very Irish Catholic crowd, and my father's people were very big in the prohibition movement." Wilson considers himself fortunate to have been raised as an atheist despite the influence of relations who included the populist leader William Jennings Bryan, a great-uncle, who would turn up at his grandparents' house at breakfast to proselytize prohibition while consuming huge amounts of food. "My father walked away from all of that and did the 'Roaring Thirties' thing. I guess that's what started his drinking."

The Wilson family tree includes other ambitious eccentrics. His uncle Mac, a professional lion tamer, would hunt mountain lions in the Southwest and bring them back to his Illinois hotel-saloon. Photographs exist of Gahan, age six or seven, surrounded by a pride of cubs. P. T. Barnum, a great-uncle of Gahan's father, Allen Barnum Wilson, also looms large in Wilson lore. While Gahan never knew him personally, Phineas Taylor possessed a brilliant sense of showmanship, and his outlandishness found its way into Gahan's own special effects. "The more I read about him, the more in awe of him I am," says Wilson, who greatly admires Barnum's genius for advertising and promotion, especially the circulars the showman used to hype his attractions. *Barnum's Advance Courier* tantalized potential ticketholders with titillating drawings of curiosities like the Sleeping Beauty, "A full life-size moving mechanical figure of a young lady of surpassing loveliness, in elegant somnific repose, her chest and respiratory organs in apparent health and vigor, and [in larger type] Breathing Precisely as if Alive!" It's an image that might have been torn from the pages of a Gahan Wilson collection.

Allen Wilson was a charismatic man of good taste, bright ideas, and poor anger management. While working as a dapper young floorwalker in Chicago's Carson Pirie Scott department store, he met Gahan's mother, Rose Marion Gahan, who was employed in the business's advertising and marketing department after attending the Art Institute of Chicago. "She was very determined and serious about wanting to be an artist," says Gahan, recalling her "Aubrey Beardsley decadent *Yellow Book* fantasy kind of drawings." Unfortunately, his mother experienced "some kind of devastating nervous breakdown that spoiled the whole damn thing. It was always quite hush-hush mysterious, not talked about. But she was quite heroic and one of these women who were way ahead of the rest of her peers."

Allen Wilson also had an eye for art. Believing that the framed paintings Carson Pirie Scott sold were "junk," he successfully assumed control of the store's art department and upgraded its inventory. Impressed by the new selection, art collector and affluent Acme Steel owner Ralph Hubbard Norton befriended Allen. Following the Wilsons' failure to independently promote their own regional art exhibitions, Norton hired Allen into Acme's product-development department, where he flourished. Young Gahan's first published cartoon, depicting tons of Acme steel being dumped atop Adolf Hitler and Hideki Tōjō, appeared in the company's in-house publication.

Gahan recalls a Dickensian visit with his father to an Acme factory outside of Chicago, where steel bars were smelted and cut down into strips, whose many uses included package strapping. "I remember being absolutely appalled by the working conditions in the factory," Gahan says. "It was horrible. You'd have great slabs of steel hurtling by on rollers until they'd crash to a halt. Then these guys would lift the slabs and hoist them onto a railroad car. What happened was they went deaf, every damn one of them. I couldn't believe it." At other times, the child learned, "guys would fall into pits of bubbling steel and completely disappear."

Allen Wilson's greatest accomplishment was a design for metal Venetian blinds patented under his name for Acme in 1942. "He worked out this very simple way to maintain strip steel's integrity, so you could bend it and it would snap right back again," says Gahan. The blinds would become ubiquitous in suburban homes and executive suites throughout the nation.

"US LOCALS DON'T CALL THEM 'ANGRY CLAMS' FOR NOTHING!"

Unpublished rough

Gahan was also affected deeply by the "death-making machinery" and toxic poisons found in the Acme steel mills scattered around the Midwest. The environmental politics apparent in many Wilson cartoons often reflect the great "pity and sorrow" he believes permeates his work on a certain level. "Really," he once told Fantagraphics Books publisher Gary Groth, "it's a terrific *joke* that we have this one really teeny fragile place and we seem to be intent on destroying it."

Despite Allen Wilson's success, "depressing" incidents involving alcohol and unpredictable rages occurred all too often in the Wilson household. The family lived in a handsome apartment on the north side of Chicago while Gahan attended high school during the forties. Late one night, Allen, a sailing aficionado, returned from his yacht club. "There was a ruckus in the hallway," recalls Gahan, "and there's my father, stinking drunk." Allen had crashed into a taxi on his way home, and a Chicago policeman had him in tow. "My father tells me to call a lawyer at the steel company. So I call him up, describe the situation, and he's there in half an hour. While we're waiting for the lawyer, a cop asked me, 'Is your dad a big deal?' And I said, 'Yeah, he's a big deal.' And off we all went to the police station, where I saw the taxi driver. He was OK, and he looked pretty smug when he saw this drunk come in. He was even happier to see this guy put in the slammer. But then it all got turned around for him, and it was a very depressing thing to see. The taxi driver thought it was going his way, but then he suddenly realized he was being fucked. It was disgusting and I was horrified."

During his late teens, Gahan attended the Todd School for Boys in Woodstock, Illinois. The school was Orson Welles's alma mater, and Gahan dined with the young genius during one of his frequent visits. Gahan also wanted to become a filmmaker. And while he enjoyed a memorable celebrity-studded two-week visit to Hollywood armed with letters of recommendation from a Chicago industrialist, he came to realize he didn't have the alpha-male gumption necessary to follow that particular career path.

His real calling, of course, was art. "As a kid I was always drawing, drawing, drawing," he says, "and everybody I know in any kind of visual art is a drawer." After attending a couple of commercial institutions, including the Chicago Academy for the Arts, Wilson followed in his mother's footsteps, enrolling in the Art Institute of Chicago, where he undertook a classic curriculum that included instruction in charcoal, oil painting, etching, lithography, life drawing, and art history. He was enthralled by his teachers, some of whom had fled Hitler's Germany, but was especially taken by the institute's museum, which was then housed in the same building as the school. Strolling from his etching class to life drawing, Wilson passed through galleries containing works by El Greco, Goya, Picasso, and his main man, Cézanne. He became the first cartoonist to graduate from the institution.

Following an abbreviated stint in the air force, thanks to a bad leg, Wilson moved to Greenwich Village in 1952 with the promise of a few months' parental support. He began peddling his wares to the scores of big and little magazines that were publishing cartoons. A self-described bohemian, Wilson lived hand-to-mouth for a couple of years, selling to outlets ranging from stag mags to the giant cartoon omnibuses. He earned $7.50 for each cartoon he sold to Ziff-Davis's *Amazing Stories* and *Fantastic*. While cartoon editors at slicker magazines such as *Collier's* and *Look* appreciated Wilson's work, they felt it hovered over readers' heads. Wilson finally got his break when *Collier's* art director Bill Chessman temporarily took over as cartoon editor. After proving himself in the weekly, Wilson soon began appearing in *Look* regularly as well, with the *Saturday Evening Post* and other top-shelf periodicals to follow.

Although he later became friends with *Mad* cofounder Harvey Kurtzman, Wilson saw too much slapstick and not enough of an edge in the humor magazine. In 1957, however, *Playboy* publisher Hugh Hefner hired Kurtzman to edit *Trump* with the intent of developing a more sophisticated version of the earlier satirical landmark. *Trump's* masthead displayed a Chicago street address, so Wilson took the opportunity to drop by the office during a visit to his parents in nearby Evanston. He was surprised and disappointed to learn that *Trump's* editorial offices were actually in New York. His portfolio, however, ended up with Hefner, whose offices he had accidentally stumbled into. Hefner, who'd been on the lookout for a Charles Addams type to offset *Playboy*'s more sexual content, shook Wilson's hand, announced, "I've been waiting for you," and hired him immediately for his four-year-old magazine.

The December 1957 issue of *Playboy* featured a black-and-white Wilson cartoon. But in March 1958, the magazine printed Wilson's first full-page color cartoon, one of which has appeared every month since. In it, a puzzled woman sweeps away part of her own shadow, a notion owing as much to Addams as to Salvador Dalí or René Magritte. In 2010, Fantagraphics Books published a three-volume box set containing the beautifully reproduced entirety of Wilson's colorful *Playboy* work. In the introduction to volume one, Hefner claims credit for the way Wilson's "eerie" *Playboy* palette is consistently dominated by a single color. "Hefner is a brilliant editor, and very tough, so I know he reproduced those things as well as he could," Wilson says. "But they were on translucent magazine paper. The colors look glaringly brilliant on the books' opaque paper, so I was in ecstasy."

Wilson's earthy palette reflects his visual influences: Goya and, less easily recognized, "those lovely Hammer horror films" from the United Kingdom, which opened his eyes to "the atmospheric, bright, spooky thing." With their neo-Victorian stage sets, Hammer films were the twentieth-century version of the penny dreadfuls that excited British readers.

Hefner, who invested in Wilson well before William Shawn did, was no less a master of self-promotion than P. T. Barnum, to Wilson's thinking. "He undertook a campaign, advancing stealthily and astutely with the Playboy clubs to provide a safe place for fantasy. You could go there, and nothing would happen, but you had a sort of romance with pretty girls. America's a different country today because of both of them." And so is cartooning, which also provides a safe space to investigate transgressive topics. *Playboy* remains the second most robust market for single-panel art after *The New Yorker*, especially for cartoonists willing and able to "sex it up"—which Wilson never did, unless you consider a woman opening her blouse to reveal a pair of bulging, monstrous eyes a turn-on.

During the sixties and seventies, Wilson sometimes spent entire days ensconced in Hefner's Chicago Playboy Mansion. Natural light was not allowed inside the house in order to maintain the illusion of an endless sybaritic night. Wilson wasn't there to indulge himself in the cornucopia of earthly delights on hand, however, but rather to work. Surprisingly, Hefner continues to edit *Playboy*'s cartoons as of this writing, and Wilson shows me fairly detailed typed notes of recent provenance. "I get away with a lot more ridiculous and grotesque stuff in *Playboy* than anywhere else," says Wilson, who at one time made enough from the magazine to live and travel in Europe for a year and a half.

Hefner, pushing ninety and still naughty, has transformed himself into something resembling a Wilson cartoon. (Not the one with the grotesque nonagenarian, of whom a concerned father remarks to his daughter, "Your mother and I think he's very nice, dear, but isn't he just a little bit old?") Wilson approves of Hefner's chemical fortification and suggests Hef might be the next step in an evolutionary process he once suggested in a cartoon in which the evolving stages of man are displayed on a staircase that continues to ascend. A lower form remarks to his business-suited apex, "I was wondering when you'd notice there's lots more steps." Wilson heartily approves of Hef's shameless reinvention as priapic geezer. "Thanks to science, he can still function sexually with the chicks, and he's brave enough to do it. He's proving that you not only can have a good time within the ordinary human life span, but that you can also extend it."

Recalling the elderly people he knew as a child, Wilson notes that "there's a point where you just stop being viable. You became this fragile thing and wore stiff, uncomfortable clothes. Beginning in your fifties, you sat and walked in an old-person way. Now you see these old bastards walking around in shorts and African hunter hats—and I love 'em for it. It's all different, and Hefner's onto that. Just as he successfully changed the way we thought about sexual freedom, now he's demonstrating that being old is not what it used to be." He adds, "I figured if I made it into my sixties I'd be doing pretty well, especially during my alcohol years."

Wilson found himself following his father's path during the 1970s. He describes his condition in a manner suggesting Poe or Lovecraft. "For a while it was manageable, but it started sliding beyond manageable and became really ghastly. I had been in control, sort of. I was doing just what my father did, which was get drunk every damn night, practically." His drinking eventually began to affect his work. "It started to fuck it up. I was in terrible trouble, in utter despair. I cannot describe how depressing it was." Wilson ended up at Silver Hill Hospital in Connecticut and describes what he saw there as "touching."

"You know what these other people are going through, and they know what you're going through, but nobody else does. There's no way they could. It's like a bunch of people on a life raft, or whatever cliché you want to use. I love these people. I kept in touch with a good many of them. For some of them it worked, for others it didn't." He maintained sobriety through Alcoholics Anonymous, which offered another version of the afflicted helping the afflicted. "It's very tricky but it worked for me, praise be. I've never been even slightly tempted to drink again, although I miss the lovely taste of wine. It was delicious."

Surprisingly, Wilson missed out on a lot of the chemical attractions of the sixties and seventies. "I never got into the dope, thank God. I had a little cocaine and didn't care for it. I did marijuana, which I didn't like at all, except for one time. I never took LSD, so that dates it. You get into this thing where, like in Eugene O'Neill's plays, there's total horrible despair. Everything's hopeless, no good, a black pit."

Although he eschewed psychedelics, the singular marijuana experience Wilson refers to provided a fascinating moment of visionary clarity that had a profound effect on his art. He was never a fan of cannabis and "particularly didn't care for the thing where time slows to an incredible crawl. You'd be at this slow-motion party and realize,

'Oh, I have to go to the bathroom.' And two hours later you're in the bathroom. You're standing there urinating for a half hour, then you come back, and God knows how long that takes." However, that one experience with a special cannabis blend at a fancy dinner party led Wilson to a heavy revelation.

"I had always been extraordinarily fond of Paul Cézanne and still am, very much so. I remember looking at his paintings while I was at the Art Institute of Chicago, sketching endlessly, and trying to understand how he magically transformed three dimensions into a flat plane. I made tiny bits of progress here and there but never really got where I wanted. But after toking away, I looked across this magnificent table full of crystal and lovely china and bottles and whatnot, and all of a sudden—I got it! And I still have it. I'm doing it now. I can look at objects and see and draw them as Cézanne did. It's a miracle that has stayed with me, totally and completely. Very often you can see Cézanne touches in my cartoons, three-dimensional objects and planes. This was given to me by whatever the hell it was that I smoked, and for that I'm very grateful."

In 1970, Wilson was recruited for *National Lampoon*, which also printed future *New Yorker* stars Sam Gross and Charles Barsotti. Wilson fit in with the *Lampoon* crew perfectly. "That was a remarkable assemblage of brilliant sons of bitches," he says. "Its spirit was insidious. It was like being part of a pirate crew. We were like some kind of religious sect. We were out to show the bastards, by God, and we did, very effectively." At the *Lampoon*, Wilson went wild, writing and drawing numerous features including "How to Spell Conspiracy" ("C is for Cover-Up / The verb and the noun / If you don't see it / Then you won't frown") and "Christmas Beware" ("Oh, little town of Bethlehem / You'd blanch to see the sight / Of your local Favorite Son / Strung up in neon light!"). Facilitated by visionary troublemakers Doug Kenney and Henry Beard, Wilson enjoyed complete artistic freedom at the *Lampoon*. It's a freedom he would never enjoy elsewhere, even at *Playboy*. "I just wish something like the *Lampoon* would happen again," bemoans Wilson. "But there's no sign of it whatsoever, even though things are much worse now than they were then."

Wilson's lifelong preoccupation with the terrors, disappointments, and ultimate tragedy of childhood flourished in *Nuts*, a monthly anti-nostalgia series that began appearing on the first page of the *Lampoon*'s funnies section in 1970. Instructed by his editors to "make it as horrible as you can," Wilson replied, "You bet!" At first he tried to do something involving monsters, "which was interesting but wasn't turning me on." Besides, he was already drawing monsters in his *Playboy* cartoons. He continued pondering the assignment. "What's *really* horrible? I wondered. What's *really* scary? Oh, shit! A little kid is scary! And in that instant I knew that I'd do a realistic strip about what the little bastards go through."

Pitched midway between *Peanuts* and *South Park*, the semiauto-biographical *Nuts* features "the kid," a chubby lad often bundled up in a bulky coat and deer-hunter cap. Each strip begins with a question that summons a Proustian memory. "Remember the first time you had to wait for something you really wanted, maybe because you had to save up for it, and how you wanted it more and more?" starts one strip depicting a model German sub that turns out to be much smaller than expected. "So long, Wolf U-boat," thinks the unnamed kid as the full-sized fantasy version of his desire sails away. Taking the child's point of view, Wilson's panels are cramped and claustro-phobic with word balloons. The strip's title is, of course, a takeoff on Charles Schulz's iconic daily comic. Wilson admires and appreciates Schulz's work, but he considers *Peanuts* a deceptively anodyne depiction of childhood.

"I always respected what Charles Schulz did—which was religious teaching. His strips were little moral fables. It's fine and dandy, but it has nothing to do with children, and that's all there is to that. But he did exactly what he set out to do, and it's quite extraordinary stuff. It did piss me off that he was pretending it was about children and it wasn't." How did Wilson's vision of childhood differ from Schulz's? "Childhood is a terrifying world. The little critters are so alive and so perceptive. They're all scared to death but so delighted when some-thing works out. Children are intensely alive and complicated. The thing that made me angry at Schulz is that he sentimentalizes the idea of childhood, which has really done a lot of harm."

Nuts makes you feel physically uncomfortable while reading it, as though the world were pressing in on you. "Everything's purposely drawn to scale," Wilson explains. "It's like the kid is being crushed and confined in this box. The frame is kid-sized, and you only see parts of the huge people and world that surround him. That's all a kid apprehends: giant projections in his immediate vicinity and every-thing else far away. Doors are big, difficult to open, and so on. But they struggle through; they're amazing. Sometimes you see a kid just crossing a busy street and you feel like, 'Good for you, kid!'"

The New Yorker didn't discover Wilson until 1980. Wilson had already discovered *The New Yorker*, of course. Artists like Addams, Arno, Thurber, Steig, Price, and Steinberg had already influenced him, although less in terms of style than in their individuality. Each had his own influences, naturally, but just as Picasso wouldn't be Picasso without Cézanne, and Arno wouldn't have been Arno with-out Daumier, Picasso was still Picasso and Arno still Arno. And Wilson, it's safe to say, wouldn't have been Wilson without Addams, whom he respected for his sense of "atmosphere" and brilliant ability to create an entire world within a series of single frames.

Wilson certainly didn't enter the magazine's orbit as a gag writer, having decided much earlier that he wouldn't pursue that path. In fact, he was "devastated," "crushed," and "shocked" to learn that Addams, Price, and Arnold Roth were using secondhand ideas. Nei-ther did Wilson alter his style to fit the *New Yorker* aesthetic, nor did Lee Lorenz ever ask him to. "If you come up with something that gooses them, they'll go along with it," Wilson says. "If you don't, they won't."

For whomever he's cartooning, Wilson compares the process to casting, designing, and illuminating a cinematic mise-en-scène. Like Arno and Addams, Wilson is extremely conscious of lighting, the dramatic effects of which he fills in after the basic drawing is completed. And his black-and-white *New Yorker* cartoons are nothing less than instamatic film noirs.

He prefers the fine line and flexibility of crow quill pens for drawings and employs a variety of techniques for his color work. "Sometimes I'll start with watercolor, which doesn't obscure the lines, and then spray it with a workable fixative," he says. "Then I can do a wash over that, or rub the cels or whatever to enrich the depth of the colors. And if you use a spray fixative, you can wipe it off and start over again without having to start from scratch." He prefers ledger bond paper that "takes the ink well" for his roughs, and tends to use watercolor paper for finishes, particularly for his *Playboy* pages.

Wilson compares cartooning to fishing: He tosses a mental line into the ocean, waits until he feels a little tug, carefully hooks it, reels it in, and flips it into his boat. The important thing, he used to tell students, is to "stay with whatever you're wrestling with, and you eventually come up with something."

He doesn't work quite as arduously as he has in the past. "Essentially, it depends on how much money is needed," he says. "I'll take a little break now and then, just wander around. I have a vague idea of who's looking for material and what I've done for them recently." Neither does he produce his drawings on a fixed schedule, preferring to tap into the flow as the spirit moves him. "I sit down to work, and when I stop, I realize all this time has passed. You're obviously dealing with some kind of mystical state. But it usually starts out with 'Who should I do stuff for now?'" He submits ten to a dozen roughs to *The New Yorker* nearly every week and "at least one solid batch" to *Playboy* each month.

While you can now write "fuck" in *The New Yorker*, the magazine's cartoons are less provocative than during the era of Arno's luscious flappers and Addams's mordant clan. Moreover, as nearly every cartoonist I've talked to points out, the magazine's layout no longer supports the mixture of vertical, L-shaped, and full-page cartoons that once were a graphic staple. Gahan Wilson's conservative critique of the magazine is no different and he still, perhaps more than any other artist, gives the magazine's art department its teeth. In a 2012 cartoon, for example, a large dog bares its fangs while clawing at the tablecloth beside an unsettled dinner guest. "Actually he's not begging," notes his host. Like so much Wilson imagery, it's like a moment captured from a play's second act, the rest of which you'll have to imagine for yourself. The only thing you can rely on is that dinner will continue.

10

The Belated Middle American: Jack Ziegler

JACK ZIEGLER DOESN'T know what makes something funny. "I got no theory at all," says the tall, bearded cartoonist. "I just start drawing and see what happens."

Lee Lorenz wrote that Ziegler's work, "if taken as a whole, constitutes a dead-on if bemused portrait of Middle America." In reality, Ziegler has only lived in Middle America—specifically, Lawrence, Kansas—since 2010. Otherwise, he's a typical coastal liberal and has called New York City, San Francisco, Las Vegas, and New Haven, New Milford, and Sharon, Connecticut, home at various times in his life. Neither does he consider himself a sociologist.

"I don't really think about what I do sociologically," he says. "I'm just trying to do stuff that amuses *me*. And I don't think about rich people or poor people or East Coast people. I'm just trying to find something funny. Which is harder and harder to do. I'm less sure of what's funny anymore. Not that I ever knew. It was always a guess."

What *is* humor, anyway? In E. B. White's introduction to *A Subtreasury of American Humor*, an influential 1941 anthology, the *New Yorker* writer-editor stated that "Humor can be dissected, as a frog can, but the thing dies in the process and the innards are discouraging to any but the pure scientific mind." Nevertheless, in 1972 the philosopher Patricia Keith-Spiegel identified more than one hundred theories of humor, most of which fit into one of eight categories—biological, superiority, incongruity, surprise, ambivalence, release, configuration, and psychoanalytic. Through these classifications, humor can be seen as either a biological relief from tension, an incongruity between expectation and reality, or a form of childlike play; Plato described the "superiority" theory as the "mixture of pleasure and pain that lies in the malice of amusement."

In 2010, the business school professor A. Peter McGraw and grad student Caleb Warren published "Benign Violations: Making Immoral Behavior Funny" in the journal *Psychological Science*. Their "benign violation" theory of humor suggests that "laughter and amusement result from violations that are simultaneously seen as benign." When violations of "personal dignity," "linguistic norms," "social norms," and "moral norms" are offset by humor, we come out ahead. As long as there's no actual harm, jokes about physical threats, social faux pas, and cultural misunderstandings actually help us get along in the world. In other words, that which makes us laugh also makes us stronger.

Like Ziegler, however, most people view humor the same way US Supreme Court justice Potter Stewart described pornography: They may not be able to define it, but they know it when they see it.

There was a period during the seventies and eighties when Ziegler's cartoons hit extremely close to home. Ziegler seemed to be furthering the hostilities James Thurber initiated in the collection of sketches known as *The War Between Men and Women*. His attitude seems to

Jack Ziegler at home in Lawrence, Kansas

have struck a cultural chord, too. In Ziegler's most popular Cartoon Bank drawing, an exasperated-looking businessman speaking to his wife from a hotel room says, "Yes, yes, yes, I miss you, too, honey. Now put the dog on." His 1987 collection is called *Marital Blitz: A Wicked Collection of Marriage-Minded Cartoons* (original title: *The Deteriorating Marriage Manual*).

The New Yorker's earliest cartoonists—including Alan Dunn, E. McNerney, and especially Peter Arno—dissected upper-class philandering by both sexes. But Ziegler's cartoons take the nascent hostility behind marriage and divorce to the outer limits. There's something almost Steinberg-ian about the balding, middle-aged man standing on a pedestal, clutching his pipe and paper, looking down upon his extremely disapproving wife, and saying, "Sorry, honey, but I got here first." And there's something almost cruel about the dinner-table scenario of a wife remarking to her husband that "I know what you're thinking. You're thinking, 'Hey, what *is* this crap?'" The book ends with a pair of respectively grim and angry suicide scenarios: "Quiet now, children. Your father has an announcement to make," says a mother to her brood as Dad holds a gun to his temple at the dinner table; in the other, a husband with a noose around his neck shouts furiously to his wife as she returns from shopping, "Well, finally! I've been standing here for hours!" And in the book's final drawing, the same balding, middle-aged man who inhabits so many of Ziegler's drawings sits across the table from his disapproving cat, looks at his food much as the above-mentioned diner does, and asks, "Cat Yummies *again*?" Who is the violator, who the violated? At this point, one approaches agreement with Denis Norden, the late British comedy writer, who defined humor as "the surprise withdrawal of sympathy."

Having contributed nearly thirteen hundred cartoons to *The New Yorker*, Ziegler has mapped a world in which nearly every form of the aforementioned categories of humor come into play. And while it's probably true that no single theory will ever explain the world of humor in all its earthly and cosmic manifestations, just as no single artistic approach to humor could do so, Ziegler's tool kit is expansive enough to suggest that he's trying.

Jack D. Ziegler arrived in the Midwest by a circuitous route that began in Brooklyn, New York, where he was born on July 13, 1942. His father, Denmore Ziegler, was born in the borough's Flatbush neighborhood (also the childhood home of Arnie Levin), while his mother, Kathleen, was raised in Forest Hills, Queens. The union of Kay and Denny, as everyone called them, was "one of those interborough marriages," Ziegler says, implying a geographic schism with comedic potential. Also, Kay was of Irish descent, Denny of German. Like a statistically intriguing number of other cartoonists' parents in this book, Kay Ziegler was a schoolteacher who'd studied art in college and dabbled in fashion design. Denny Ziegler was a salesman who worked for J. S. & W. R. Eakins, Inc., a pigment and dye company noted for its "Velvetized" products. Jack's earliest art supplies were liberated from the Eakins supply room.

Forest Hills has long been a divided neighborhood, with upscale Forest Hills Gardens on one side of Queens Boulevard and middle-

and lower-middle-class homes on the other, where the Zieglers lived. Jack's upbringing was "normal." He attended Our Lady Queen of Martyrs, a parochial school that didn't provide art classes. He nevertheless drew constantly with his fountain pen and blue ink.

Jack collected baseball cards and EC comics like *Weird Science* and *Tales from the Crypt*. By the time he was eleven years old, Jack was taking the subway into Manhattan regularly with his best friend, Brian McConnachie. The two would haunt the used magazine stores near Forty-Second Street and Eighth Avenue in search of choice back issues. "Then I'd have to sneak 'em into the house," Ziegler says. "I'd have a stack under my shirt. They didn't know I was going into the city."

The two boys' adventures also included impromptu visits to local comics artists whose addresses they'd looked up in the phone book. They called on Bernard "Bernie" Krigstein, a fine artist known mostly for the handful of remarkable stories he illustrated for EC in 1954 and 1955. "I don't think he had a lot of patience for us, because we kind of just showed up at his door."

The pair also dropped in at both EC and Atlas Comics, the publishing company that evolved into Marvel Comics. Delighted by the boys' enthusiasm, the Atlas staff made them feel at home. *Blackhawk* artist Charles Nicholas "Chuck" Cuidera even let them watch him draw. "It was really quite something."

The Zieglers subscribed to *Life, Look, Time,* and the *New York Daily News.* "My father didn't like the *New York Times*," Jack says. "I had the feeling he might've been a Republican, but we never talked about that." Brian's parents always subscribed to *The New Yorker,* though, and their residence provided Jack a looser, more playful home away from home. "His mother was kinda nuts," he says, laughing. "She was an ex-showgirl, a lot of fun—and funny. She was always puttin' show tunes on the Victrola." Brian's father owned a small film company in Manhattan that produced industrial shorts. Brian grew up to become a writer and actor. After working at *National Lampoon* during its early-seventies heyday, he went on to write for *Shining Time Station, SCTV Network,* and *Saturday Night Live.* His acting credits

"HOW ABOUT — FOR GOD'S SAKE — THIS ONE?"

Previously unpublished rough

include roles in *Caddyshack* and *Sleepless in Seattle,* as well as Woody Allen's *Husbands and Wives* and *Bullets over Broadway.*

Ziegler's first exposure to comics was the *Daily News*'s funny pages. He later bought the *Saturday Evening Post* and *New Yorker* for their cartoons. His work was inspired directly by the comic characters of his youth: Nancy, Sluggo, Archie, the Lone Ranger, Tonto, and Buck Rogers have all popped up in his drawings, as have imaginary spin-offs like Toasterman, Pancakeboy, and Mr. Overeasy. The comics of his youth affected his work on a formal level as well.

Considering the high ratio of rejection to acceptance in the field, becoming a successful cartoonist, especially on a freelance basis, requires rigorous self-control if not quite an appetite for rejection. "You actually have to have quite a bit of discipline to sit down each day and do what you do," Ziegler says. "A lot of people who claim to be writers or artists, they get up at noon or three in the afternoon or whenever. I gotta get up early to do what I do. It's a job."

Jack undoubtedly learned about self-control at Our Lady Queen of Martyrs, with its disciplinarian nuns, and later at Xavier High School, a Jesuit all-boys institution specializing in military science and located in Manhattan's Chelsea neighborhood. Although he didn't consider turning pro until long after he left college, Jack published his first cartoons in *Xavier*, the school magazine. He liked his fellow students and received a "decent" education there. The only downside he recalls is that "it was a pain in the ass" to wear a uniform on the subway into Greenwich Village during the late fifties. Xavier students wore one of two uniforms. The more formal consisted of "spiffy" dress blues with white stripes down the pants legs and gold buttons, a visor hat, a white shirt, and a black tie. The other was the "OD" (olive drab) combo of brown tie, brown jacket, brown pants, and lighter brown shirt commonly associated with Dwight D. Eisenhower's military years. "The Greenwich Village beatniks really enjoyed seeing us boys come down the street," says Ziegler, who was required to join Xavier's Reserve Officers' Training Corps (ROTC) program to graduate.

"I enjoyed high school more than I did college," Ziegler says of his subsequent years at Fordham University. He snagged a plum job as a CBS page, which he also enjoyed more than college. When classes were over, Ziegler would hop on the subway to Studio 50 (now the Ed Sullivan Theater) near Times Square. Alongside "a bunch of out-of-work writers and actors, and some students," he ushered for *The Garry Moore Show*, *The Jackie Gleason Show*, and *The Ed Sullivan Show*. He was on duty when the Beatles made their American debut on *The Ed Sullivan Show* in February 1964 and for many of the Brit rockers who followed. "There were screaming girls in the audience, but it was pretty well controlled. They didn't print too many tickets, so we in fact had to find people on the street for the dress rehearsal." His "phenomenal" job lasted through most of college.

After graduation, Ziegler worked in the mailroom of D'Arcy Advertising on Park Avenue. Chances were that he would be drafted into the army with a good chance of being sent to Vietnam, "and I had no great desire to do that." He found an army reserve unit that required eighteen months of service rather than the customary six months. After basic training, he was sent to the Department of Defense Language Institute in Monterey, California, where he studied Russian for a year before being sent back to a reserve unit in New

York—"the best way I knew to not have to do Vietnam." Ziegler acquired a taste of California while avoiding deployment. After immersing himself in Russian, he would wind down at the Bullseye, "a great little bar with a great jukebox. If you had to do the army, Monterey was not a bad gig."

He left Monterey in March 1967 and returned to New York and a job at CBS Radio. He drew only sporadically, as a "hobby," while working for network transmission facilities at Black Rock, the CBS's midtown monolith. While attending Brian McConnachie's Chicago wedding, he met a teacher named Jean Ann Rice, whom he married the following April. The couple rented an apartment on West Fifty-Fifth Street for about a year before buying a Volkswagen bus and driving to San Francisco because, Ziegler recalls, "I thought I'd like to actually see California while not being in the army."

At this point we are at the equivalent of ten panels into Jack Ziegler's "Autobio," a two-page, twenty-six-panel spread he drew for *The New Yorker*'s December 1998 cartoon issue. The Zieglers' VW bus appears elevated above the highway as it heads west with the moon hovering in the distance. Preceding it is a panel in which Ziegler replicates himself thrice with the same slightly shell-shocked expression under a caption reading "College, the Army, and marriage followed in quick succession." The following three panels, however, are joyous and expansive, as our newly relocated, patchouli-scented hero auditions his air-guitar chops at a Grateful Dead show in his "buckskin jacket, leather pants, and hippie vest." The next panel reads simply: "Didn't get the gig." Life assumes hyperspeed on the facing page, with Ziegler acquiring a dog and kids before returning back east to the "sub-sub-suburbs" of rural Connecticut.

Ziegler's four years in San Francisco, from 1969 to 1972, were a youthful oasis prior to the onset of adult responsibilities. Jack found employment at KTVU, a TV station in Oakland, while Jean Ann worked at a department store and taught. The couple bought a German shepherd puppy on the street, and Jack inhaled but did not trip. They spent a few years in a nice apartment near North Point, where

Jean Ann became pregnant with the first of the couple's three children. "The rent was cheap, but not cheap enough for one person's income," Ziegler says, "so we had to move again."

A music fan at one of the era's rock epicenters, Ziegler frequented the Fillmore and the Matrix. He memorably caught the Velvet Underground three times in a single week at the latter. "The last night I was there, the audience was me and maybe two other people." He attended Altamont with his friend Walter, an arson-inclined army acquaintance straight out of *Catch-22*. "He hated the army worse than I did," Ziegler says. "He used to set fire to his barracks and then run upstairs and pretend to be asleep, so they wouldn't suspect him." Jack and Walter enjoyed Altamont and were far enough back that they couldn't see a member of the Hells Angels security team stab gun-wielding Meredith Hunter to death. They did, however, see a man hanging from a wire onstage, working his way hand over hand from one mountain of speakers to another, until he fell. Walter, who was quite high himself, "was deeply invested in this guy making it to the other speakers," Ziegler recalls, "and when he didn't, that was the end of Walter." Otherwise, they had a pretty good time, only learning about Hunter's murder during their drive home.

Jack and Jean Ann's final San Francisco apartment was on Stanyan Street, adjacent to Golden Gate Park. "That's when I started doing cartoons and figured I should move back east if I wanted to be serious about this." San Francisco was, of course, ground zero for the underground comix movement, but Ziegler admits that although he tried to gear his work toward the cosmodelic, "I was never particularly good at it." He met with *Rolling Stone* magazine's first art director, Robert Kingsbury, who was looking for a cartoonist, "but he couldn't figure out what kind of cartoons he wanted, and the stuff I showed him wasn't it. I thought what I was doing was good but it was pretty crappy, as I look back on it." He also spent six months on a novel that, again, "I thought was good when I was writing it but turns out it wasn't."

Meanwhile, Brian McConnachie, despite being a "terrible" artist with good ideas, according to Ziegler, had started selling his writing

AT THE LAFF-A-MINIT

Previously unpublished rough

and cartoons to *National Lampoon* back in New York. His contributions included a 1972 spread boasting "The Worst Cartoons in the
World." He reported back to Ziegler in San Francisco: "I can't even
draw and I'm selling cartoons—but you can actually draw. Maybe
this is something you wanna think about." So Ziegler did, realizing finally that he had a knack for the single-panel cartoon and that
"maybe this would be a way to make a living without having to sell
my soul in some awful job." After unsuccessfully submitting drawings
to various magazines by mail, Ziegler visited McConnachie and, after
a week, decided to return to New York. "If I'm ever gonna make this
work," he thought, "it's not gonna happen in San Francisco." Sending
his wife and daughter ahead, Ziegler drove back across the country
with Blanche the dog in a U-Haul truck, his VW hitched behind.

In December 1972, the Ziegler family landed in Mattituck, Long
Island, moving into a (thankfully insulated) summer cottage belong-
ing to McConnachie's mother. Jack began making the rounds of
Manhattan magazines, dropping off his batch at *The New Yorker* each
week and picking it back up, unappreciated, the next. He only sold
about ten drawings to *National Lampoon*, but Michael O'Donoghue

provided some advice Ziegler took to heart: "He told me I was drawing way too realistically. As I look back on those drawings, they were really wrong. They weren't cartoony enough. They weren't reduced down to their lowest common denominator or whatever you want to call it. There were wrinkles in the clothing, y'know? People were too tall and there shouldn't be any tall cartoon people."

In the spring, Jack and Jean Ann moved to New Haven, and Jack began selling to *The New Yorker*.

Charles Addams illustrated the first idea Ziegler sold to *The New Yorker*. "It's Edgar Allan Poe sitting at a table and trying to think of something to write. He's imagining different animals saying 'Nevermore'—one's a turtle, I think, and one was . . . I can't even remember, maybe a dog or a cat—before hitting the obvious." The animals Ziegler misremembers are actually a depressed pig, an angry moose, and a frightened turtle, with Poe himself looking especially forlorn. And as excited as Ziegler was to make his first sale to the magazine, "I would've much preferred to be able to do it myself."

As it happened, Lorenz, who joined the magazine's staff in 1973, was on the lookout for new artists. And in December Ziegler was delighted to find one of Lorenz's infamously illegible notes among that week's rejects. "Dear Mr. Ziegler," read the unsigned missive, "would you mind stopping back to discuss one of your ideas with me? Thank you." Natasha, a "dark, smoldering vixen" of a receptionist, buzzed Ziegler into an anteroom, where he sat down beside the "real"—i.e., published—*New Yorker* cartoonists.

Ziegler described his first encounter with Lorenz in "Spec Work," an unpublished memoir: "The caption and layout were fine, he said, but some adjustments would be required in the body of the drawing. Could I perhaps make the fellow on the phone older and a tad more Biblical? And the inner workings of the conveyer belt seemed, well, not quite mechanical enough. Just a few lines added onto the finished drawing should do it." Ziegler, who describes Lorenz's comments as more "fact-checking" than editing, returned home, finished his rough sketch, and sent it back. "They rejected that one, too." The third time was the charm. Ziegler's first *New Yorker* drawing, published February 11, 1974, depicts a bearded man in a toga sitting at a desk and talking on the phone as a conveyor belt churns out birds saying "Moo!" The caption reads: "Hello? Beasts of the Field? This is Lou, over in Birds of the Air. Anything funny going on at your end?" This was the first of several conveyor belt cartoons Ziegler would draw over the years, as though he were still attempting to get it right. One, for example, depicts a line worker putting in his order to the coffee service: "The usual." In another, hazmat-suited men funnel candies into an endless line of jars labeled GENERIC YUMMIES.

Two weeks after its acceptance, Ziegler received a check for $305. He sold another one a month later, for which he received only $215. The difference was due to what Lorenz termed "the formula." *The New Yorker*, he explained, paid for cartoons by the square centimeter each occupied in print.

While Lorenz was buying Ziegler's cartoons regularly, they were not appearing in the magazine. The bottleneck turned out to be Carmine Peppe, who, after starting at *The New Yorker* as an office boy in 1925, went on to become its de facto art editor in the thirties and, eventually, its miracle-working "makeup editor" in charge of the magazine's layout and overall look.

"He didn't like my work, apparently," says Ziegler. "But he was the layout guy, and this was in the days when they really knew how to lay out the magazine; the cartoons were always printed exactly the size they should be, as opposed to today, where it's like 'Who's doing it?' Anyway, Carmine was great at that. But he didn't like my stuff. I never met him. But I had always heard that if they bought something from a new person they would print it pretty quickly. So the weeks went by, and then a couple of months, and I finally said to Lee, 'I was wondering if that first drawing is ever going to appear.' And he didn't realize it hadn't. Meanwhile, I've started selling fairly regularly to the magazine, and nothing is appearing. It turned out that Carmine thought that if they printed my stuff, it would be the end of the magazine and that it would just destroy *The New Yorker* as we know it. Which it did, apparently," he adds with a laugh. "Eventually,

"Hello? 'Beasts of the Field?' This is Lou over in 'Birds of the Air.' Anything funny going on at your end?"

Previously unpublished rough

Lee spoke to Carmine and said, 'Listen, we have to start printing his stuff.' William Shawn spoke to him, too, and insisted they start printing it 'because we're going to be buying this kind of stuff.' I started appearing gradually from then on, but he was still holding a lot back. I was selling a lot and very little was getting printed. But eventually they started printing my stuff on a regular basis."

In an unpublished memoir, former cartoon editor James Geraghty wrote that when Shawn "sensed I really liked something that he didn't, he would buy it, but not use it, and here, he was devious." Shawn would ask Peppe to remove cartoons he had purchased, but didn't care for, from the dummy issue prior to publication. Peppe apparently felt he had the same privilege after Lorenz replaced Geraghty. As it turns out, Ziegler's "Beasts of the Field" cartoon popped out quite nicely in the middle of an Edna O'Brien short story, surrounded in the section by an elegant ink-washed drawing by Lorenz ("And what sector of the economy are you folks from?" asks the wife of one prosperous couple to a another during a reunion) and a magnificently minimal Charles Barsotti cartoon ("Hamill and Royko are right up there, all right," says one young Manhattan sophisticate to another at a bar, "but for my money Breslin is still the master").

"I thought my stuff looked OK," Ziegler says. "I knew how to draw. But I look back on those early drawings and they're not really anything like what I draw now. Because the more you do it, the more comfortable you get. You kind of fall into your style. I didn't quite have what has become recognizably mine until much later. I wanted to *be* George Booth or George Price. I wasn't going to copy them, but their drawings were so *right*." Booth is a particular favorite of Ziegler's. "His drawings are *so funny*, even without the captions. It's the way people interact, the way they look at each other, or the rooms and buildings he draws. There's the dogs, a guy in a bathtub . . . and it's all so *dry*."

The New Yorker operates as an amorphous chorus of individual voices composing a loosely defined (cosmopolitan, sophisticated, liberal, bourgeois) aesthetic. Shawn sought artists with distinct styles and somewhat broader socioeconomic focuses. "They didn't want somebody who was trying to do '*New Yorker*' cartoons, whatever that is, but individual voices," says Ziegler, "which they found in a number of people such as myself, Roz Chast, Charley Barsotti, and certainly George Booth. I was doing stuff that I thought was funny, too. I wasn't trying to gear it to the *New Yorker* audience—I was just trying to do stuff I would like to *see* in *The New Yorker*. I still don't know what stuff of mine is funny to other people, because it's such a subjective thing. To this day, I just do what works for me, and I don't even think about *The New Yorker*—although I do send them everything I draw."

Things started to happen fast once Ziegler began selling to the magazine. Best of all, he was able to make a living. Soon he was appearing in the *Saturday Evening Post, Saturday Review, Writer's Digest,* and "a couple of girly mags." Not *Playboy*, however, which rejected his work for years. "Michelle Urry, the cartoon editor, didn't think my drawings were sexy enough. She was like, 'What can we do to make you think sexy?'" He eventually sold work to *Oui* (1972–81), *Playboy*'s bid to lure a younger audience with more explicit photography than its parent publication.

Over the decades, Ziegler has been one of the more social cartoonists among a comradely bunch. Roz Chast has referred to him as the Tuesday group's "lunch-meister," which Ziegler denies. During the eighties, the regular lunch crew often included Ziegler, Chast, Bill Woodman, Bob Mankoff, Richard Cline, Sam Gross, Boris Drucker, and a few others. Their regular hangout was the Green Man, an Irish bar, but Ziegler would occasionally arrive in the city early and wander around the neighborhood looking for other lunch venues "to shake things up." Brian McConnachie would occasionally join them—"He's much more social than I am," Ziegler says—and suggest spontaneous outings to the racetrack or a ball game, or a trip on the Circle Line.

Ziegler was an important formal innovator in the single-panel gag form.

His ingenious alternative to the traditional cartoon caption, inspired by comic strips, consisted of enclosing the caption somewhere in the panel rather than below it. For many years, up to half of Ziegler's cartoons eschewed captions completely in favor of more economical interior descriptions, gags, or comments. "It depended on the drawing," he explains. "I just felt it was better to do this drawing *this* way than with a standard caption, because it requires less explanation. I was just trying to make it simpler instead of being long-winded. I started out doing pretty normal things. But as I kept doing it, I had ideas that just didn't work in a normal fashion and needed a more logical way to present themselves. It was a way to do it that just looked right." Ziegler's relocated captions also advanced the process that led from script-like dialogues under the illustrations, as in magazines like *Punch,* to the shorter, pithier, single-line captions that typified *New Yorker* cartoons by the 1930s.

The interior captions often add another level of reference to Ziegler's cartoons as well. While a man wearing an apron and holding a spatula and addressing his shrink in a word balloon from the couch might also work as a caption ("It all began when I was a boy. The aroma of Mom's freshly baked bread was everywhere, choking me with its calm, soothing and nutritious lies . . ."), it's all the more effective offset by a punning interior caption reading "Angst over easy."

"I've always thought his gags were better than his art," opines Dan Piraro, whose *Bizarro* cartoons often employ the Ziegler-ian interior caption. "His art is fine, funny, gets the idea across, and ultimately very professional. But to be honest, it never seemed inspiring in and of itself. The way he structures a gag, however, is something I have intentionally emulated. He's terrific at that, and few people in the history of the genre have been better."

There's something endearingly retro about Ziegler's word balloons, captions, and other design elements from the world of comics. Readers sometimes complain about how often a *New Yorker* cartoon's clothing, architecture, or furniture seems stuck in the past. Businessmen especially tend to appear as they did in the thirties, forties, or fifties. And like Bruce McCall, who has made anachronism his stock in trade, Ziegler's stock imagery references the bulbous appliances, clothing, and headwear of his childhood. "I drew people in fedoras

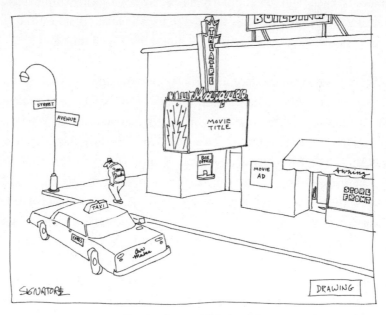

Previously unpublished rough

into the nineties and didn't think about it," he says. "But people haven't worn fedoras since the sixties. To this day, I'll draw a parking meter, fire hydrant, or mailbox that's strictly out of the fifties and sixties—because they look more interesting. If you want to draw a car, are you gonna draw a Toyota? No, you're gonna draw a Buick, an old Chevy, or a Cadillac with fins."

Ziegler's characters are aging, too, he says, relieving him of the problem of drawing older persons he experienced at thirty. "One drawing I did for the magazine had a bunch of executives at a conference table, but I couldn't get them to look old enough. After several attempts, Lee [Lorenz] handed it to Whitney Darrow Jr. to draw. Now, of course, I have no problem drawing old people."

Like all *New Yorker* cartoonists, Ziegler occasionally goes through spells when, for whatever reason, its editors aren't buying his work. Does it freak him out? "Always does," he says with a laugh. "If you don't sell for quite a while, you start getting really nervous. And then they start buying again, and all your worry was for naught." With only a limited number of slots in the magazine, room has to be budgeted for both regulars and newcomers. And with something approximating a .075 percent acceptance rate for all cartoons submitted, the chances of a drawing being bought any week are daunting.

Jack and Jean Ann Ziegler raised their three children in New Milford, Connecticut, before separating in the early nineties. In 1994, Jack met Kelli Gunther, a jazz singer, and the pair married in Las Vegas two years later. A year after returning to Connecticut, the couple was watching a TV documentary about Cirque du Soleil, which they had enjoyed in Vegas, and were inspired to move to Nevada. "So we moved there, and of course everybody thought we were crazy. 'Las Vegas?! Are you fucking insane?'" After seven years, the aridity gave Jack an unstoppable nosebleed that was only cauterized properly after multiple trips to the emergency room. Forced to leave Vegas for moister climes, the couple returned to Connecticut and purchased a home in the rural town of Sharon. "Within two weeks of being there, we realized this was a terrible mistake," Ziegler says. "We had a great house eventually, because we did a lot of work on it, but neither one of us really wanted to be back in the Northeast. Sharon was nothing but trouble for me. I think I panicked in Las Vegas and just wanted to go someplace that had humidity. I went off the deep end there." Since Kelli had long desired to move to Kansas, where her family lived, they sold their home and moved to Lawrence in 2010.

"Before we moved here we knew we were splitting up," says Ziegler of his latest relocation. "Kelli still lives in town here, and we're very friendly. This is where I want to be at this point. It's a good town. And it's humid enough! I know things are winding down at *The New Yorker*, and it's cheap here. You couldn't say the same thing about Sharon. I got a great place for next to nothing." He'd also like to find a publisher for the memoir he began writing during one of the hiatuses imposed upon artists with a substantial backlog of work. "It all goes back to that goddamn Carmine Peppe," he says half seriously. "Because everything kind of got bunched and backed up when he wouldn't print my stuff. At one point I had fifty drawings in the bank that hadn't run and I never quite caught up."

Like nearly all cartoonists, Ziegler is also a huge fan of the medium and its creators. Original drawings by Sidney Harris, Richard

Previously unpublished rough

McCallister, Brian McConnachie, and others line a hallway in the lower level of his house. When cartoonist Victoria Roberts comes up in conversation, Ziegler opens up a scrapbook into which he has affixed her most recent *New Yorker* drawing. For years he has cut out and collected images, accumulating a large personal anthology. He scoffs at Saul Steinberg's disdain for cartoonists, with the exception of Charles Addams. "He never liked cartoonists 'cause he was really an artist, and cartoonists for the most part are fairly annoying: a dour, morose group of people." His book also contains examples of Ariel Molvig's absurdist visual puns, Julia Suits's tiny-headed suburbanites, and Matthew Diffee's frequently Ziegler-ian two-person setups.

"At *The New Yorker*, you can just draw what you want to draw. And ninety percent of it's gonna be rejected, but so what? It's just fun to do it. It's like I retired when I turned thirty. That's the last time I worked for a normal paycheck. It's been great to have had almost forty years of doing pretty much what I'd be doing if I didn't have a job." And he continues to draw, simply to see what will happen.

11

Neckless: The Short, Sharp World of Zachary Kanin

"You wanted to role-play—I can't help it if a doctor would be medically obligated to say something about your weight."

WHAT MODERN GUY can't relate to the Zachary Kanin cartoon in which a king sits forlornly on his throne and muses to an expressionless guard, "I want to be feared as a tyrant, loved as a father, and revered as a god, but I also want them to think I'm funny"?

With his knack for absurd gags and self-deprecating humor, Kanin is in many ways the new face of *New Yorker* cartooning. He also numbers among a small subcategory of artists who draw for the magazine to supplement their day jobs, which, in his case, involves a steady gig as a writer for *Saturday Night Live*. Over a six-month period in 2012, Kanin, who would not turn thirty until the following year, had more cartoons published in *The New Yorker* than any other artist. His more than two hundred published panels represent the current state of gag cartooning while alluding subtly to the tradition's past masters.

The comedic rule of three prevails in a couple of Kanin cartoons, inspired, perhaps, by Roz Chast. The notion that "Some Things Are Better Left Unembroidered" is illustrated by a trio of pillows declaring, respectively, that MY GRANDCHILDREN ARE ALL UGLY, HOME IS WHERE THE BEDBUGS ARE, and YES, THESE PILLOWS HAVE BEEN USED FOR SEX. A roster of "Budget Sideshow Attractions" includes "The bearded hot dog!," "The world's *youngest* man!," and "The two-headed pencil!" And a Charles Addams–esque sense of the macabre, with perhaps a tinge of Jack Ziegler, takes on contemporary flirtation with a four-eyed, double-nosed man in a bar saying to an uninterested woman, "Play coy if you like, but no one can resist a perfectly symmetrical face." Or Addams again when a pair of young kids delightedly anticipates jumping on a spiderwebbed trampoline while its huge spinner lurks behind a nearby tree.

Addams, Chast, and Ziegler have all admittedly influenced Kanin. "Jack and Roz are a little more experimental, which I definitely like," he says, "and I read a lot of B. Kliban growing up. I really like the idea of experimenting with what constitutes a cartoon, although I don't do that as much anymore and instead am sort of figuring out how to tell a joke concisely. But it's still fun when I can come up with something nontraditional and not just a scene with a punch line."

Kanin's cartooning style isn't particularly easy to describe, and he often feels at a loss when asked to characterize it. If the best *New Yorker* cartoonists create distinctive and unique worlds, Kanin's is a slightly surreal place where things have gone sometimes seriously awry. The word "weird" comes to mind, he says, but at the end of the day they really consist only of things that make him laugh. "I like it when they're dark, but they're not always dark, and I feel like everyone has a pretty big smile on their face even when they are. And I like it when they're goofy." These qualities combine in cartoons like the desert scene depicting a tattered clown squirting his equally dehydrated companion, who says, "I don't know whether to be mad that

Zachary Kanin at home in Brooklyn

you had water this whole time or impressed with your commitment to the joke"—as slick a piece of meta-comedy as you'd want.

Many cartoons concern the comeuppance of authority. But look at Kanin's work long enough and you begin to feel like he's on a one-man emasculation crusade. A woman brings nail polish rather than a nail file to her incarcerated man. "Come out with your hands up—you're surrounded by men with megaphones," says one of many such men circling a house. Three men with saws work on boards suspended over cinder blocks in an image captioned "Remedial Karate." And "Not to diminish what you've achieved in the last eighteen months of training, but it appears that the javelin roll is not an Olympic sport," says a guy to a pair of athletes. Kanin doesn't necessarily agree with this reading of his work, however.

"I think it's less de-macho-izing than . . . I'm probably trying to think of what would be the worst way to do something. That's probably what most of my cartoons and humor are like: Here's our goal and then what's the stupidest way people could not accomplish that goal and really miss the mark. That's the most fun for me, when people have a goal and they're just so bad at achieving it."

Many of his cartoons result from visual puzzles he sets up for himself. "I had one—and this was definitely not one of my funnier cartoons—but it was a toreador standing on a ladder with a giraffe rather than a bull. A toreador with an animal that's not a bull is like half of a cartoon idea; but putting him on the ladder . . . that was an idea I felt good about.

"And I don't really draw necks. That's the best way to describe my pictures: None of the people really have necks."

The bearded and very youthful-looking Kanin resides with his wife, Christina Angelides, an efficient-energies advocate for the Natural Resources Defense Council, in a brownstone building in Brooklyn's upwardly mobilized Park Slope neighborhood. A wall of bookshelves contains mostly graphic novels and other comics collections by Frank Miller, Daniel Clowes, Ron Regé Jr., Geoff Johns, and many others. A large blackboard boasts a Kanin sketch of a bearded naked man in repose, a poof of gas emerging from the contented gent's nether regions.

A former *Harvard Lampoon* president, Zach Kanin has enjoyed a life of privilege. Don't look for parental schoolteachers, although one younger brother, Jonah, teaches in Los Angeles; the other, Frank, attends Georgetown University Law Center. Like the cartoonist formerly known as Curtis Arnoux Peters, Zach is a modern American aristocrat. His father, Dennis R. Kanin, is principal owner of New Boston Ventures; he cofounded the real estate development company after serving as Massachusetts senator Paul Tsongas's chief of staff. Zach's mother, Carol Kanin, is finance director for the late senator's widow, Representative Niki Tsongas. Carol Kanin's father, Frank Licht, was governor of Rhode Island from 1969 to 1973. And Christina Angelides's father, Phil Angelides, was a California State treasurer and chairman of the Financial Crisis Inquiry Commission, and is currently president of Riverview Capital Investments in Sacramento.

Unlike Arno, Kanin came under no pressure to change his name in order to protect his family from the shame of his cartooning career. But like Arno, who led a jazz band after leaving Yale, Kanin briefly led his own music group, an Americana act called Tony Ferrante and the Animal Kingdom, until *SNL* began to gobble up his time. (Kanin's dog howls in pain whenever he practices harmonica, an image that wouldn't be out of place in a Kanin cartoon.)

Zachary Joshua Kanin was born in Washington, DC, on September 20, 1983. His family moved to Newton, Massachusetts, some eighteen months later. Like his father, a compulsive doodler, Kanin has been drawing for as long as he can recall.

"In preschool I would draw a lot of people with sharp teeth that were just lines. Eventually I realized that other kids used triangles, and I was like, 'That looks *much* better than just a straight line!'" The kindergarten and first grade journals he kept at Ward Elementary School in Newton turned into sequential illustrated stories in something akin to panels. Second grade brought *Attack of the Killer Piranhas*, a series of chapter books (sometimes involving elaborate torture chambers) consisting of chapters precisely two pages long—"even if it was in the middle of a word," he says, and laughs. "So if the last word of one chapter was 'play-,' the next started with '-ground.'" A few years later, Kanin started to draw his first real comic book, *Super Stupid*, about a "really dumb" superhero with a paunch, and by fifth grade he was distributing Xerox copies of *Mutt Mangler*, a collaborative effort.

Kanin read *The Far Side, Bloom County, Calvin and Hobbes, Garfield, Dilbert,* and *Doonesbury.* Like many young fans of his cohort, he got into superhero comics around the time of 1992's "Death of Superman" story line. After collecting comics for several years, he "sort of stopped," and it wasn't until the late '00s that he began to read more of the "adult, sad stuff" published by the likes of Fantagraphics Books and Drawn and Quarterly. "I'm pretty obsessed with that," says Kanin, who still gets a kick out of mainstream comics as well.

Gary Larson's *The Far Side* was his first single-panel obsession. "Either *The Far Side* or *Beyond the Far Side* was probably the first single-panel book I got. I was always reading it and can remember taking it to a restaurant and getting barbecue sauce on it. We always read *The New Yorker*, too. Charles Addams's stuff was fun because every couple of years I would go back, look at them, and be like, 'Now I get these ten cartoons I didn't get as a kid.' With the *Bloom County* and *Doonesbury* books, I was basically reading about what was funny in 1975, or whenever, and making jokes about Jimmy Carter and Tammy Faye Bakker to my parents." He laughs. "They thought it was funny, but I'd have no idea what I was talking about."

Literal-minded Dennis Kanin often became the butt of dinner-table humor. "My mom would say outlandish things to us that we all knew were jokes, and he'd get very upset when he didn't know she was joking," Zach says. But it's only fun and games until someone starts vomiting. "We would start riffing, and then my youngest brother would laugh so hard that our mom would start screaming that we had to stop or else he was going to throw up, which he occasionally did." This only egged his older brother on, of course, because "it's sort of hard to stop when you're that close to the ultimate goal."

After a year at Bigelow Middle School, Zach transferred to the all-boys Roxbury Latin School in seventh grade. His father and brothers have all attended Roxbury, the country's oldest continuously operating school (est. 1645) and a historic conduit to elite universities. He describes himself as a class clown, just this side of disruptive. He learned to "really embrace the weirdness of whatever I was thinking" at creatives-oriented Wingate Kirkland summer camp on Cape Cod.

Zach began studying cartooning with a local artist during middle school. His earliest single-panel efforts included one in which a bee asks a flower, "Was it good for you, too, dear?" In another, a chicken entering a KFC with a HELP WANTED sign in the window declares, "I'm gonna get this job if it's the last thing I do"—"And it was," reads Zach's kicker.

Although he was occasionally publishing cartoons in Roxbury's student paper, the *Tripod*, Kanin's artistic horizons were broadening. "I wanted to be a cartoonist when I entered Roxbury Latin, but I was thinking more about painting and writing by the time I left," he says. Kanin followed his father's path to Harvard. A nominal English ma-

"O.K., I know it's a long shot, but if we can each convert one lion ..."

Kanin

Previously unpublished rough

jor thanks to the field's relatively few requirements, Kanin took more art than lit courses. He studied painting with cartoon-inspired Sue Williams and joined the *Harvard Lampoon* in the spring of 2002.

Kanin arrived at the *Harvard Lampoon* as an artist and describes his early writing efforts as "horrible." But he soon began carving out an increasingly important role for himself in this noted shortcut to the world of film and TV comedy writing. "It was weird," he says, "because you knew about all the people who had come from the *Lampoon* who were working in TV, and that was an exciting part of being there. But at the same time, there was a real vibe of it *not* being a preprofessional sort of place for one of those jobs. But we looked up to the people who had them. I think I took it more seriously than other people did. I think kids do treat it more preprofessionally now, and that's probably smart. They're using it. On the other hand, I sort of liked the purity of it, that you do this funny stuff only while you're there without worrying about where it's taking you."

In 2004, the *Harvard Lampoon*, under Kanin's editorship, published a parody of *H Bomb*, a somewhat controversial student erotica magazine whose publication he beat by a month to widespread attention thanks to his marketing efforts. "There's a lot of love in it," Kanin told the *Hartford Courant* at the time. "We agree with [*H Bomb*'s editors] that Harvard is a very stuffy place. It makes light of the thing, but parody is the sincerest form of flattery, I've heard." Full of tacky nudity, the *Lampoon*'s cover featured Kanin himself in tweed, with glasses and a pipe, waving a small school pennant while making a slightly shocked face in response to the bare breast beside him. "That was one of those things where everyone's like, 'I hate the *Lampoon* but I really like this.' Well, I'll take it."

A week before graduation, a human resources person from *The New Yorker* called the *Harvard Lampoon* office to ask if anyone might be interested in becoming cartoon editor Bob Mankoff's assistant. "I answered the phone, so I was like, 'Yeah, I'll do it,'" Kanin recalls. His interview with Mankoff consisted of the editor talking to him "for like an hour and a half, and then he was like, 'I didn't ask you any questions. Go write an essay.'" Kanin's response included a section analyzing successful and unsuccessful drawings from the magazine's cartoon archive. He recalls praising Richard Decker's 1931 drawing of escaped convicts running from a prison to a waiting cab they direct to "The Waldorf!" He was less thrilled by cartoons that "just sort of insert a buzzword from pop culture of the day into a regular setting, and that's the joke. But we're all guilty of doing that sometimes," he admits.

At the time, the assistant art editor's duties consisted of reading the mail and sorting out submissions from regular contributors. Kanin would then go through the hundreds of unsolicited submissions the magazine received each week and pick out anything showing promise amid the slush. Another large part of the gig involved sifting through the thousands of Caption Contest entries the magazine receives every week, which took him two or three days. His administrative duties included answering phone calls and e-mails, and he provided quality control for images and links on the magazine's website, which has become more elaborate since he worked there.

The assistant art editor was also supposed to attend the weekly art meetings at which the cartoon editor and editor in chief decided the next issue's lineup. During the first meeting of his first week on the job, however, Kanin was asked to cast the deciding vote on a cartoon that Mankoff ("my boss") and David Remnick ("my boss's boss") couldn't agree on. "They asked me, and I was like, 'Um . . .' And they never asked me to come to a meeting again." He laughs and adds, "But I also started submitting cartoons pretty soon after so it would've been weird to have me at the meetings anyway."

Slogging through the slush pile, Kanin never felt on the lookout for "*New Yorker*–style" cartoons but rather a well-drawn joke. The "*New Yorker*–style" part arrives automatically simply because it's published in *The New Yorker* and the caption's written in italics. And that style is ever evolving. "In the last ten years or so, a whole new group of cartoonists has appeared who are less New York–y or upper class," he says. "They're more about jokes, or gags, and I probably fall into that category. I definitely don't draw cartoons with an audience in mind—not that anyone does. I think everyone just draws what they think is funny, or, if not, they know how to construct a joke."

Kanin began submitting his own cartoons his second week at work. Technically, he'd mailed his first *New Yorker* submission to Tina Brown while he was in the second grade: "Hey, Tom," says one hunter to another, standing over Donald Duck lying in a pool of blood, "I think you better take a look at this one." Kanin had recently learned how to draw Donald Duck and Mickey Mouse during a trip to Disney World. His earlier rejection behind him, Kanin sold his first cartoon in September 2005. His timely rendition of "The 40-Year-Old Virgin Olive Oil," as its interior caption reads, consists of a half-empty uncorked bottle with flies buzzing about it. "It's not one for the ages but I was happy about it," he says.

During the editor's 2006 Christmas party, Mankoff offered his assistant a cartooning contract. "I called my parents after the party, and I was really excited. My mom shook my dad awake and told him, 'It's like winning an election!' She had to put it in those terms. But we were all excited because it basically meant that I could leave the job and make a living cartooning." Kanin's hitch ended in August 2007.

Kanin

Previously unpublished rough

"Bob sort of pushes you along after two years because he only has so many stories and he needs a new audience," Kanin says with a laugh. "He was really very encouraging."

By that time, Kanin had published a Shouts & Murmurs piece. "One Small Step" (June 4, 2007) riffed on the story of Sunita "Suni" Williams, the astronaut who ran the equivalent of a marathon on the space station treadmill, imagining her accomplishing other feats, such as climbing Mount Everest on a Stairmaster. It demonstrated how Kanin could take an idea and run with it à la *SNL*'s version of sketch comedy.

Mankoff also helped Kanin sell a book. *The Short Book: Tall Stories, Freakish Facts & the Long & Short of Being Small in a Great Big World* was published by Black Dog & Leventhal in 2007, two months after Kanin left the magazine. His future wife helped with research while the couple lived in a dank basement in Upper Manhattan. "I told her, 'Come to New York, you're going to have a great time!' And she sat on my bed researching for me. But there was a Ping-Pong table, so we were OK." Chockablock with gags and Kanin illustrations, *The Short Book* was an exemplary comedy-world calling card: "Being short is tough," Kanin writes in his foreword. "But it's also fun. And strange. And exciting! It is sometimes thoughtful, occasionally interesting, and once in a blue moon it is languid." Thurber and Benchley would have approved. And as a takeoff on Kanin's own diminutive stature, it's a brilliant example of self-effacing overcompensation.

Since leaving the magazine in a staff capacity (cartoonist Farley Katz followed as Mankoff's next assistant), Kanin has written one Talk of the Town piece about a meeting of the Society of Professional Investigators and another about a clothing store for short men. He parodied the magazine's journalistic tradition in two-page spreads such as "The Shocking Truth about Vampires," an interview in which we learn that vampires awaken only at night because they are workaholics, and 2012's "October Surprise!," which imagined election-year revelations such as Barack Obama's "all-nude" issue of the *Harvard Law Review* (complete with echoes of Kanin's *Harvard Lampoon* triumph) and a birth certificate proving Mitt Romney to be a forty-six-year-old woman from Des Moines.

In 2006, Kanin and a couple of his *Harvard Lampoon* friends became real campaign humorists when they supplied his future father-in-law, Phil Angelides, with campaign-trail jokes during his unsuccessful run for governor of California. Kanin is unsure whether his material was used—"a lot of them were real complicated"—but he takes credit, or blame, for suggesting that Angelides repeatedly ask where the cameras are located during a radio interview with Adam Carolla.

"I find it hard to do cartoons about politics," Kanin says. "David Sipress is really good at it. He can have a take on something and simplify it, which is a talent I'm starting to learn at *Saturday Night Live* because we have to deal with the news. You can't be vague there; you have to have an actual take on something. As I get older, I'll probably be interested in actually saying something with my cartoons. But for now I'm wary of having any real messages." He did a couple of vaguely political cartoons for *Time* magazine. In one, published prior to Obama's first election, someone leans out of the voting booth to ask, "Which one's the terrorist again?"

While Kanin has explored longer-form cartooning, it hasn't exactly stuck. Somewhere in a file cabinet, he has several dozen roughly drawn pages of an unfinished graphic novel about God, the Bible, and the Apocalypse that might make a good bromance. "There's a lot of funny stuff in it, which is why I stuck with it, but I was a lot happier once I stopped," he says.

In the summer of 2011, after hearing that a couple of *SNL* writers were on their way out, Kanin submitted a package of sketches to the show. On September 20, 2011, the Tuesday before the first show of *SNL*'s thirty-seventh season, Kanin sat down in the writers' room around noon and worked until seven o'clock the following morning. Writing for television being an infinitely more collaborative effort than cartooning, Kanin is part of two small groups who like to work together.

Sketches Kanin worked on include "Maya Angelou's I Know Why the Caged Bird Laughs," wherein the sainted writer pranks friends Cornel West and Morgan Freeman; "Dying Wish," in which expiring soldier Alec Baldwin requests a friend to "Tell my son there's no Santa Claus . . . And explain to him how sex works"; and what was possibly the most-watched Hulu clip of the year, "The Real Housewives of Disney," with Lindsay Lohan as leader of a gaggle of bitchy fairy-tale princesses. Being a *New Yorker* cartoonist gives Kanin a certain quirky cachet, he allows. "A lot of times people will show me their doodles as a joke, like, 'Is this good?' Yeah, it's cool."

Kanin usually types out his gags before drawing them, but that doesn't necessarily mean his captions come first. When working on a batch, he says he first comes up with several general categories to play around with. "I try to keep it varied. It might be a type of person, a profession, a place, an animal, or something like kissing someone's ass. I'll give myself ten minutes with each category to type as many jokes as I can. I let my mind wander. Some of them will have no cap-

"Just a few more minutes folks ..."

Kanin

Previously unpublished rough

tion and others are basically just a punch line. And then I move on.
Sometimes a punch line comes first and sometimes the idea does. I
don't always stick to the original categories; it's mainly a way to make
sure I sit down and think of ideas for a solid hour."

Since he began working for *SNL*, Kanin draws three or so smaller
batches at a time during breaks in the show's schedule, which he submits over as many weeks. These smaller batches consist of six to eight
cartoons, as opposed to the twelve he'd usually do. His bigger batches
might include "five that I don't even understand," in the hopes that
the competition's not too great that week and the editors will find
something interesting in them. But "I don't have a lot of throwaway
ones anymore," he says. His new schedule also dulls the sting of rejection. "When you stay up all night Monday and Tuesday drawing and
find out that it was all for nothing, that'll really get you. But if I stay
up all night Thursday through Sunday of one week, and then three
weeks later one of my batches didn't sell, I don't care." Kanin admits
that "a nice thing about having another job now is that I still feel
really good when I do sell, but I don't feel so bad when I don't."

Resubmission has always been part of the game, too, and Kanin resubmits something nearly every month. "For a long time, Bob discouraged resubmitting. Then he recently said, 'Hey, you guys know you can resubmit?' We're like, 'Yeah, we know. We've been doing that for years.'" Kanin adds that "if you turn in ten cartoons, and six of them are good, and they buy one, or two at most, then you have four or five really good ones left." In other words, there could be gold in those rejects. Unlike other cartoonists, however, Kanin doesn't go so far as to re-caption rejected cartoons before resubmitting them—but only because "I'm not organized enough. I'll usually have three or four captions for a cartoon, pick the best one, and save the other ones for later." But he doesn't always get back to them.

Kanin draws his roughs, which appear very similar to his finishes, with a felt pen on computer paper. He then puts the rough on a light box and traces over it with a black Uni-Ball Micro pen to sharpen his lines, cleans up his inks for shading, and turns it in. He used to use a nib pen but came to prefer Uni-Balls because "the line was freer from the constant dipping. I don't know if the line quality is as good but the drawing definitely feels better when I have more control over it." He uses Strathmore 300 paper for roughs and 400 for finishes. Early on, Mankoff would occasionally ask for revisions like "make this thing look how it's supposed to look," but today Kanin gets only the occasional grammar query from the copy department.

Every cartoon needs a setting such as a doctor's office, restaurant, or prison, but Kanin generally eschews familiar setups like the desert island, slave ships, and the Grim Reaper as being too much like meta-cartooning, or a "game within a game." (In his classic Grim Reaper cartoon, Death kills a man and his cat, and then stops to kill a houseplant as he thinks, "God, I'm such a perfectionist.") Tracing clichés back to their origins, on the other hand, can sometimes make you forget how commonplace they actually are.

"I was watching a History Channel show about the whaling ship *Essex,* which was capsized by a whale in the Pacific in 1820 [the incident inspired Melville's *Moby-Dick*]. The survivors took a lifeboat to an island. Three of them were like, 'We're going to stay here. We don't think you're ever going to make it to land.' The rest did make it to land, but they had to eat one another along the way. And you think, 'Man, what if you were on that desert island? That would be crazy. I wonder if there are any jokes about that? Oh, wait a sec, that's the most common thing ever!' It's just a cliché now, a cartoon game. We've lost all sense that this is a terrifying experience that's happened to people." With doctors, at least, there are actual stakes involved. Plus, he adds, not completely seriously, "I can't really draw palm trees. You might know it's a palm tree, but I'm never really satisfied with the coconuts."

For cartoonists such as Kanin, Gross, Ziegler, and others, much of their work is about stripping an idea to its essence. And looked at in a certain way, all cartoons may actually be the same cartoon. "I've drawn a lot of astronaut cartoons but haven't sold any of them," says Kanin. "It's so easy: You just draw the helmet, you don't have to draw the face, and the landscapes are always the same. I draw a lot of beached whales, again real easy. Cowboys, beached whales, doctors, astronauts: They're all versions of a desert island, I guess."

Kanin used to say his cartoons answer a question nobody is asking. "But then Christina pointed out how that didn't really mean anything, so I stopped saying it." He holds to no particular theory about humor, either. "I'm definitely one of those people who feels that if you think about it too much you can't do it." He mentions the principle of incongruity—or as Kant put it, "the sudden transformation of a strained expectation into nothing"—but doesn't sound especially enthusiastic about it.

The miracle of cartooning is the ability to set up an unexpected situation and resolve it in a single line, image, or combination thereof to show why it's wrong—such as God using an angel's halo as a cup holder as another angel remarks, "Oh, that's what those are for!" Another strategy is to misdirect a reader in the first half of a sentence and then take a sharp left turn—usually with a deftly applied "but." In Kanin's case, this would lead to the sort of situation in which a mother says to a guest, "I'm Jewish and Don is Catholic, but we're raising the kids as wolves," while a pair of children leap about the floor.

There's darkness on the edge of Kanin's world, but the violations are always benign. "A nice thing about cartoons," he says, "is that you can transgress all the way, because it's just a drawing." Readers don't always agree, as when *The New Yorker* published a panel in which two men with scalpels hover above an infant lying on a table as one says to the other, "There's gotta be an easier way to get candy from a baby." Kanin received a lot of hate mail for that one, including re-criminations for advocating infanticide. "In what way does this advocate that?" he wonders. "It goes without saying that no babies were harmed in the cartoon. I'm just saying that those guys are under the impression there's going to be candy in there."

In truth, many of Kanin's favorite cartoons contain elements of implied physical pain. Asked to name some of his favorite drawings, he mentions one in which a mother says, "I can feel the baby kicking," as the child she's holding in her hands kicks her in the face. In another, a dad swings a group of kids sideways in a painful parody of Newton's cradle. His most recent favorite involves only emotional pain: An angry woman sits on the bed with her arms crossed as her stethoscope-sporting husband in his underwear says, "You wanted to role-play—I can't help it if a doctor would be medically obligated to say something about your weight."

Kanin, however, doesn't believe humor comes from a dark, un-happy place—at least not his. "I definitely talk about things I've done, or that are happening to me, in the worst possible light to try to find the humor that way. Like when you're having a bad day and stub your toe, forget to pay a bill, and so on. I'll try to do that kind of pile-ons with situations I'm in and find the humor that way. But my life's pretty good," he says with a laugh. "I don't have a lot of real complaints."

12

The Doctor of Dots: Robert Mankoff

WHAT LEMMINGS BELIEVE

WHEN IT COMES to single-panel cartooning, *New Yorker* cartoon editor Robert Mankoff is the drawing world's most prestigious gatekeeper of gags. Nearly every week a thousand cartoons, give or take, find their way into Mankoff's domain on the twenty-first floor of the Condé Nast Building in midtown Manhattan. Inhabiting a small yet prestigious closed-door office amid a maze of open cubicles, Mankoff, with the help of assistant editor Marc Philippe Eskenazi, hones that pile down to forty or fifty finalists that will eventually be winnowed down to the sixteen or seventeen cartoons bought by David Remnick, who, as the magazine's editor, has final say on what ends up in print.

Mankoff is one of cartooning's more public faces. He delivered a popular TED Talk in 2013, and he appears on television and lectures regularly in a manner that combines his education in psychology with his former ambition to be a stand-up comedian. His sixties bona fides are still apparent in his long white hair and short beard, but he seems as comfortable in a suit and tie as in the cheerful Hawaiian shirt he's sporting the morning I visit his office. He's both artist and entrepreneur, a combination that landed him his *New Yorker* position in 1997 after drawing professionally for two decades.

Mankoff's signature cartooning style is a version of stippling, drawing with dots. At one point during our conversation, he begins to sketch a face consisting solely of these while barely glancing at pen and paper. He first drew this way in high school and soon became attached to its photographic qualities—apparent in *Wall Street Journal* artist Hai Knafo's signature stippled "hedcuts" of the past three decades, which, unlike Mankoff's drawings, are copied from photographs. "There was an accidental quality to the forms that came out," Mankoff says of the style. "It's actually fairly hard to do. I found it meditative, like a type of knitting while sketching." His earlier cartoons were in a more orthodox style, but his idiosyncratic stippling was an attention getter that also came naturally. "I figured that anybody who opened up my envelope was at least going to look at it," he says.

Influenced by Saul Steinberg and other European cartoonists, Mankoff's early style was eccentric, cerebral, and "sort of mannerist." They were caption-free pantomime cartoons embracing ideas more symbolic than mirthful. "At the time, I felt that was the purest type of cartooning to do, the most universal." Indeed, Mankoff's first book—*Elementary: The Cartoonist Did It*, published in 1980—consists only of nonverbal images, beginning with the cover drawing of Holmes and Watson investigating a murder committed with a man-sized quill pen. Mankoff's style developed through the eighties, and eventually he became a more verbal, joke-oriented cartoonist. He eventually felt he was limiting himself by only drawing pantomimes, which were also, he admits, a "very hard type of cartooning" to do.

More than one longtime *New Yorker* artist has expressed nostalgia for the days when Lee Lorenz had Bob Mankoff's job and William

Robert Mankoff in his New Yorker office

Shawn was editing the magazine. They have other beefs, too, which Mankoff addressed during our conversation. He's an eloquent spokesman for the medium. In addition to editing and cartooning, Mankoff has also been posting weekly on *The Cartoon Bureau*, a *New Yorker* blog. He feels he has found his voice—a thematically entwined blend of words and imagery—in the blog form. Outside the magazine, he has been working with the University of Michigan, conducting research into the psychology, economics, and sociology of humor with the help of data gathered through *The New Yorker*'s popular Caption Contest.

But comedy, as we all know by now, is not pretty. And the hardest part of his position at the magazine, Mankoff admits, is dealing with rejection—i.e., managing the 99.9 percent of submitted cartoons that don't make it into the magazine. "I've been on both sides," he says, "and, frankly, rejecting is easier than being rejected. That's why I wanted this job!"

. . .

For most purposes, Mankoff's workweek begins on Tuesday. Between the hours of 11 a.m. and 12:30 p.m., his office is open to any cartoonist who makes an appointment. Mankoff sees between fifteen and thirty artists during that period, both established and prospective. "I'm always open to having new people in the magazine, and I pretty much see everyone," he says, although the chances of a walk-in making it into the magazine remain lottery-like at best—not that some very assured and otherwise accomplished would-be cartoonists haven't given it a shot. Norman Mailer once dropped by with a collection of drawings, later published as *Modest Gifts: Poems and Drawings* (2003). ("Aptly titled," declares Mankoff.) A nuclear physicist once visited the office with three cartoons he was convinced were the best ever. A "strange assortment" of people tends to show up, Mankoff says, including recent retirees who've long wanted to give it a shot. Mankoff tends to be affable but blunt. "'This is really not going to work,' I'll say. 'This takes more time and energy than you've really got or will want to devote to it.' And while I'm in no way ageist, I know from a practical standpoint that the amount of time you're gonna put into this is gonna wear you out."

By Tuesday, the cartoon office will have received about five hundred cartoons from the fifty artists with *New Yorker* contracts and a similar amount, roughly, from outsiders. After his assistant makes an initial pass through the slush pile, Mankoff winnows down the hundreds of potential publishable images to forty or fifty. He tries to include at least one cartoon from each of the regulars. "Even if I'm not particularly crazy about any of them, I still want to show people's cartoons to David. Maybe I'm wrong; he has a different opinion." He also tries to get a rich mixture of both fantasy- and reality-based cartoons, classic situations, clichés (desert-island gags and their ilk), as well as "stuff you've never seen before," all of which he will present to Remnick.

On Wednesday at 2:30 p.m., Mankoff, Remnick, and managing editor Silvia Killingsworth assemble for the weekly cartoon meeting. "We have three baskets: yes, no, and maybe," Mankoff says. "I'll show the cartoons to David, who will make the ultimate decision. I've done what I do; let him do what he does. David has a very good sense of humor and he's a very busy guy. He's like Obama: He's got a million things to do and cartoons are just one of them. You want to present him with good choices and good advice, but he can't go that wrong. Silvia will also chime in with her opinions. Sometimes Remnick will ask, 'Do you really like this?' I'll say, 'Yeah.' He'll say, 'I don't.' I'll say, 'Please, this is really good.'" Although Mankoff and Remnick often disagree about cartoons, that entails less drama than you might imagine. "The truth—and David would know this—is that when I bring those fifty to him, and we pick sixteen or seventeen, there'd be some overlap but also enormous diversity of people's opinions no matter who was editor."

On the rare occasions when Remnick is absent, Mankoff and Killingsworth will usually bring in another person "to make it more social." The guests sometimes include visiting writers, such as Lawrence Wright, former managing editor Amelia Lester, and senior editor Henry Finder. "I've already seen the cartoons, so I'm not going to be laughing at them," Mankoff says with a straight face. "David's seeing them for the first time, but he's only one person, and a person by himself doesn't laugh at cartoons. You need a third person to laugh or to just have the aspect of an audience."

Unlike William Shawn, who would bloat the reserves with cartoons purchased to keep a struggling artist or two afloat, the contemporary *New Yorker* has a strict budget and sticks to it. "We know how much we have in reserve and how much we've bought for the year," Mankoff affirms. Accepted roughs, as always, are marked with a simple "OK."

To avoid embarrassing repetitions, the roughs Remnick OKs (including one that will provide Caption Contest bait) will be checked against a database. When artists generate hundreds of ideas per year, it's not unusual to repeat either their own or someone else's ideas unconsciously. Indeed, artists often include variations of the same idea within their own weekly batches of cartoons.

Every rough then goes to *The New Yorker*'s renowned fact-checking department to ensure that accuracy is maintained even within the reality- or fantasy-based cartoon realm. Next, Mankoff will e-mail each artist whose work was OKed a reproduction of the drawing and whatever comments he might have regarding how it should be improved for the sake of clarity or humor. He then contacts the rest of the regulars to say that all the OKs have gone out and "sorry if you didn't get one," perhaps dropping in some office news. If an artist hasn't sold something in a while, Mankoff might call him or her and offer encouragement. "Cartoonists, like anybody else, have ups and downs," he notes, "and you want to encourage people to go on even though they've been going through a dry spell."

But who edits the editor? As a cartoonist himself, Mankoff goes through much the same procedure whenever he submits his own cartoons to the magazine. "I show them to David Remnick," Mankoff says, "and he's perfectly willing to reject them."

The New Yorker has bought more than 950 Mankoff cartoons since he sold his first drawing to Lee Lorenz in 1977. Although he was selling cartoons elsewhere, *The New Yorker* was "Harvard" to those lesser institutions. After submitting at least ten cartoons a week to the magazine for about two years, Mankoff was discouraged and feared his work would never appear in the magazine—until Lorenz and Shawn bought a "rather strange" cartoon from him. Mankoff's *New Yorker* debut was a beautifully detailed stipple drawing of a gentleman enjoying his coffee and reading a daily paper generated by a printing press a few feet away. One could read this as a commentary on the illusion of immediacy binding consumer to product; an earlier version depicted a reporter typing directly into a printing press delivering finished newspapers on the other end. Mankoff, who still finds the image "lovely," was surprised *The New Yorker* bought it at all.

"It was interesting that they would accept something like this," he says. "That drawing style is so intensive, and eventually caused me such physical pain, that I modified it." He now uses fewer dots per square centimeter, which he regrets. "I liked the hours I spent doing it the original way," he says.

His very first sale was to Norman Cousins's *Saturday Review of*

Literature (now just *Saturday Review*) in 1975. In that drawing, an un-stippled Superman sits in a personnel office while a guy reads his ré-sumé: "Faster than a speeding bullet . . . More powerful than a loco-motive . . . No shorthand?" In a sideways manner, it even suggests the way Mankoff, who never intended to be a cartoonist, more or less fell into the trade when plan A—to become a professor of psychology—went awry.

Robert Mankoff was born in the Bronx on May 1, 1944. His par-ents were part of an extended Jewish family. A dozen family mem-bers shared the top floor of a single-family home in the Bronx and later a small house in Queens. Bob's father, Lou Mankoff, trained to be an electrician in vocational high school but did "all sorts of things" during the Depression, including learning to lay linoleum. After serving in World War II, he opened his own carpet and lino-leum store. Bob describes his father as a "very intelligent guy" who educated himself at the New York Public Library but had higher as-pirations for his son.

After attending the High School of Music & Art (now Fiorello H. LaGuardia High School of Music & Art and Performing Arts), an alternative public school then located on 135th Street, Mankoff was admitted to Syracuse University in 1962. He majored in psychol-ogy but "didn't really attend classes too much . . . it was the sixties." It was also the Vietnam War, and Mankoff worked for New York City's welfare department to avoid the draft, eventually ending up on wel-fare himself. Graduate school seemed like another viable way to put off service, so he enrolled in Atlanta University (now Clark Atlanta University), the historically black university being one of the very few schools that would accept his lackluster Syracuse grades. Mankoff didn't last at Atlanta and eventually joined the National Guard. (Years later, Mankoff visited the school while on a book tour publi-cizing *The Complete Cartoons of "The New Yorker*," which he edited. "I gave a talk and someone asked if I had ever been to Atlanta before. And I said, 'As a matter of fact, I have. I was one of two white stu-dents here in 1967.' So they introduced me that way, and I said, 'Ex-cuse me. "Caucasian American" students.'")

Published originally in Elementary: The Cartoonists Did It, *1980*

Having failed as a welfare worker, a speed-reading teacher at a Catholic high school, and a doctoral candidate in psychology (at age thirty, he dropped out of City University of New York without completing his dissertation), Mankoff decided to pursue a career in cartooning. "A lot of cartoonists of my generation followed circuitous paths," he says. "They ended up being *New Yorker* cartoonists partly through talent, but there was also a certain amount of serendipity and accident involved." Upon being informed of his son's goal of becoming a professional cartoonist, his father replied, "You know, they already have people who do that."

Lou Mankoff needn't have worried; the practice of cartooning was only part of Bob Mankoff's concern with the form. In 1992, Mankoff founded the Cartoon Bank to license published and unpublished (i.e., rejected) cartoons by *New Yorker* artists for textbooks, newsletters, advertising, and other media. "Cartoonists aren't very good at representing their own work," Mankoff says, and he hoped to supply the marketing apparatus for them to make more money from their work. With some eighty-five thousand cartoons in its inventory, the Cartoon Bank leveraged *New Yorker* talent in a way the magazine's owners must have envied. The magazine had only first publication rights to the cartoons, after which they reverted back to the artists, and Mankoff was capitalizing on their potentially lucrative afterlife. He ran the business with his third wife, Cory Scott Whittier, with whom he lives in Hastings-on-Hudson in Westchester County.

In 1997, Mankoff sold the Cartoon Bank to *The New Yorker*, and Condé Nast took the operation online. Lee Lorenz was also about to retire, and Mankoff was interested in his job. Mankoff had the administrative skills to operate the Cartoon Bank, and making him cartoon editor must have seemed like a synergistic no-brainer. However, his editorial responsibilities gradually overtook his oversight of the Cartoon Bank, whose administration fell to other parts of Condé Nast.

As cartoon editor, Mankoff was soon obliged, as Lorenz had been, to refresh the magazine's stable of artists—"although I didn't realize it for a while, because it was a smoothly running operation." Mankoff credits Lorenz with enlisting a new generation of unorthodox cartoon innovators into the magazine. James Geraghty, Lorenz's predecessor, "wasn't going to resonate to that type of humor," Mankoff says. "So when you think of the types of careers we had, part of it depended on Lee himself becoming cartoon editor in 1972 and needing a new crew of people to do it." Lorenz hired Arnie Levin in 1973; Jack Ziegler, Roz Chast, Michael Maslin, Mankoff, and others soon followed. "People were getting older, retiring, passing away, and whatnot," Mankoff continues. "Which is what I've also been confronted with."

Mankoff hired half of the magazine's current crop of artists and considers it an eclectic assortment. "Many different people are represented for their strengths and skills," he says. "You don't really compare apples to oranges to kumquats when you're looking through this stuff. Whether it's a Michael Crawford cartoon or a P. C. [Peter] Vey, they have different sensibilities. You can't arrange them on some cardinal scale. They're all within their own domain, in a way." Mankoff blogs like he talks; and as he talks, he likes to provide examples, picking up cartoons off his desk almost randomly to make his point. "Peter Vey is going to have a particular rhythm. It's almost as if he's riffing." Mankoff holds up a drawing in which one character says to another, "It's good to spend a few minutes with someone I can easily forget," and explains: "All of his captions start one way and go another, like a garden path. They have a contradictory, loopy nature to them." As the academic in Mankoff begins to emerge, you sometimes imagine drawings dropping into tagged bins.

"One of the ways I look at it," he continues, "is that cartoonists operate either within the realm of fantasy or reality. Bill Haefeli, who does a lot of cartoons about couples, often gay couples, is very observational." A Haefeli cartoon situation, he says, might be a little unlikely—"That's why it's a joke"—but it could happen in real life. Zach Kanin's cartoon situations, on the other hand, transcend reality. "There's no way a log is reading about Joan of Arc to a little kid in bed and saying that 'fifteen completely innocent logs perished in the fire.' It's a complete fantasy."

When it comes to cartooning at *The New Yorker*, context is key. "Each of these cartoons is its own container. One context is *The New Yorker* itself; another is cartooning; another is the cartoonist. And each of those can be appreciated on its own terms. You can open the magazine without ever having seen the other cartoons—but most people have seen these cartoons and have feelings or preconceptions regarding *The New Yorker*, the artists, and the art form. There's a history, a grammar, and people understand and enjoy that language. There's an overall enjoyable experience to *New Yorker* cartooning, and that's what I try to help the magazine achieve."

As for the age-old question as to what exactly constitutes a *New Yorker* cartoon, Mankoff is somewhere between the "I know it when I see it" school and Andy Warhol's definition of art as anything you find in a museum. In reality, however, "there is no such thing as a *New Yorker* cartoon," he says with a chuckle. "It's partly like a bottle of wine you know is good although you might not think it's better than any other wine if you were to do a blind taste test. The context of a cartoon appearing in *The New Yorker* makes it a *New Yorker* cartoon." There are family resemblances, he admits, as well as cartoons that would never appear elsewhere because they're "unusual or difficult to understand or have a whole other element to them that is not middle-of-the-road."

New Yorker cartoons, he believes, are characterized by adventurousness. "Most panel cartoons absolutely wanna please," but at least some *New Yorker* cartoons demand that the reader makes an effort to meet it in the middle. The difference, he suggests, lies between something like Michael Maslin's cartoon of a French army knife that's all corkscrews and Roz Chast's 1980 cartoon "Lotsa Ducks." In the latter, a group of five birds is surrounded by profiles of ordinary citizens saying, "Some buncha ducks!," "Gee whillikers!," "One heckuva lot!," and so on—all of which Mankoff reads with dramatic relish.

"I started cartooning because I was scared to do stand-up," says Mankoff of the road not taken. "I would have to play Brown's Hotel or someplace else in the Borscht Belt, which were places I'd gone growing up. And that filled me with fear, because that wasn't the kind of comedy I wanted to do. If I'd been born a little later, I think I would have been involved in that type of scene: crazier comedy, more incongruous and stuff. But when I was ready to do it, writing it, I was also cartooning, which isn't as scary as stand-up." Anyone who's seen Mankoff's TED Talk or other videos online knows he has sturdy stand-up chops, especially when combined with his academic interests.

Incongruity is an academic notion that pops up often in Mankoff's presence. In comedy theory it signifies the inconsistency between what we expect from a situation and what is delivered. "That's the way humor works, for the most part," says Mankoff. A line nearly always misattributed to Groucho Marx sends you in one direction with "I've had a lovely evening" and then pulls the rug out from under you by concluding, "but this wasn't it." Incongruity is a classic comic principle that, combined with diminishment (not to mention inversion),

Previously unpublished

explains many a *New Yorker* refrigerator trophy. When Jack Ziegler draws an enormous toaster, to provide one of Mankoff's examples, his image defies our expectation while mocking (diminishing) the very idea of bigness. Similarly, Ziegler's "Mormon Tabernacle Toaster" has many, many slots for toast. Most of the jokes in *The New Yorker* are fairly basic, admits Mankoff. But the standard gags set readers up for the knottier outliers. "Sometimes you put in one that's pretty strange so that one even stranger can be accepted," although this isn't necessarily done intentionally.

Captionless cartoons were common in *The New Yorker*'s earliest years and into the forties. Mankoff sees the *New Yorker* aesthetic as running roughly parallel to motion pictures and, later, television. Pantomime cartoons reflected the influence of silent movies on that generation, especially in terms of physical comedy, which was virtually absent by the forties. "If you look at cartoons of the forties and fifties," he says, "the people in the cartoons don't make jokes. They don't think what they're saying is funny, but *we* think what they're saying is funny." Moving to one of three screens on his desk ("there's usually a lot more"), he pulls up an atmospherically rich 1947 cartoon by Perry Barlow. A young, feather-hatted woman surrounded by men at a baseball game looks at her watch and says to her date, "For good-ness' sake! Why didn't they tell us there'd be an extra inning?" In this cartoon, Mankoff notes, "She's not making a joke; we're making fun of her." In the ensuing decades, however, television, and sitcoms in particular, have naturalized a new form of self-aware, everyone's-a-comedian humor. Today, Mankoff says, "people are saying the lines. They're wisecracking just like the people in sitcoms." He brings up a cleanly rendered Alex Gregory cartoon in which a very contempo-rary woman says, "I started my vegetarianism for health reasons, then it became a moral choice, and now it's just to annoy people." "She's making a joke, y'know what I mean? She's the actor in the sitcom."

That notion extends to Mankoff's own greatest hit, which depicts a businessman standing behind his desk, phone to ear, gazing down at his planner, and saying, "No, Thursday's out. How about never—is never good for you?" It is *The New Yorker*'s most widely reprinted car-toon and has appeared in countless textbooks and other publications (although Matthew Diffee's image of Che Guevara sporting a Bart Simpson T-shirt has likely sold more shirts). Its caption, Mankoff notes, appears in *The Yale Book of Quotations*. "Let me put it this way: I know the cartoon that's going to be mentioned in my obituary," he says accurately, especially since it's also the title of his 2014 memoir. "But in no way is 'Thursday's out' anywhere close to my favorite of my cartoons." The far more elegant drawing labeled "What Lemmings Believe," in which a flock of lemmings ascends into the sky rather than plunges from the edge of a cliff, reflects his feelings about reli-gion and "is deeply resonant for me."

As cartoon-department pooh-bah and the public face for *New Yorker* cartooning, Mankoff accepts praise and takes flak for his domain— both from within and without its borders. Many artists, for example, object to the cookie-cutter way cartoons are laid out in the maga-zine. For decades, cartoons would appear amid the magazine's three-column grid in diverse sizes and shapes: full pages, half-page horizontals, half-page verticals, two-and-a-half-column cutaways, and even, occasionally, jumping from page to page. They were printed larger, in general, and more exactly retained the proportions in which they were drawn. Today, however, *New Yorker* cartoons uniformly fit into two columns and rarely extend more than a half page vertically regardless of their original size.

The difference between artistic intent and the strictures of design become apparent if you compare drawings printed in *The New Yorker*'s Cartoons of the Year collections, which retain their original specifications, to what appeared in the magazine. "I know artists have that complaint," Mankoff responds to the charge of cookie-cutter-ism. He admits that "truly, some of the cartoons don't look very good that way, no doubt about that," and expects his colleagues to be encouraged by the 2013 redesign that allows for more layout options, which has translated to some upsizing. He points to the "constraints" of full-page photographs and illustrations, which limit the number of cartoons that can be run in an era of diminished page counts compared with the magazine's sixties and seventies heyday, when it was twice the size it is today.

To those who argue that *New Yorker* cartoons are not as beautifully illustrated as they once were, Mankoff responds that if you wanted to see truly beautiful illustrations, go back to the *Punch* magazine of 1895. "There you'll see full-blown, very complicated drawings. So even the *New Yorker* cartoon style we admire from the forties and fifties is a much-simplified style." He compares the artists of the forties and fifties to singers like Bing Crosby and Frank Sinatra who interpreted material written by nonperforming tunesmiths. So even when cartoonists such as Alan Dunn and James Stevenson were drawing their hearts out, "a lot of their jokes were very mild."

New Yorker cartoonists came to resemble the singer-songwriters of the seventies and eighties, such as Bob Dylan and the Beatles, whose creative energy offset their technical limitations. That being said, Mankoff points out that Matthew Diffee, Drew Dernavich, and Harry Bliss are just a few of the current crop who come from fine-arts backgrounds. "Times change and cartoons change with them," he says. "If you look on the Internet in terms of drawing styles, it's a more direct, primitive style people actually go for, like Keith Haring." Mankoff believes that cartooning—"this particular form of haiku"—is better than ever, more interesting, with the energy of the modern world. "Years from now when they're saying the *New Yorker* cartoons aren't as good as they used to be, they'll be looking at *these* cartoons," he offers with a chuckle.

An early adopter of computer technology, Mankoff owns an iPhone containing all seventy-five thousand *New Yorker* cartoons. ("That's not an app; that's something I did.") Moreover, the magazine's very popular back-page Caption Contest has provided huge amounts of data for his research, especially into the "subjective diversity" of humor as generated by its holistic context: source, audience expectation, general mood, and so on. How does this pertain to the Caption Contest, which averages five thousand entries per week? It's raw data for Mankoff, who uses categories discerned by his assistant, and a computer program, to generate a random sample of five hundred entries that maps out the comic landscape of any particular contest. "Like everything else at *The New Yorker*, we're very thorough." Mankoff has determined that those five hundred entries contain 99 percent of all the themes and ideas submitted to the contest. From those about a dozen will appear on an online survey sent to forty to fifty insiders, who rate each caption as "not funny," "sort of funny," or "funny." The three highest scorers become the finalists, and the winner is chosen in an online poll.

The sheer volume of comedic material a cartoon editor deals with could take a toll on anyone's sense of humor. Mankoff's curiosity transcends disgust but he does admit that looking at comedy too closely "can be a little numbing," adding that "going to the International Society for Humor Studies conference is not something that's humorous itself. It's pretty dry." Anyone who thinks that cartooning is all laughs has never had to do it for a living. "I understand that when I look at a hundred cartoons, I'm not going to think they're very funny. I'm sure not gonna have any natural response to them, such as laughing. So I

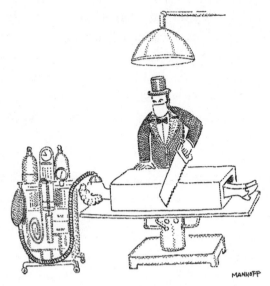

Previously unpublished

have to waive all that and use intellectual guidelines, factoring in sa-tiation effects, sequential effects, all these things.

"I actually do very few cartoons anymore. I think I'm going to get back to it, but for the last year I've sort of been on sabbatical. One thing's for sure: I've published a lot fewer cartoons since I've been car-toon editor than I published before, and I feel good about that. Here's the reason," Mankoff explains in a tone of confidentiality: "I have a lot to do now. To be a cartoonist, you have to devote an enormous amount of time to woolgathering, to sitting and drawing. If you don't do that, you don't deserve to get the cartoon."

And that's the magic of cartooning, in a nutshell: simply an artist poised over a blank sheet of paper, waiting for something brain-ticklingly funny to happen. A cartoonist's studio is that magical sweatshop where words and image come together in a manner that seems preordained and perfectly natural, yet just a tad uncanny. 'Twas ever thus. Although the style and content of its drawings have changed radically over the ninety years since *The New Yorker* published Alfred Frueh's subway sketch, the single-panel cartoon's elegant minimalism has remained essentially the same, albeit in a greatly diminished market. But wouldn't it be fantastic if publishers once again commissioned cartoons to carbonate the "longreads" of our technologically transitional time? Until they do, we'll continue to savor these sparkly little worlds on the pages, and screens, of *The New Yorker*—before looking at anything else, of course.

Acknowledgments

Here's to the artists, first and foremost, who so graciously gave me their time, thoughts, and memories. Cartoonists tend to be kind, funny, and generally wonderful people, and I encourage you to befriend and support them. Special thanks to Bob Mankoff for help negotiating the bureaucratic byways of Condé Nast.

This book grew out of the Know Your *New Yorker* Cartoonists column I impetuously pitched *Comics Journal* editor Dan Nadel, who wisely and readily agreed to run it. Those interviews would have been *much* harder to publish without the transcription assistance of Toby Liebowitz, Jack McKean, Kristen Bisson, Ben Horak, Kara Krewer, Janice Lee, Madisen Semet, Rolando A. López, Ao Meng, Hans Anderson, Oren Ashkenazi, Ian Burns, Kara Krewer, and the Unknown Intern.

Matt Groening, Lynda Barry, Ivan Brunetti, Calvin Trilling, Dan Piraro, Sarah Booth, Dione Booth, Paul Winters, Gary Groth, and the staff of the New York Public Library's Manuscripts and Archives Division all came through with the right stuff at the right time. I'm also grateful to my seemingly unflappable editor, Ed Park; inspiringly meticulous copy editor, Nancy Tan; and afropop-appreciative agent, Sarah Lazin.

Thanks as well to the friends, colleagues, and family who provided feedback, assistance, encouragement, and inspiration along the way, especially Susan Bernofsky, Craig Bromberg, Paul Dalen, Bob Eckstein, Vanessa Gould, Dan Levy, Rick Meyerowitz, Gary Panter, David Shenk, Robert Sietsema, Art Spiegelman, Nathaniel Wice, and my cartoon-critiquing daughters, Penelope and Violet.

Illustration Credits

Pages in **bold** refer to previously unpublished work.

1: Lorenz/New Yorker Collection/www.cartoonbank.com
3: Richard Gehr
5: Lee Lorenz
13: Lee Lorenz and Ricky Serro
15: Lee Lorenz
19: Richard Gehr
21: Sam Gross
22: Richard Gehr
26, 30 (published originally in *National Lampoon*), **33, 38**: Sam Gross
40: Chast/New Yorker Collection/www.cartoonbank.com
43: Richard Gehr
47, 53, 56: Roz Chast
59: Booth/New Yorker Collection/www.cartoonbank.com
60–61: George Booth
62: Sarah Booth
64–74: George Booth

75: Koren/New Yorker Collection/www.cartoonbank.com

77: Richard Gehr

80 (published originally in *The Jester*), **83, 87, 90, 93**: Edward Koren

94: Barsotti/New Yorker Collection/www.cartoonbank.com

96: Richard Gehr

99, 102, 105, 107, 109: Charles Barsotti

111: Levin/New Yorker Collection/www.cartoonbank.com

113: Mel Flythe

117, 121: Arnie Levin

125: Richard Gehr

129: Roberts/New Yorker Collection/www.cartoonbank.com

131: Richard Gehr

134: Victoria Roberts, *My Day*, Chatto & Windus, 1984

137: Victoria Roberts, *Australia Felix*, Chatto & Windus, 1988

141: Victoria Roberts, *Biographees*, Chatto & Windus, 1986

143: Victoria Roberts, *After the Fall*, W. W. Norton & Company, 2012

145: Wilson/New Yorker Collection/www.cartoonbank.com

147: Richard Gehr

151: Gahan Wilson

162: Ziegler/New Yorker Collection/www.cartoonbank.com

164: Richard Gehr

167, 171, 174, 177, 179: Jack Ziegler roughs

181: Kanin/New Yorker Collection/www.cartoonbank.com

183: Richard Gehr

187, 190, 193: Zachary Kanin roughs

197: Mankoff/New Yorker Collection/www.cartoonbank.com

199: Richard Gehr

204 (from *Elementary: The Cartoonists Did It*, Avon, 1980), **208, 212**: Robert Mankoff